Vegetarian Cookbook for Beginners

Elevate Your Vegetarian Diet with Fresh and Flavorful Recipes. Your Complete Guide to Healthy Eating | 30-Days Meal Plan Included

Katy Annabel

Copyright 2022 – Katy Annabel © All rights reserved.
The content contained within this book may not be reproduced, duplicated or transmitted without direct written permission from the author or the publisher.
Under no circumstances will any blame or legal responsibility be held against the publisher, or author, for any damages, reparation, or monetary loss due to the information contained within this book. Either directly or indirectly.

Legal Notice:
This book is copyright protected. This book is only for personal use. You cannot amend, distribute, sell, use, quote or paraphrase any part, or the content within this book, without the consent of the author or publisher.

Table of Content

Author 8
Introduction 9
Top 3 reasons to practice a vegetarian diet 10
Breakfast 11
1. Tofu Scramble 11
2. Veggie Omelette 11
3. Avocado Toast 12
4. Quinoa Porridge 12
5. Smoothie Bowl Recipe 13
6. Lentil And Sweet Potato Hash 13
7. Chia Seed Pudding 13
8. Grilled Vegetable And Feta Sandwich 14
9. Vegetable Frittata 14
10. Spinach And Feta Breakfast Burrito 15
11. Mushroom And Goat Cheese Tart 15
12. Tomato And Basil Breakfast Tart 16
13. Sweet Potato And Black Bean Breakfast Burrito..16
14. Cauliflower And Chickpea Fritters 17
15. Broccoli And Cheddar Breakfast Quiche 17
16. Zucchini And Feta Fritters 18
17. Eggplant And Mozzarella Breakfast Stack 18
18. Carrot And Ginger Breakfast Smoothie 19
19. Beet And Goat Cheese Breakfast Salad 19
20. Chickpea And Spinach Breakfast Scramble 20
21. Sweet Potato And Kale Breakfast Hash 20
22. Vegan Breakfast Tacos 20
23. Vegan Breakfast Casserole 21
24. Vegan Breakfast Sandwich 21
25. Vegan Breakfast Muffins 22
26. Crispy Tofu Breakfast Scramble 22
27. Breakfast Polenta With Roasted Vegetables 23
28. Vegan Breakfast Enchiladas 23
29. Vegan Banana Pancakes 24
30. Vegan Breakfast Sausage Patties 24
31. Vegan Breakfast Strata 25
32. Vegan Breakfast Tacos With Tofu Scramble 25
33. Vegan Breakfast Burrito Bowl 26
34. Vegan Breakfast Smoothie Bowl 26
35. Vegan Breakfast Quinoa Bowl 26
36. Vegan Breakfast Parfait 27
37. Vegan Breakfast Risotto 27
38. Vegan Breakfast Waffles 28
39. Vegan Breakfast Pastry 28
40. Vegan Breakfast Sandwich With Tempeh Bacon.29
41. Vegan Breakfast Oatmeal Bake 29
42. Vegan Breakfast Chia Pudding 30
43. Vegan Breakfast Bagel 30
44. Vegan Breakfast Tofu Scramble Tacos 30
45. Vegan Breakfast Muffins With Zucchini And Carrot 31
46. Vegan Eggless French Toast 31
47. Vegan Breakfast Omelets 32
48. Vegan Breakfast Tofu Scramble With Turmeric ..32
49. Vegan Breakfast Hashbrowns 32
50. Vegan Breakfast Hashbrowns 33
Lunch 34
51. Grilled Vegetable Wrap 34
52. Black Bean And Sweet Potato Tacos 34
53. Spinach And Feta Stuffed Portobello Mushrooms 34
54. Quinoa And Black Bean Salad 35
55. Avocado And Tomato Toast 35
56. Lentil And Vegetable Curry 36
57. Chickpea And Spinach Stew 36
58. Vegetable And Tofu Stir Fry 37
59. Cucumber And Hummus Sandwich 37
60. Broccoli And Cheddar Soup 38
61. Grilled Eggplant And Zucchini Sandwich 38
62. Pasta Primavera 39
63. Roasted Vegetable And Feta Quiche 39
64. Spicy Black Bean And Sweet Potato 40
65. Vegetable And Lentil Shepherd's Pie 40
66. Creamy Tomato And Basil Soup 41
67. Grilled Vegetable And Mozzarella Panini 41
68. Chickpea And Vegetable Curry 42
69. Vegetable And White Bean Chili 42
70. Vegetable And Pesto Pizza 43
71. Grilled Vegetable And Feta Skewers 43
72. Vegetable And Bean Burritos 44
73. Vegetable And Tofu Pad Thai 44
74. Caprese Salad With Grilled Eggplant 45
75. Creamy Mushroom And Wild Rice Soup 45
76. Spicy Sweet Potato And Black Bean Burrito Bowl 46
77. Vegetable And Chickpea Tagine 46
78. Grilled Vegetable And Pesto Panini 47
79. Vegetable And Tofu Korma 47

80.	Tomato And Basil Pasta Salad	48
81.	Grilled Vegetable And Hummus Wrap	48
82.	Vegetable And Lentil Shepherd's	49
83.	Lentil And Vegetable Stew	49
84.	Vegetable And Quinoa Fried Rice	50
85.	Vegetable And Ricotta Calzones	50
86.	Vegetable And Cheese Strata	51
87.	Vegetable And Tofu Teriyaki	52
88.	Vegetable And Cashew Stir Fry	52
89.	Vegetable And Black Bean Enchiladas	53
90.	Vegetable And White Bean Soup	54
91.	Vegetable And Tofu Lettuce Wraps	54
92.	Vegetable And Feta Frittata	55
93.	Vegetable And Chickpea Curry	55
94.	Vegetable And Pesto Linguine	56
95.	Vegetable And Chickpea Shawarma	56

Main Recipes 58

96.	Lentil Soup	58
97.	Vegetable Curry	58
98.	Spaghetti With Marinara Sauce	59
99.	Grilled Portobello Mushrooms	59
100.	Ratatouille	59
101.	Vegetable Stir-Fry	60
102.	Spinach And Feta Stuffed Shells	60
103.	Black Bean Tacos	61
104.	Falafel	61
105.	Vegetable Lasagna	62
106.	Vegetable Paella	63
107.	Eggplant Parmesan	63
108.	Vegan Shepherd's Pie	64
109.	Vegetable Paella	64
110.	Vegetable Pad Thai	65
111.	Vegetable Biryani	65
112.	Grilled Eggplant Salad	66
113.	Vegetable And Tofu Fried Rice	67
114.	Vegetable And Quinoa Salad	67
115.	Vegetable Korma	68
116.	Vegetable Risotto	68
117.	Vegetable Pot Pie	69
118.	Roasted Cauliflower Soup	69
119.	Vegan Chili	70
120.	Vegetable Enchiladas	71
121.	Grilled Vegetable Skewers	71
122.	Roasted Vegetable And Hummus Wrap	72
123.	Vegetable And Bean Enchiladas	72
124.	Vegetable And Cashew Cream Pasta	73
125.	Vegetable And Black Bean Burger	73
126.	Vegetable And Lentil Dahl	74
127.	Vegetable And Tofu Korma	74
128.	Vegetable And Tofu Scramble	75
129.	Vegetable And Lentil Shepherd's Pie	75
130.	Vegetable And Pesto Quiche	76
131.	Vegetable And Tofu Broccoli Stir Fry-	76
132.	Vegetable And Ricotta Stuffed Shells	77
133.	Vegetable And Black Bean Quesadilla	77
134.	Vegetable And Tofu Fried Rice	78
135.	Vegetable And Tofu Curry	78
136.	Vegetable And Lentil Soup	79
137.	Vegetable And Tofu Pad Thai	79
138.	Vegetable And Tofu Satay	80
139.	Vegetable And Tofu Tikka Masala	80
140.	Vegetable And Tofu Enchiladas	81
141.	Vegetable And Tofu And Vegetable Pot Pie	81
142.	Vegetable And Tofu And Vegetable Biryani	82

Salad 84

143.	Greek Salad Recipe	84
144.	Classic Caprese Salad	84
145.	Caesar Salad	84
146.	Arugula And Parmesan Salad	85
147.	Spinach And Strawberry Salad	85
148.	Broccoli And Cheddar Salad	85
149.	Roasted Beet And Goat Cheese Salad	86
150.	Kale And Quinoa Salad	86
151.	Cucumber And Tomato Salad	87
152.	Sweet Potato And Black Bean Salad	87
153.	Potato Salad	87
154.	Carrot And Raisin Salad	88
155.	Avocado And Corn Salad	88
156.	Cabbage And Apple Salad	89
157.	Three Bean Salad	89
158.	Chickpea And Cilantro Salad	89
159.	Eggplant And Tomato Salad	90
160.	Zucchini And Olive Salad	90
161.	Artichoke And Parmesan Salad	90
162.	Green Bean And Almond Salad	91
163.	Beet And Orange Salad	91
164.	Squash And Feta Salad	92
165.	Cauliflower And Blue Cheese Salad	92
166.	Radish And Cottage Cheese Salad	93
167.	Pea And Mint Salad	93

#	Recipe	Page
168.	Asparagus And Lemon Salad	93
169.	Mushroom And Walnut Salad	94
170.	Tomato And Mozzarella Salad	94
171.	Cauliflower And Raisin Salad	94
172.	Watercress And Potato Salad	95
173.	Leek And Fennel Salad	95
174.	Radicchio And Pear Salad	96
175.	Lentil And Spinach Salad	96
176.	Endive And Roquefort Salad	96
177.	Cucumber And Dill Salad	97
178.	Pea And Pecorino Salad	97
179.	Apple And Celery Salad	97
180.	Carrot And Cashew Salad	98
181.	Zucchini And Basil Salad	98
182.	Cauliflower And Parmesan Salad	98
183.	Beet And Horseradish Salad	99
184.	Eggplant And Walnut Salad	99
185.	Fennel And Orange Salad	99
186.	Cabbage And Cheddar Salad	100
187.	Carrot And Parsley Salad	100
188.	Radish And Mint Salad	100
189.	Spinach And Blue Cheese Salad	101
190.	Potato And Leek Salad	101
191.	Black Bean And Mango Salad	102
192.	Tomato And Basil Salad	102
193.	Artichoke And Olive Salad	102
194.	Cabbage And Peanut Salad	103
195.	Carrot And Ginger Salad	103
196.	Squash And Cranberry Salad	103
197.	Cucumber And Cilantro Salad	104
198.	Eggplant And Bell Pepper Salad	104
199.	Broccoli And Almond Salad	104
200.	Zucchini And Pine Nut Salad	105
201.	Beet And Walnut Salad	105
202.	Green Bean And Pesto Salad	105
203.	Radish And Avocado Salad	106
204.	Cauliflower And Pistachio Salad	106
205.	Asparagus And Parmesan Salad	106
206.	Pea And Lemon Salad	107
Smoothie		108
207.	Green Goddess Smoothie	108
208.	Beryllioses Smoothie	108
209.	Mango Madness Smoothie	108
210.	Tropical Dream Smoothie	108
211.	Carrot Ginger Smoothie	109
212.	Peach Melba Smoothie	109
213.	Spinach Apple Smoothie	109
214.	Cucumber Melon Smoothie	109
215.	Chocolate Banana Smoothie	110
216.	Avocado Lime Smoothie	110
217.	Pineapple Coconut Smoothie	110
218.	Strawberry Basil Smoothie	110
219.	Blueberry Almond Smoothie	111
220.	Beetroot Apple Smoothie	111
221.	Kale Kiwi Smoothie	111
222.	Grapefruit Rosemary Smoothie	112
223.	Raspberry Ginger Smoothie	112
224.	Orange Mango Smoothie	112
225.	Pomegranate Pear Smoothie	112
226.	Acai Berry Smoothie	113
227.	Cauliflower Turmeric Smoothie	113
228.	Sweet Potato Pie Smoothie	113
229.	Radish Cucumber Smoothie	113
230.	Broccoli Walnut Smoothie	114
231.	Asparagus Lemon Smoothie	114
232.	Zucchini Basil Smoothie	114
233.	Sweet Pea Mint Smoothie	114
234.	Cabbage Ginger Smoothie	115
235.	Apple Cinnamon Smoothie	115
236.	Lemon Ginger Smoothie	115
237.	Cacao Avocado Smoothie	115
238.	Banana Oat Smoothie	116
239.	Pineapple Spinach Smoothie	116
240.	Sweet Potato Cinnamon Smoothie	116
241.	Mango Lassi Smoothie	116
242.	Carrot Orange Smoothie	117
243.	Strawberry Kale Smoothie	117
244.	Papaya Pineapple Smoothie	117
245.	Blackberry Lemon Smoothie	117
246.	Peach Mango Smoothie	118
247.	Cucumber Melon Mint Smoothie	118
248.	Chocolate Hazelnut Smoothie	118
249.	Avocado Cacao Smoothie	118
250.	Pineapple Coconut Lime Smoothie	119
251.	Papaya Paradise Smoothie	119
252.	Beetroot Ginger Smoothie	119
253.	Kale Banana Smoothie	119
254.	Blackberry Vanilla Smoothie	120
255.	Orange Mango Ginger Smoothie	120
256.	Raspberry Lime Smoothie	120

#	Recipe	Page
257.	Acai Berry Blueberry Smoothie	120
258.	Sweet Potato Pie Spiced Smoothie	121
259.	Cauliflower Turmeric Coconut Smoothie	121
260.	Broccoli Walnut Smoothie With Vanilla	121

Snacks 122

#	Recipe	Page
261.	Baked Sweet Potato Fries	122
262.	Grilled Zucchini And Bell Pepper Skewers	122
263.	Stuffed Portobello Mushrooms	122
264.	Black Bean And Corn Quesadillas	123
265.	Chickpea And Avocado Salad	123
266.	Spinach And Feta Stuffed Phyllo Cups	124
267.	Cucumber And Dill Yogurt Dip	124
268.	Eggplant Parmesan Bites	124
269.	Grilled Eggplant Roll-Ups	125
270.	Lentil And Beetroot Patty	126
271.	Zucchini And Carrot Fritters	126
272.	Spicy Sweet Potato And Black Bean Taquitos	127
273.	Tomato And Basil Bruschetta	127
274.	Vegan Mac And Cheese	128
275.	Creamy Tomato And Lentil Soup	128
276.	Mushroom And Lentil Pâté	128
277.	Cauliflower And Cashew Cheese	129
278.	Sweet Potato And Black Bean Chili	129
279.	Vegan Sushi Rolls	130
280.	Vegan Chili Cheese Fries	130
281.	Grilled Eggplant And Halloumi Skewers	131
282.	Carrot And Ginger Soup	131
283.	Vegan Lentil Shepherd's Pie	132
284.	Stuffed Sweet Potatoes	132
285.	Indian-Style Lentil And Vegetable Stew	133
286.	Vegan Lentil And Vegetable Shepherd's Pie	133
287.	Sweet Potato And Black Bean Chili	134
288.	Vegetable And Lentil Curry	135
289.	Vegan Lentil And Vegetable Stew	135
290.	Roasted Cauliflower And Chickpea Salad	136
291.	Grilled Eggplant And Zucchini Rolls	136
292.	Grilled Eggplant And Zucchini Skewers	137
293.	Roasted Portobello Mushroom And Red Pepper Skewers	137
294.	Vegetable And Lentil Lasagna	137
295.	Vegan Lentil And Vegetable Pot Pie	138
296.	Vegetable And Lentil Stir Fry	139
297.	Vegetable Pie	139
298.	Vegan Lentil And Vegetable Spaghetti	140
299.	Vegan Lentil And Vegetable Spaghetti Sauce	140
300.	Vegan Lentil And Vegetable Pizza	141
301.	Vegan Lentil And Vegetable Shepherd's Pie	141
302.	Vegan Lentil And Vegetable Curry Pasta	142
303.	Vegan Lentil And Vegetable Curry Pizza	142

Dinner 144

#	Recipe	Page
304.	Lentil And Vegetable Curry	144
305.	Vegetable Lasagna	144
306.	Eggplant Parmesan	145
307.	Chickpea And Spinach Stew	145
308.	Zucchini And Corn Fritters	146
309.	Quinoa And Black Bean Burrito Bowls	146
310.	Pesto Pasta Salad	147
311.	Cauliflower And Chickpea Curry	147
312.	Lentil And Beetroot Patty	148
313.	Grilled Zucchini And Bell Pepper Skewers	148
314.	Vegetable Samosas	149
315.	Roasted Brussels Sprouts With Balsamic Glaze	149
316.	Roasted Cauliflower Bites	150
317.	Carrot And Ginger Soup	150
318.	Vegetable And Lentil Pot Pie	151
319.	Black Bean And Sweet Potato Chili	151
320.	Grilled Eggplant And Bell Pepper Sandwich	152
321.	Falafel Balls With Tahini Sauce	152
322.	Stuffed Bell Peppers With Quinoa And Black Beans	153
323.	Spinach And Ricotta Stuffed Shells	153
324.	Vegetable And Paneer Korma	154
325.	Stuffed Okra With Peanut And Tamarind Sauce	154
326.	Chana Masala	155
327.	Tofu And Broccoli Stir-Fry	155
328.	Grilled Eggplant Rolls With Ricotta And Basil	156
329.	Sweet Potato And Black Bean Tacos	156
330.	Cauliflower And Pea Curry	157
331.	Lentil And Vegetable Shepherd's Pie	158
332.	Vegetable Moussaka	158
333.	Lentil And Pumpkin Curry	159
334.	Stuffed Eggplant With Quinoa And Feta	159
335.	Vegetarian Chili Cheese Fries	160
336.	Pan-Seared Portobello Mushrooms With Balsamic Glaze	160
337.	Vegetable And Cashew Korma	161
338.	Vegetarian Lentil And Vegetable Pot Pie	161
339.	Black Bean And Sweet Potato Enchiladas	162
340.	Tomato And Eggplant Gratin	163
341.	Vegetable And Lentil Soup	163

342.	Vegetarian Lentil And Vegetable Curry	164
343.	Vegetable And Lentil Curry Pot Pie	164
344.	Vegetable Jalfrezi	165
345.	Vegetarian Lentil And Vegetable Curry Pie	166
346.	Vegetable And Paneer Tikka Masala	166
347.	Vegetable And Lentil Dal	167
348.	Vegetable And Paneer Biryani	167
349.	Vegetable And Lentil Frittata	168
350.	Vegetable And Lentil Chili	169
351.	Vegetable And Lentil Stew	169
352.	Vegetable And Lentil Curry	170
353.	Vegetable And Lentil Lasagna	170
354.	Vegetable And Lentil Enchiladas	171
355.	Vegetable And Lentil Burrito Bowls	172
356.	Vegetable And Lentil Stir-Fry	172
357.	Vegetable And Lentil Korma	173
358.	Vegetable And Lentil Curry Pie	173

Desserts 175

359.	Vegan Chocolate Mousse	175
360.	Fruit Sorbet	175
361.	Vegan Apple Crisp	175
362.	Vegan Chocolate Chip Cookies	176
363.	Vegan Carrot Cake	176
364.	Vegan Banana Bread	177
365.	Vegan Strawberry Cheesecake	178
366.	Vegan Pumpkin Pie	178
367.	Vegan Chocolate Brownies	179
368.	Vegan Lemon Bars	179
369.	Vegan Pecan Pie	180
370.	Vegan Blueberry Cobbler	180
371.	Vegan Ice Cream	181
372.	Vegan Tiramisu	181
373.	Vegan Crème Brûlée	182
374.	Vegan Peanut Butter Cups	182
375.	Vegan Key Lime Pie	183
376.	Vegan Chocolate Truffles	183
377.	Vegan Almond Butter Cups	184
378.	Vegan Berry Crisp	184
379.	Vegan Apple Pie	184
380.	Vegan Vanilla Cupcakes	185
381.	Vegan Pumpkin Cheesecake	186
382.	Vegan Chocolate Cake	186
383.	Vegan Chocolate Pudding	187
384.	Vegan Oatmeal Cookies	187
385.	Vegan Cinnamon Rolls	188
386.	Vegan Peach Cobbler	188
387.	Vegan Lemon Tart	189
388.	Vegan Gingerbread Cookies	189
389.	Vegan Pecan Tart	190
390.	Vegan Red Velvet Cake	191
391.	Vegan Chocolate Chip Muffins	191
392.	Vegan Baked Apple	192
393.	Vegan Chocolate Fondue	192
394.	Vegan Rice Pudding	192
395.	Vegan Chocolate Banana Bread	193
396.	Vegan Chocolate Orange Truffles	193
397.	Vegan Scones	194
398.	Vegan Cheesecake	194
399.	Vegan Chocolate Hazelnut Tart	195
400.	Vegan Apple Tart	195
401.	Vegan Apple Crumble	196
402.	Vegan Chocolate Cream Pie	196
403.	Vegan Mango Sorbet	197
404.	Vegan Raspberry Sorbet	197
405.	Vegan Banana Cream Pie	198
406.	Vegan Blueberry Muffins	198
407.	Vegan Chocolate Macarons	199
408.	Vegan Chocolate Banana Ice Cream	200
409.	Vegan Blackberry Sorbet	200
410.	Vegan Orange Tart	200

30-Days Meal Plan 202

Conclusion 203

Author

Hi everyone, I'm Katy. I decided to write this recipe book because I've personally experienced the benefits of a vegetarian diet. It all started when I decided to change my lifestyle and become a vegetarian. My love for animals and my desire to live in a more sustainable and aware world dictated this choice.

Over time, I have noticed an improvement in my health and increased energy and vitality. I was so impressed with the benefits that I decided to share my experience with the world. I created this cookbook to show everyone that the vegetarian diet is healthy, balanced, and delicious.

Each recipe in this book has been created with care and love to offer my readers a balanced and healthy food choice. I hope this book can be a source of inspiration for all who want to take care of their health. In addition, it can help spread awareness that a vegetarian diet is essential for health, the environment, and animals.

Thank you for purchasing my vegetarian diet book. I have reserved a bonus chapter that you can download directly to your device for free.

To do this, just scan this QR code or click here.

Enjoy the reading.

Introduction

Welcome to this vegetarian diet cookbook, where you will learn how to cook delicious and nutritious dishes that will help you improve your health, respect the environment and become more aware of the food you eat. The vegetarian diet is an increasingly popular food choice, offering many benefits for health, the environment, and food awareness.

In addition to being a healthy, balanced, and nutrient-rich choice, a vegetarian diet can reduce environmental impact and support sustainable agriculture. In this way, you will have the opportunity to contribute to protecting the environment and conserving natural resources while improving your overall health.

This book will guide you to discover delicious vegetarian recipes that will delight your palate and help you lead a healthy lifestyle. You'll learn how to prepare balanced meals that suit your tastes and nutritional needs and discover how to use healthy, sustainable ingredients to create meals that will leave you feeling great.

We are excited to share these recipes and encourage you to experiment with new ingredients and cooking styles. We are sure that once you learn how to cook delicious vegetarian recipes, you will improve your health and become more aware of the food you eat and help create a more sustainable world.

Top 3 reasons to practice a vegetarian diet

Now let's see what the 3 main reasons for actively following the vegetarian diet are:

1. Feel fit like never before: The vegetarian diet is a real panacea for our bodies! It is rich in vegetables, fruits, legumes, nuts, and seeds, which provide a wide range of essential nutrients such as protein, fiber, iron, calcium, and vitamins. Eating well-balanced foods helps you maintain a healthy weight, reduce your risk of chronic diseases like diabetes, heart disease, and certain types of cancer, and feel energized to tackle the day. So there's no reason to feel fatigued or down when following a vegetarian diet - you'll be ready to discover how easy and rewarding it is to feel healthy!

2. Making a difference for the environment: Practicing a vegetarian diet is good for ourselves and our planet! The intensive farming of animals for meat production has significant impacts on the environment, including water pollution, deforestation, biodiversity loss, and greenhouse gas emissions. On the other hand, choosing to eat foods of plant origin reduces this negative impact and contributes to a more sustainable future for all of us. You will feel proud that you are making a difference every time you eat a vegetarian meal!

3. Discover the world of flavors: The vegetarian diet is a culinary adventure full of surprises! You will have the opportunity to experiment with new recipes, ingredients, and tastes, making you discover how fun and tasty it is to eat healthily. There's no need to give up your favorite dishes anymore, as plenty of vegetarian alternatives are just as delicious. Experimenting with vegetarian cooking will help you become more creative and impress your guests with your delicious dishes. What's better than learning to cook, have fun, and care for yourself and the planet simultaneously?

Breakfast

1. Tofu Scramble

Cooking Time: 20 minutes **Prep. Time:** 10 minutes **Servings:** 4

Ingredients:
- 1 block of firm tofu, drained and crumbled
- 1 tbsp olive oil
- 1 small onion, diced
- 1 bell pepper, diced
- 1 tbsp nutritional yeast
- 1 tsp turmeric powder
- 1 tsp cumin powder
- Salt and pepper, to taste
- Optional: diced tomatoes, spinach, mushrooms, etc.

Instructions:
1. Heat the olive oil in a pan over medium heat.
2. Add the onion and bell pepper and sauté for about 5 minutes, until softened.
3. Add the crumbled tofu, nutritional yeast, turmeric, cumin, salt and pepper to the pan and stir.
4. Cook for about 5-7 minutes, until the tofu is heated through and starting to brown.
5. If desired, add in diced tomatoes, spinach, mushrooms, or any other vegetables you like.
6. Cook for an additional 3-5 minutes, until the vegetables are cooked to your liking.
7. Taste and adjust seasoning as needed.
8. Serve hot, as is or with toast, in a burrito or as a breakfast bowl.

Nutritional Value: Calories: 120 Protein: 8g Fat: 8g Carbohydrates: 6g Fiber: 2g

2. Veggie Omelette

Cooking Time: 10 minutes **Prep. Time:** 5 minutes **Servings:** 1

Ingredients:
- 2 eggs
- 1/4 cup diced bell peppers (red, yellow, and green)
- 1/4 cup diced mushrooms
- 1/4 cup diced onions
- Salt and pepper, to taste
- 1 tablespoon olive oil

Instructions:
1. In a small mixing bowl, whisk together the eggs and set aside.
2. In a large skillet, heat the olive oil over medium heat.
3. Add the diced bell peppers, mushrooms, and onions to the skillet and sauté for 2-3 minutes, or until they are slightly softened.
4. Pour the eggs into the skillet and season with salt and pepper.
5. Use a spatula to gently scramble the eggs and vegetables together.
6. Once the eggs are cooked through, use the spatula to fold the omelette in half.
7. Serve hot and enjoy!

Nutritional Value: Calories: 191 Protein: 12g Fat: 15g Carbohydrates: 5g Fiber: 1g Sugar: 3g

3. Avocado Toast

Cooking Time: 5 minutes **Prep. Time:** 5 minutes **Servings:** 1

Ingredients:
- 1 ripe avocado
- 1/4 teaspoon salt
- 1/4 teaspoon black pepper
- 1/4 teaspoon garlic powder
- 1/4 teaspoon onion powder
- 1/4 teaspoon cayenne pepper (optional)
- 1 slice of bread (preferably whole grain or sourdough)
- Optional: 1 tomato, diced
- Optional: 1/4 teaspoon of lemon or lime juice

Instructions:
1. Toast the bread to your desired level of crispiness.
2. While the bread is toasting, cut the avocado in half, remove the pit and scoop out the flesh into a bowl.
3. Mash the avocado with a fork or a potato masher, to your desired consistency.
4. Mix in the salt, pepper, garlic powder, onion powder and cayenne pepper (if using) until well combined.
5. If you are using, squeeze lemon or lime juice over the avocado and mix it.
6. Once the bread is toasted, spread the avocado mixture on top of it.
7. If you are using, add diced tomatoes on top of the avocado spread.
8. Enjoy your avocado toast while it's still warm.

Nutritional Value: Calories: 250 Protein: 4g Fat: 18g Carbohydrates: 19g Fiber: 7g

4. Quinoa Porridge

Cooking Time: 15 minutes **Prep. Time:** 5 minutes **Servings:** 2

Ingredients:
- 1 cup quinoa
- 2 cups water
- 1/4 tsp salt
- 1/2 tsp vanilla extract
- 1 tsp cinnamon powder
- 1/4 cup maple syrup
- 1/2 cup milk (any kind)
- 1/4 cup chopped nuts (almonds, walnuts, pecans, etc.)
- 1/4 cup dried fruits (raisins, cranberries, blueberries, etc.)

Instructions:
1. Rinse the quinoa in a fine-mesh strainer under cold running water for about 2 minutes.

2. In a medium saucepan, bring the quinoa, water, and salt to a boil.
3. Reduce the heat to low, cover, and simmer for about 15 minutes, or until the quinoa is cooked and the water is absorbed.
4. Remove from heat and stir in vanilla extract, cinnamon powder, maple syrup, milk, chopped nuts and dried fruits.
5. Serve the quinoa porridge hot and enjoy!

Nutritional Value: Calories: 400 Protein: 9g Fat: 12g Carbohydrates: 67g Fiber: 5g

5. Smoothie Bowl Recipe

Cooking Time: 5 minutes **Prep. Time:** 5 minutes **Servings:** 1

Ingredients:
- 1 banana
- 1 cup frozen berries (strawberries, blueberries, raspberries)
- 1/2 cup Greek yogurt
- 1/4 cup almond milk
- 1 tablespoon honey (optional)
- 1/4 teaspoon vanilla extract
- Toppings: granola, nuts, seeds, fresh fruit, etc.

Instructions:
1. In a blender, add the banana, frozen berries, Greek yogurt, almond milk, honey (if using) and vanilla extract.
2. Blend on high until the mixture is smooth and creamy.
3. Pour the smoothie into a bowl.
4. Add your desired toppings such as granola, nuts, seeds, fresh fruit etc.
5. Serve and enjoy!

Nutritional Value: Calories: 310 Protein: 12g Fat: 6g Carbohydrates: 57g Fiber: 8g Sugar: 38g

6. Lentil And Sweet Potato Hash

Cooking Time: 30 minutes **Prep. Time:** 10 minutes **Servings:** 4

Ingredients:
- 1 medium sweet potato, peeled and diced
- 1 cup cooked brown or green lentils
- 1 small onion, diced
- 2 cloves of garlic, minced
- 1 teaspoon paprika
- 1/2 teaspoon cumin powder
- 1/4 teaspoon turmeric powder
- Salt and pepper, to taste
- 2 tablespoons olive oil
- Optional: diced tomatoes, spinach, mushrooms, etc.

Instructions:
1. Preheat a large skillet over medium heat and add the olive oil.
2. Add the diced sweet potato and cook for about 10 minutes, until it starts to soften and brown.
3. Add the onion, garlic, paprika, cumin, turmeric, salt, and pepper to the skillet and cook until the onion is translucent, about 3-5 minutes.
4. Stir in the cooked lentils and cook for an additional 5 minutes, until heated through.
5. If desired, add in diced tomatoes, spinach, mushrooms, or any other vegetables you like and cook for an additional 3-5 minutes, until the vegetables are cooked to your liking.
6. Taste and adjust seasoning as needed.
7. Serve hot, as is or with toast, in a burrito or as a breakfast bowl.

Nutritional Value: Calories: 250 Protein: 12g Fat: 8g Carbohydrates: 33g Fiber: 8g

7. Chia Seed Pudding

Cooking Time: 0 minutes **Prep. Time:** 5 minutes + overnight soak **Servings:** 1

Ingredients:
- 1/4 cup chia seeds

- 1 cup almond milk or any milk of your choice
- 1 tablespoon honey or any sweetener of your choice
- 1/4 teaspoon vanilla extract
- toppings of your choice (fresh fruit, nuts, seeds, etc)

Instructions:
1. In a medium mixing bowl, combine the chia seeds, almond milk, honey, and vanilla extract.
2. Stir well to ensure that the chia seeds are evenly distributed in the mixture.
3. Cover the bowl with plastic wrap or a lid and refrigerate overnight, or for at least 4 hours.
4. Before serving, give the pudding a quick stir to break up any clumps.
5. Divide pudding into serving bowl and add toppings of your choice such as fresh fruit, nuts, seeds, etc.
6. Serve and enjoy!

Nutritional Value: Calories: 225 Protein: 7g Fat: 15g Carbohydrates: 18g Fiber: 12g Sugar: 5g

8. Grilled Vegetable And Feta Sandwich

Cooking Time: 15 minutes **Prep. Time:** 10 minutes **Servings:** 1

Ingredients:
- 2 slices of whole wheat bread
- 1/4 cup crumbled feta cheese
- 1/4 cup sliced mushrooms
- 1/4 cup sliced bell peppers (red, yellow, green)
- 1/4 cup sliced red onion
- 1/2 teaspoon olive oil
- Salt and pepper, to taste
- Optional: lettuce leaves, tomato, avocado, or any other toppings of your choice

Instructions:

1. Preheat your grill or a grill pan over medium heat.
2. Brush the sliced mushrooms, bell peppers, and red onion with olive oil and season with salt and pepper.
3. Grill the vegetables for about 5-7 minutes or until they are tender and slightly charred.
4. While the vegetables are cooking, butter one side of each slice of bread.
5. Once the vegetables are cooked, assemble the sandwich by layering the grilled vegetables, crumbled feta cheese, and any additional toppings (lettuce, tomato, avocado, etc.) on one slice of bread.
6. Place the other slice of bread on top, buttered side down.
7. Grill the sandwich for about 2-3 minutes per side, or until the bread is golden brown and crispy.
8. Remove from the grill and let the sandwich cool for a few minutes before slicing in half and serving.

Nutritional Value: Calories: 310 Protein: 14g Fat: 15g Carbohydrates: 31g Fiber: 5g Sugar: 8g

9. Vegetable Frittata

Cooking Time: 25 minutes **Prep. Time:** 10 minutes **Servings:** 4

Ingredients:
- 6 large eggs
- 1/4 cup milk
- Salt and pepper, to taste
- 2 tablespoons olive oil
- 1 small onion, diced
- 2 cloves of garlic, minced
- 1 cup chopped vegetables of your choice (such as bell peppers, mushrooms, spinach, tomatoes)
- 1/4 cup grated cheese (cheddar, feta, or parmesan)

Instructions:

1. Preheat the oven to 375°F (190°C).
2. In a mixing bowl, whisk together the eggs, milk, salt, and pepper.
3. Heat the olive oil in a 10-inch oven-safe skillet over medium heat.
4. Add the onion and garlic and cook until softened, about 3-5 minutes.
5. Add the chopped vegetables and cook until they are tender, about 5-7 minutes.
6. Pour the egg mixture into the skillet and stir gently to combine the vegetables and eggs.
7. Cook on the stovetop for 2-3 minutes, or until the bottom of the frittata is set.
8. Sprinkle the grated cheese on top of the frittata.
9. Transfer the skillet to the oven and bake for about 15-20 minutes, or until the eggs are set and the cheese is golden brown.
10. Let it cool for a few minutes before slicing and serving.

Nutritional Value: Calories: 200 Protein: 12g Fat: 15g Carbohydrates: 3g Fiber: 1g

10. Spinach And Feta Breakfast Burrito

Cooking Time: 15 minutes **Prep. Time:** 5 minutes **Servings:** 1
Ingredients:
- 1 large flour tortilla
- 2 eggs
- 1/4 cup crumbled feta cheese
- 1/4 cup chopped spinach
- 1/4 cup diced bell pepper (red, yellow, green)
- Salt and pepper, to taste
- 1 tablespoon olive oil

Instructions:
1. Heat a skillet over medium heat and add olive oil.
2. In a small mixing bowl, whisk together the eggs and set aside.
3. Add diced bell pepper to the skillet, sauté for 2-3 minutes or until they are slightly softened.
4. Add the chopped spinach and sauté for an additional 1-2 minutes or until wilted.
5. Pour the eggs into the skillet and season with salt and pepper.
6. Use a spatula to gently scramble the eggs and vegetables together.
7. Remove from heat and add crumbled feta cheese
8. Place a large flour tortilla on a plate and spoon the egg and vegetable mixture in the center of the tortilla.
9. Roll the tortilla tightly around the filling, tucking in the sides as you roll.
10. Slice in half and serve.

Nutritional Value: Calories: 356 Protein: 17g Fat: 23g Carbohydrates: 20g Fiber: 3g Sugar: 2g

11. Mushroom And Goat Cheese Tart

Cooking Time: 30 minutes **Prep. Time:** 15 minutes **Servings:** 4
Ingredients:
- 1 sheet of pre-made puff pastry, thawed
- 1 tbsp olive oil
- 8 oz sliced mushrooms (cremini or button mushrooms)
- 1 small onion, diced
- 2 cloves of garlic, minced
- 1 tsp thyme leaves
- Salt and pepper, to taste
- 1/4 cup crumbled goat cheese
- 1 egg, beaten (for egg wash)

Instructions:
1. Preheat the oven to 400F (200C) and roll out the puff pastry sheet on a lightly floured surface to a rectangle shape.
2. Place the puff pastry on a baking sheet lined with parchment paper.

3. In a skillet, heat the olive oil over medium heat. Add the mushrooms, onion, garlic, thyme, salt, and pepper. Cook for about 10 minutes, or until the mushrooms are browned and the onions are translucent.
4. Spread the mushroom mixture over the puff pastry, leaving a 1-inch border around the edges.
5. Sprinkle the crumbled goat cheese over the mushroom mixture.
6. Fold the edges of the puff pastry over the filling, creating a rustic look.
7. Brush the beaten egg over the edges of the pastry.
8. Bake in the preheated oven for 15-20 minutes, or until the pastry is golden brown and puffed.
9. Remove from the oven and let it cool for a few minutes before slicing and serving.

Nutritional Value per Serving: Calories: 200 Protein: 6g Fat: 16g Carbohydrates: 12g Fiber: 1g

12. Tomato And Basil Breakfast Tart

Cooking Time: 40 minutes **Prep. Time:** 10 minutes **Servings:** 4
Ingredients:
- 1 sheet of puff pastry, thawed
- 1/2 cup grated mozzarella cheese
- 1/4 cup grated Parmesan cheese
- 4-5 fresh tomatoes, thinly sliced
- 1/4 cup chopped fresh basil
- Salt and pepper, to taste
- 1 tablespoon olive oil
- 1 egg, beaten (for egg wash)

Instructions:
1. Preheat your oven to 375°F (190°C) and line a baking sheet with parchment paper.
2. Roll out the puff pastry sheet on a lightly floured surface to a thickness of 1/8 inch.
3. Place the puff pastry sheet on the prepared baking sheet.
4. Brush the puff pastry sheet with the beaten egg.
5. Sprinkle mozzarella cheese, Parmesan cheese, and chopped basil over the puff pastry sheet, leaving a 1/2-inch border around the edge.
6. Arrange the sliced tomatoes on top of the cheese and basil.
7. Drizzle the tomatoes with olive oil and season with salt and pepper.
8. Fold the edges of the puff pastry up and over the tomatoes, pinching the edges to seal.
9. Brush the edges with the beaten egg.
10. Bake for 25-30 minutes or until the puff pastry is golden brown and the tomatoes are tender.
11. Let it cool for a few minutes before slicing and serving.

Nutritional Value: Calories: 318 Protein: 10g Fat: 24g Carbohydrates: 16g Fiber: 1g Sugar: 2g

13. Sweet Potato And Black Bean Breakfast Burrito

Cooking Time: 25 minutes **Prep. Time:** 10 minutes **Servings:** 4
Ingredients:
- 2 medium sweet potatoes, peeled and diced
- 1 tbsp olive oil
- 1 small onion, diced
- 2 cloves of garlic, minced
- 1 tsp cumin powder
- 1/2 tsp smoked paprika
- 1/4 tsp chili powder
- Salt and pepper, to taste
- 1 can black beans, drained and rinsed
- 4 large flour tortillas
- Optional: diced tomatoes, avocado, cilantro, cheese, etc.

Instructions:
1. Preheat a large skillet over medium heat and add the olive oil.
2. Add the diced sweet potato and cook for about 10 minutes, until it starts to soften and brown.
3. Add the onion, garlic, cumin, smoked paprika, chili powder, salt, and pepper to the skillet and cook until the onion is translucent, about 3-5 minutes.
4. Stir in the black beans and cook for an additional 5 minutes, until heated through.
5. Warm up the tortillas according to package instructions.
6. Spread a little bit of the sweet potato and black bean mixture on each tortilla, leaving a small border around the edges.
7. If desired, add diced tomatoes, avocado, cilantro, cheese, or any other toppings you like.
8. Roll up the tortillas, tucking in the sides as you go, to form a burrito.
9. Heat a large skillet over medium heat, and cook each burrito for about 2 minutes per side, or until lightly browned and heated through.
10. Serve the burritos hot and enjoy!

Nutritional Value per Serving: Calories: 300 Protein: 12g Fat: 5g Carbohydrates: 54g Fiber: 8g

14. Cauliflower And Chickpea Fritters

Cooking Time: 15 minutes **Prep. Time:** 10 minutes **Servings:** 4
Ingredients:
- 1 head of cauliflower, grated
- 1 cup cooked chickpeas, mashed
- 1/4 cup all-purpose flour
- 2 cloves of garlic, minced
- 1/4 cup chopped fresh parsley
- 1/4 cup chopped fresh cilantro
- 2 eggs, beaten
- Salt and pepper, to taste
- 1/4 cup vegetable oil for frying

Instructions:
1. In a large mixing bowl, combine the grated cauliflower, mashed chickpeas, flour, garlic, parsley, cilantro, eggs, salt, and pepper.
2. Mix well until the ingredients are well combined.
3. Heat the vegetable oil in a large skillet over medium-high heat.
4. Using a spoon or an ice cream scoop, drop heaping tablespoons of the cauliflower mixture into the hot oil.
5. Fry the fritters for 2-3 minutes per side, or until they are golden brown and crispy.
6. Using a slotted spoon, transfer the fritters to a paper towel-lined plate to drain off any excess oil.
7. Serve hot and enjoy!

Nutritional Value: Calories: 320 Protein: 12g Fat: 20g Carbohydrates: 27g Fiber: 8g Sugar: 5g

15. Broccoli And Cheddar Breakfast Quiche

Cooking Time: 45 minutes **Prep. Time:** 15 minutes **Servings:** 6
Ingredients:
- 1 unbaked 9-inch pie crust
- 1 tbsp olive oil
- 1 small onion, diced
- 2 cloves of garlic, minced
- 1 cup chopped broccoli florets
- 3 large eggs
- 1 cup milk
- 1/2 cup heavy cream
- 1 tsp dried thyme
- Salt and pepper, to taste
- 1 cup shredded cheddar cheese

Instructions:
1. Preheat the oven to 375F (190C).
2. In a skillet, heat the olive oil over medium heat. Add the onion, garlic, and broccoli and sauté for about 5 minutes, or until the vegetables are softened.
3. In a large bowl, whisk together the eggs, milk, cream, thyme, salt, and pepper.
4. Spread the sautéed vegetables in the bottom of the pie crust.
5. Pour the egg mixture over the vegetables.
6. Sprinkle the shredded cheddar cheese over the top.
7. Bake the quiche in the preheated oven for 35-40 minutes, or until the crust is golden brown and the filling is set.
8. Remove from the oven and let it cool for a few minutes before slicing and serving.

Nutritional Value: Calories: 300 Protein: 12g Fat: 21g Carbohydrates: 16g Fiber: 1g

16. Zucchini And Feta Fritters

Cooking Time: 15 minutes **Prep. Time:** 10 minutes **Servings:** 4

Ingredients:
- 2 medium zucchinis, grated
- 1/2 cup crumbled feta cheese
- 1/4 cup all-purpose flour
- 2 cloves of garlic, minced
- 1/4 cup chopped fresh dill
- 2 eggs, beaten
- Salt and pepper, to taste
- 1/4 cup vegetable oil for frying

Instructions:
1. In a large mixing bowl, combine the grated zucchinis, crumbled feta cheese, flour, garlic, dill, eggs, salt, and pepper.
2. Mix well until the ingredients are well combined.
3. Heat the vegetable oil in a large skillet over medium-high heat.
4. Using a spoon or an ice cream scoop, drop heaping tablespoons of the zucchini mixture into the hot oil.
5. Fry the fritters for 2-3 minutes per side, or until they are golden brown and crispy.
6. Using a slotted spoon, transfer the fritters to a paper towel-lined plate to drain off any excess oil.
7. Serve hot and enjoy!

Nutritional Value: Calories: 222 Protein: 14g Fat: 14g Carbohydrates: 22g Fiber: 14g

17. Eggplant And Mozzarella Breakfast Stack

Cooking Time: 20 minutes **Prep. Time:** 15 minutes **Servings:** 4

Ingredients:
- 1 large eggplant, sliced into 1/4-inch rounds
- Salt and pepper, to taste
- 1/4 cup all-purpose flour
- 2 large eggs
- 1/2 cup breadcrumbs
- 1/4 cup grated Parmesan cheese
- 1 cup marinara sauce
- 4 slices of mozzarella cheese
- Fresh basil leaves, chopped, for garnish

Instructions:
1. Preheat the oven to 400F (200C).
2. Season the eggplant slices with salt and pepper.
3. Place the flour in one shallow dish, and beat the eggs in another shallow dish. In a third shallow dish, mix together the breadcrumbs and grated Parmesan cheese.
4. Dip each eggplant slice in the flour, then the beaten eggs, and finally in the breadcrumb mixture.
5. Place the eggplant slices on a baking sheet lined with parchment paper.

6. Bake for about 15-20 minutes, or until the eggplant is golden brown and crispy.
7. To assemble the stacks, start with a slice of eggplant on the bottom, then a spoonful of marinara sauce, a slice of mozzarella cheese, another slice of eggplant, more marinara sauce, and another slice of mozzarella cheese.
8. Repeat the process until you have used all of the eggplant slices.
9. Bake the stacks in the oven for an additional 5 minutes, or until the cheese is melted and bubbly.
10. Garnish with fresh basil leaves and serve hot.

Nutritional Value: Calories: 250 Protein: 10g Fat: 16g Carbohydrates: 15g Fiber: 4g

18. Carrot And Ginger Breakfast Smoothie

Cooking Time: 5 minutes **Prep. Time:** 5 minutes **Servings:** 1
Ingredients:
- 1 cup frozen carrots
- 1/2 banana
- 1/2 inch fresh ginger, peeled and grated
- 1/2 cup plain Greek yogurt
- 1/2 cup orange juice
- 1/4 cup almond milk or any milk of your choice
- 1 tablespoon honey (optional)
- 1/4 teaspoon vanilla extract

Instructions:
1. In a blender, add the frozen carrots, banana, ginger, Greek yogurt, orange juice, almond milk, honey (if using) and vanilla extract.
2. Blend on high until the mixture is smooth and creamy.
3. Pour the smoothie into a glass and serve immediately.

Nutritional Value: Calories: 222 Protein: 12g Fat: 4g Carbohydrates: 42g Fiber: 6g Sugar: 27g

19. Beet And Goat Cheese Breakfast Salad

Cooking Time: 20 minutes **Prep. Time:** 10 minutes **Servings:** 4
Ingredients:
- 1 lb beets, peeled and diced
- 1 tbsp olive oil
- Salt and pepper, to taste
- 4 cups mixed greens
- 1/4 cup crumbled goat cheese
- 1/4 cup chopped toasted walnuts
- 1/4 cup dried cranberries
- 2 tbsp balsamic vinegar
- 1 tbsp honey
- 1 clove of garlic, minced

Instructions:
1. Preheat the oven to 375F (190C).
2. Toss the beets with olive oil, salt, and pepper.
3. Spread the beets out on a baking sheet and roast for 20-25 minutes, or until they are tender.
4. While the beets are roasting, in a small bowl, whisk together the balsamic vinegar, honey, and minced garlic.
5. In a large bowl, combine the mixed greens, roasted beets, crumbled goat cheese, toasted walnuts, and dried cranberries.
6. Drizzle the dressing over the salad and toss to combine.
7. Serve the salad immediately and enjoy!

Nutritional Value per Serving: Calories: 250 Protein: 6g Fat: 18g Carbohydrates: 16g Fiber: 3g

20. Chickpea And Spinach Breakfast Scramble

Cooking Time: 10 minutes **Prep. Time:** 5 minutes **Servings:** 1
Ingredients:
- 2 eggs
- 1/4 cup cooked chickpeas
- 1/4 cup chopped spinach
- 1/4 cup diced bell pepper (red, yellow, green)
- Salt and pepper, to taste
- 1 tablespoon olive oil
- Optional: diced tomatoes, avocado, or any other toppings of your choice

Instructions:
1. In a small mixing bowl, whisk together the eggs and set aside.
2. In a large skillet, heat the olive oil over medium heat.
3. Add the diced bell pepper to the skillet, sauté for 2-3 minutes or until they are slightly softened.
4. Add the chopped spinach, cooked chickpeas and sauté for an additional 1-2 minutes or until wilted.
5. Pour the eggs into the skillet and season with salt and pepper.
6. Use a spatula to gently scramble the eggs and vegetables together.
7. Once the eggs are cooked through, remove from heat and add any desired toppings.
8. Serve and enjoy!

Nutritional Value: Calories: 315 Protein: 17g Fat: 22g Carbohydrates: 16g Fiber: 7g Sugar: 4g

21. Sweet Potato And Kale Breakfast Hash

Cooking Time: 25 minutes **Prep. Time:** 10 minutes **Servings:** 4
Ingredients:
- 2 medium sweet potatoes, peeled and diced
- 1 tbsp olive oil
- 1 small onion, diced
- 2 cloves of garlic, minced
- 1/2 tsp smoked paprika
- 1/4 tsp cumin powder
- Salt and pepper, to taste
- 1 bunch of kale, stems removed and leaves chopped
- 4 large eggs
- Optional: diced tomatoes, avocado, cilantro, cheese, etc.

Instructions:
1. Preheat a large skillet over medium heat and add the olive oil.
2. Add the diced sweet potato and cook for about 10 minutes, until it starts to soften and brown.
3. Add the onion, garlic, smoked paprika, cumin, salt, and pepper to the skillet and cook until the onion is translucent, about 3-5 minutes.
4. Stir in the kale and cook for an additional 5 minutes, until the kale is wilted and tender.
5. Create 4 wells in the hash, and crack an egg into each one.
6. Cover the skillet and cook for about 3-4 minutes or until the egg whites are set and the yolks are still runny.
7. If desired, add diced tomatoes, avocado, cilantro, cheese, or any other toppings you like.
8. Serve the hash hot and enjoy!

Nutritional Value: Calories: 244 Protein: 8g Fat: 4g Carbohydrates: 34g Fiber: 9g

22. Vegan Breakfast Tacos

Cooking Time: 15 minutes **Prep. Time:** 10 minutes **Servings:** 4
Ingredients:

- 8 corn tortillas
- 1 block of firm tofu, crumbled
- 1/4 cup diced bell peppers (red, yellow, green)
- 1/4 cup diced onions
- 1/4 cup diced mushrooms
- 1/4 cup diced tomatoes
- 1 tablespoon olive oil
- 1 teaspoon chili powder
- 1/2 teaspoon ground cumin
- Salt and pepper, to taste
- Optional: chopped fresh cilantro, avocado, or any other toppings of your choice

Instructions:
1. Heat a skillet over medium heat and add olive oil.
2. Add diced bell peppers, onions, and mushrooms to the skillet and sauté for 2-3 minutes or until they are slightly softened.
3. Add the crumbled tofu, diced tomatoes, chili powder, cumin, salt and pepper to the skillet.
4. Cook, stirring occasionally, for an additional 5-7 minutes or until the tofu is heated through and the vegetables are tender.
5. While the filling is cooking, warm the tortillas in the oven or on a skillet.
6. Once the tortillas are warm and pliable, add the tofu and vegetable filling.
7. Add any desired toppings such as chopped fresh cilantro, avocado, or salsa.
8. Fold the tortillas in half and serve warm.

Nutritional Value: Calories: 246 Protein: 13g Fat: 12g Carbohydrates: 26g Fiber: 5g Sugar: 3g

23. Vegan Breakfast Casserole

Cooking Time: 45 minutes **Prep. Time:** 15 minutes **Servings:** 6
Ingredients:

- 8 oz firm tofu, pressed and crumbled
- 1 tbsp olive oil
- 1 small onion, diced
- 2 cloves of garlic, minced
- 1 red bell pepper, diced
- 1/2 cup sliced mushrooms
- 1/2 cup diced tomatoes
- 1 tsp dried oregano
- 1 tsp smoked paprika
- Salt and pepper, to taste
- 4 cups torn whole wheat bread
- 2 cups unsweetened non-dairy milk
- 2 tbsp nutritional yeast
- 1 tbsp Dijon mustard
- 1 tbsp tahini
- Optional: diced avocado, fresh herbs, hot sauce

Instructions:
1. Preheat the oven to 375 °F (190C).
2. In a skillet, heat the olive oil over medium heat. Add the onion, garlic, red bell pepper, mushrooms, diced tomatoes, oregano, smoked paprika, salt, and pepper. Cook for about 8-10 minutes or until the vegetables are softened.
3. In a large mixing bowl, combine the bread, non-dairy milk, nutritional yeast, Dijon mustard, and tahini. Stir well.
4. Add the crumbled tofu, and vegetables to the bread mixture, stir well.
5. Pour the mixture into a greased

Nutritional Value: Calories: 350 Protein: 15g Fat: 18g Carbohydrates: 22g Fiber: 4g

24. Vegan Breakfast Sandwich

Cooking Time: 10 minutes **Prep. Time:** 5 minutes **Servings:** 1
Ingredients:

- 2 slices of whole wheat bread
- 1 vegan sausage patty
- 1/4 cup diced tomatoes

- 1/4 cup diced avocado
- 1/4 cup sliced mushrooms
- 2 tablespoons vegan mayonnaise
- 1 teaspoon Dijon mustard
- Salt and pepper, to taste

Instructions:
1. Heat a skillet over medium heat and cook the vegan sausage patty according to package
2. While the vegan sausage patty is cooking, prepare the sandwich by spreading the vegan mayonnaise and Dijon mustard on one side of each slice of bread.
3. On the bottom slice of bread, add the diced tomatoes, avocado, sliced mushrooms, and cooked vegan sausage patty.
4. Sprinkle with salt and pepper to taste.
5. Top with the other slice of bread, and press down gently.
6. Heat the skillet and place the sandwich on it, and cook for about 2-3 minutes per side, or until the bread is golden brown and crispy.
7. Remove from the skillet and let it cool for a few minutes before slicing in half and serving.

Nutritional Value: Calories: 437 Protein: 16g Fat: 32g Carbohydrates: 28g Fiber: 8g Sugar: 5g

25. Vegan Breakfast Muffins

Cooking Time: 20 minutes **Prep. Time:** 15 minutes **Servings:** 12 muffins

Ingredients:
- 2 cups all-purpose flour
- 2 tsp baking powder
- 1 tsp baking soda
- 1/2 tsp salt
- 1/4 tsp ground cinnamon
- 1/4 tsp ground nutmeg
- 1/2 cup brown sugar
- 1/2 cup unsweetened applesauce
- 1 cup unsweetened non-dairy milk
- 1 tsp vanilla extract
- 1/4 cup chopped pecans or walnuts (optional)
- 1/4 cup dried cranberries or raisins (optional)

Instructions:
1. Preheat the oven to 375F (190C) and line a muffin tin with paper liners.
2. In a large mixing bowl, combine the flour, baking powder, baking soda, salt, cinnamon, and nutmeg.
3. In a separate bowl, mix together the brown sugar, applesauce, non-dairy milk, and vanilla extract.
4. Add the wet ingredients to the dry ingredients and mix until just combined.
5. Fold in the chopped pecans or walnuts and dried cranberries or raisins if desired.
6. Spoon the batter into the prepared muffin tin, filling each cup about 2/3 full.
7. Bake for 20-25 minutes, or until a toothpick inserted into the center of a muffin comes out clean.
8. Remove from the oven and let cool in the tin for 5 minutes before transferring

Nutritional Value: Calories: 344 Protein: 13g Fat: 21g Carbohydrates: 44g Fiber: 3g Sugar: 6g

26. Crispy Tofu Breakfast Scramble

Cooking Time: 20 minutes **Prep. Time:** 10 minutes **Servings:** 2

- **Ingredients:**
- 1 block of firm tofu, pressed and cubed
- 2 tablespoons cornstarch
- 1/4 teaspoon salt
- 1/4 teaspoon black pepper
- 1/4 cup vegetable oil
- 1/4 cup diced onion
- 1/4 cup diced bell peppers (red, yellow, green)
- 1/4 cup sliced mushrooms

- 1/4 cup diced tomatoes
- 1 tablespoon soy sauce
- 1 teaspoon nutritional yeast (optional)
- Optional: chopped fresh cilantro, avocado, or any other toppings of your choice

Instructions:
1. In a shallow dish, whisk together the cornstarch, salt, and pepper.
2. Add the cubed tofu to the dish and toss until evenly coated in the cornstarch mixture.
3. Heat the vegetable oil in a large skillet over medium-high heat.
4. Add the tofu cubes to the skillet and cook for about 2-3 minutes per side, or until they are crispy and golden brown.
5. Remove the tofu from the skillet and set it aside.
6. In the same skillet, add diced onion, bell peppers, mushrooms and sauté for 2-3 minutes or until they are slightly softened.
7. Add diced tomatoes, soy sauce, nutritional yeast (if using) and sauté for an additional 1-2 minutes.
8. Add the cooked tofu back to the skillet and toss gently to combine.
9. Serve in plates and add toppings of your choice such as chopped fresh cilantro, avocado, or salsa.

Nutritional Value: Calories: 250 Protein: 12g Fat: 20g Carbohydrates: 11g Fiber: 4g Sugar: 4g

27. Breakfast Polenta With Roasted Vegetables

Cooking Time: 40 minutes **Prep. Time:** 20 minutes **Servings:** 4

Ingredients:
- 1 cup coarse cornmeal
- 4 cups water
- Salt and pepper, to taste
- 1 tbsp olive oil
- 1 small onion, diced
- 2 cloves of garlic, minced
- 1 red bell pepper, diced
- 1 small eggplant, diced
- 1/2 cup sliced mushrooms
- 1 tsp dried thyme
- 1/4 cup grated Parmesan cheese (optional)
- Optional: diced tomatoes, avocado, cilantro, cheese, etc.

Instructions:
1. Preheat the oven to 375F (190C).
2. In a large pot, bring the water to a boil. Slowly add the cornmeal while whisking constantly.
3. Reduce the heat to low and simmer for 20-25 minutes, or until the polenta is thick and creamy.
4. Season with salt and pepper to taste.
5. Spread the polenta into a greased 9x13 inch baking dish and set aside.
6. In a separate baking sheet, toss the onion, garlic, red bell pepper, eggplant, mushrooms, thyme, salt, pepper and olive oil.
7. Roast for about 20-25 minutes or until vegetables are tender

Nutritional Value: Calories: 299 Protein: 16g Fat: 19g Carbohydrates: 35g Fiber: 8g Sugar: 2g

28. Vegan Breakfast Enchiladas

Cooking Time: 30 minutes **Prep. Time:** 20 minutes **Servings:** 4

Ingredients:
- 8 corn tortillas
- 1 cup diced sweet potatoes
- 1 cup diced bell peppers (red, yellow, green)
- 1 cup diced onions
- 1 can of black beans, drained and rinsed
- 1 cup of your favorite enchilada sauce

- 1/4 cup diced fresh cilantro
- 1/4 cup diced fresh parsley
- 1/4 cup diced fresh jalapeño
- 1/4 cup diced fresh tomatoes
- Salt and pepper, to taste
- 1 tablespoon olive oil
- Optional: vegan cheese, diced avocado, or any other toppings of your choice

Instructions:
1. Preheat the oven to 375°F (190°C).
2. Heat a skillet over medium heat and add olive oil.
3. Add diced sweet potatoes, bell peppers, and onions to the skillet and sauté for 8-10 minutes, or until they are slightly softened.
4. Add black beans, salt, and pepper, cook for an additional 2-3 minutes.
5. Remove the skillet from the heat, and add cilantro, parsley, jalapeño, and tomatoes to the skillet and stir until well combined.
6. Spread a thin layer of enchilada sauce on the bottom of a baking dish.
7. Place a tortilla on a plate and add 2-3 tablespoons of the sweet potato and black bean mixture to the center and serve. Enjoy

Nutritional Value: Calories: 324 Protein: 16g Fat: 19g Carbohydrates: 34g Fiber: 8g Sugar: 1g

29. Vegan Banana Pancakes

Cooking Time: 10 minutes **Prep. Time:** 10 minutes **Servings:** 4
Ingredients:
- 1 cup all-purpose flour
- 1 tbsp sugar
- 2 tsp baking powder
- 1/4 tsp salt
- 1 cup unsweetened non-dairy milk
- 1 ripe banana, mashed
- 1 tbsp vegetable oil
- 1 tsp vanilla extract

Instructions:
1. In a large mixing bowl, whisk together the flour, sugar, baking powder, and salt.
2. In a separate bowl, mix together the non-dairy milk, mashed banana, vegetable oil, and vanilla extract.
3. Add the wet ingredients to the dry ingredients and stir until just combined.
4. Heat a non-stick skillet over medium heat.
5. Using a 1/4 cup measuring cup, scoop the batter onto the skillet.
6. Cook for 2-3 minutes per side, or until the pancakes are golden brown and cooked through.
7. Serve with your favourite toppings such as syrup, fruit, or nut butter.

Nutritional Value per Serving: Calories: 200 Protein: 3g Fat: 7g Carbohydrates: 32g Fiber: 1g

30. Vegan Breakfast Sausage Patties

Cooking Time: 20 minutes **Prep. Time:** 10 minutes **Servings:** 4
Ingredients:
- 1 cup cooked and crumbled tempeh
- 1/4 cup diced onions
- 1/4 cup diced mushrooms
- 1/4 cup diced bell peppers (red, yellow, green)
- 1/4 cup breadcrumbs
- 1 tablespoon soy sauce
- 1 teaspoon smoked paprika
- 1 teaspoon dried thyme
- 1/4 teaspoon black pepper
- 1 tablespoon olive oil for frying

Instructions:
1. In a mixing bowl, combine the crumbled tempeh, diced onions, mushrooms, bell peppers, breadcrumbs, soy sauce, smoked paprika, dried thyme, and pepper.
2. Mix well until the ingredients are well combined.

3. Shape the mixture into 4 patties, about 1/2 inch thick.
4. Heat the olive oil in a large skillet over medium-high heat.
5. Add the patties to the skillet and cook for 4-5 minutes per side, or until they are golden brown and crispy.
6. Remove from heat and let them cool for a few minutes before serving.

Nutritional Value: Calories: 140 Protein: 10g Fat: 7g Carbohydrates: 12g Fiber: 3g Sugar: 2g

31. Vegan Breakfast Strata

Cooking Time: 45 minutes **Prep. Time:** 15 minutes **Servings:** 6

Ingredients:
- 8 oz firm tofu, pressed and crumbled
- 1 tbsp olive oil
- 1 small onion, diced
- 2 cloves of garlic, minced
- 1 red bell pepper, diced
- 1/2 cup sliced mushrooms
- 1/2 cup diced tomatoes
- 1 tsp dried oregano
- 1 tsp smoked paprika
- Salt and pepper, to taste
- 6 cups torn whole wheat bread
- 2 cups unsweetened non-dairy milk
- 2 tbsp nutritional yeast
- 1 tbsp Dijon mustard
- 1 tbsp tahini
- Optional: diced avocado, fresh herbs, hot sauce

Instructions:
1. Preheat the oven to 375F (190C).
2. In a skillet, heat the olive oil over medium heat. Add the onion, garlic, red bell pepper, mushrooms, diced tomatoes, oregano, smoked paprika, salt, and pepper. Cook for about 8-10 minutes or until the vegetables are softened.
3. In a large mixing bowl, combine the bread, non-dairy milk, nutritional yeast, Dijon mustard, and tahini. Stir well.
4. Add the crumbled tofu, and vegetables to the bread mixture, stir well.
5. Pour the mixture into a greased 9x13 inch baking dish.
6. Bake for 45 minutes, or until the top is golden brown and the casserole is cooked through.
7. Remove from the oven and let cool for a few minutes before slicing and serving.
8. If desired, you can add diced avocado, fresh herbs, or hot sauce to the top before serving.

Nutritional Value: Calories: 300 Protein: 12g Fat: 12g Carbohydrates: 32g Fiber: 3g

32. Vegan Breakfast Tacos With Tofu Scramble

Cooking Time: 20 minutes **Prep. Time:** 10 minutes **Servings:** 4

Ingredients:
- 1 block of firm tofu, drained and crumbled
- 1 tbsp olive oil
- 1/2 small onion, diced
- 1/2 red bell pepper, diced
- 1/2 tsp ground cumin
- 1/4 tsp turmeric
- Salt and pepper, to taste
- 8 corn tortillas
- Salsa, avocado, fresh cilantro, or any other toppings of your choice

Instructions:
1. Heat the olive oil in a large skillet over medium heat. Add the onion and red bell pepper and sauté for about 5 minutes or until softened.
2. Crumble the tofu into the skillet and add the cumin, turmeric, salt, and pepper.

Cook for an additional 5-7 minutes or until the tofu is heated through.
3. While the tofu scramble is cooking, warm the tortillas in the oven or on a skillet.
4. Once everything is ready, assemble the tacos by placing some of the tofu scramble in each tortilla and adding your desired toppings such as salsa, avocado, cilantro, or any other you like.
5. Serve immediately and enjoy!

Nutritional Value: Calories: 200 Protein: 12g Fat: 10g Carbohydrates: 17g Fiber: 3g

33. Vegan Breakfast Burrito Bowl

Cooking Time: 15 minutes **Prep. Time**: 10 minutes **Servings**: 2

Ingredients:
- 1 cup cooked brown rice
- 1 cup diced tomatoes
- 1 cup diced bell peppers (red, yellow, green)
- 1 cup diced onions
- 1 cup diced avocado
- 1 can of black beans, drained and rinsed
- 1/4 cup diced fresh cilantro
- 1/4 cup diced fresh parsley
- 1/4 cup diced fresh jalapeño
- 1/4 cup diced fresh tomatoes
- Salt and pepper, to taste
- 1 tablespoon olive oil
- Optional: vegan sour cream, vegan cheese, or any other toppings of your choice

Instructions:
1. Heat a skillet over medium heat and add olive oil.
2. Add diced bell peppers, onions, and sauté for 2-3 minutes or until they are slightly softened.
3. Add diced tomatoes, black beans, salt, and pepper and sauté for an additional 1-2 minutes.
4. Remove the skillet from the heat, and add cilantro, parsley, jalapeño, and diced tomatoes to the skillet and stir until well combined.
5. In a serving bowl, add cooked brown rice and top it with the skillet mixture.
6. Add diced avocado and any desired toppings such as vegan sour cream, vegan cheese, or salsa.
7. Stir everything together and serve.

Nutritional Value: Calories: 449 Protein: 14g Fat: 18g Carbohydrates: 63g

34. Vegan Breakfast Smoothie Bowl

Prep. Time: 5 minutes **Servings**: 1

Ingredients:
- 1 banana, frozen
- 1/2 cup frozen berries (strawberries, blueberries, raspberries, etc.)
- 1/2 cup unsweetened non-dairy milk
- 1/4 cup rolled oats
- 1 tbsp chia seeds
- 1 tsp honey or maple syrup (optional)
- Toppings: fresh fruit, granola, nuts, seeds, coconut flakes, etc.

Instructions:
1. In a blender, combine the banana, frozen berries, non-dairy milk, rolled oats, chia seeds, and honey or maple syrup (if using).
2. Blend until smooth and creamy.
3. Pour the smoothie into a bowl.
4. Add your desired toppings such as fresh fruit, granola, nuts, seeds, coconut flakes, etc.
5. Serve and enjoy immediately.

Nutritional Value: Calories: 300 -Protein: 8g Fat: 8g Carbohydrates: 50g Fiber: 8g

35. Vegan Breakfast Quinoa Bowl

Cooking Time: 20 minutes **Prep. Time**: 10 minutes **Servings**: 2

Ingredients:
- 1 cup cooked quinoa
- 1 cup diced tomatoes
- 1 cup diced bell peppers (red, yellow, green)
- 1 cup diced onions
- 1 cup diced avocado
- 1 can of black beans, drained and rinsed
- 1/4 cup diced fresh cilantro
- 1/4 cup diced fresh parsley
- 1/4 cup diced fresh jalapeño
- 1/4 cup diced fresh tomatoes
- Salt and pepper, to taste
- 1 tablespoon olive oil
- Optional: vegan sour cream, vegan cheese, or any other toppings of your choice

Instructions:
1. Heat a skillet over medium heat and add olive oil.
2. Add diced bell peppers, onions, and sauté for 2-3 minutes or until they are slightly softened.
3. Add diced tomatoes, black beans, salt, and pepper and sauté for an additional 1-2 minutes.
4. Remove the skillet from the heat, and add cilantro, parsley, jalapeño, and diced tomatoes to the skillet and stir until well combined.
5. In a serving bowl, add cooked quinoa and top it with the skillet mixture.
6. Add diced avocado and any desired toppings such as vegan sour cream, vegan cheese, or salsa.
7. Stir everything together and serve.

Nutritional Value: Calories: 449 Protein: 14g Fat: 18g Carbohydrates: 63g Fiber: 15g Sugar: 7g

36. Vegan Breakfast Parfait

Prep. Time: 10 minutes **Servings:** 1

Ingredients:
- 1/2 cup vegan yogurt
- 1/2 cup fresh berries (strawberries, blueberries, raspberries, etc.)
- 1/4 cup granola
- 1 tbsp chia seeds
- 1 tsp honey or maple syrup (optional)

Instructions:
1. In a parfait glass or bowl, add a layer of vegan yogurt.
2. Add a layer of fresh berries on top of the yogurt.
3. Sprinkle a layer of granola over the berries.
4. Repeat the layers until you reach the top of the glass or bowl.
5. Sprinkle chia seeds and drizzle honey or maple syrup (if using) on top.
6. Serve and enjoy immediately.

Nutritional Value: Calories: 250 Protein: 8g Fat: 8g Carbohydrates: 37g Fiber: 7g

37. Vegan Breakfast Risotto

Cooking Time: 30 minutes **Prep. Time:** 10 minutes **Servings:** 4

Ingredients:
- 1 cup Arborio rice
- 2 cups vegetable broth
- 1 cup diced bell peppers (red, yellow, green)
- 1 cup diced onions
- 1 cup diced mushrooms
- 1/4 cup nutritional yeast
- 2 cloves of garlic, minced
- 2 tablespoons olive oil
- Salt and pepper, to taste
- Optional: diced tomatoes, avocado, or any other toppings of your choice

Instructions:
1. In a large skillet, heat the olive oil over medium heat.

2. Add the diced bell peppers, onions, and mushrooms, and sauté for 2-3 minutes or until they are slightly softened.
3. Stir in the minced garlic and sauté for an additional 1-2 minutes.
4. Add the Arborio rice to the skillet and stir to coat the rice in the oil.
5. Slowly pour in the vegetable broth, one ladleful at a time, stirring constantly.
6. Allow the liquid to be absorbed before adding more.
7. Continue stirring and adding broth until the risotto is creamy and the rice is cooked through, about 20 minutes.
8. Stir in the nutritional yeast, salt, and pepper to taste.
9. Serve in plates and add toppings of your choice such as diced tomatoes, avocado or any other toppings you like.

Nutritional Value: Calories: 288 Protein: 10g Fat: 9g Carbohydrates: 41g Fiber: 12g Sugar: 2g

38. Vegan Breakfast Waffles

Cooking Time: 10 minutes **Prep. Time:** 10 minutes **Servings:** 4
Ingredients:
- 1 cup all-purpose flour
- 1 tsp baking powder
- 1/4 tsp salt
- 1/4 tsp ground cinnamon
- 1 cup unsweetened non-dairy milk
- 1/4 cup unsweetened applesauce
- 1 tbsp vegetable oil
- 1 tsp vanilla extract
- Vegan butter or oil for the waffle iron

Instructions:
1. In a large mixing bowl, whisk together the flour, baking powder, salt, and cinnamon.
2. In a separate bowl, mix together the non-dairy milk, applesauce, vegetable oil, and vanilla extract.
3. Add the wet ingredients to the dry ingredients and stir until just combined.
4. Preheat your waffle iron and grease it with vegan butter or oil.
5. Pour the batter into the waffle iron, following the manufacturer's **Instructions:** for your waffle iron.
6. Cook the waffles until golden brown, about 3-5 minutes.
7. Serve with your favorite toppings such as syrup, fresh fruit, or powdered sugar.

Nutritional Value Calories: 200 Protein: 4g Fat: 8g Carbohydrates: 28g Fiber: 1g

39. Vegan Breakfast Pastry

Cooking Time: 25-30 minutes **Prep. Time:** 15 minutes **Servings:** 8
Ingredients:
- 2 cups all-purpose flour
- 1 tablespoon sugar
- 1 teaspoon salt
- 1/2 cup cold vegan butter
- 1/4 cup ice water
- 1 cup diced veggies (bell peppers, onions, mushrooms, etc.)
- 1/4 cup diced vegan cheese (optional)
- 1/4 cup diced fresh herbs (parsley, cilantro, etc.)
- Salt and pepper, to taste
- 1 tablespoon olive oil

Instructions:
1. In a large mixing bowl, combine the flour, sugar, and salt.
2. Cut the cold vegan butter into small cubes and add it to the bowl.
3. Using a pastry cutter or your fingers, cut the butter into the flour mixture until it resembles coarse crumbs.

4. Slowly add the ice water, 1 tablespoon at a time, and mix until a dough forms.
5. Knead the dough for a minute or two, then wrap it in plastic wrap and refrigerate for at least 30 minutes.
6. In a skillet, heat the olive oil over medium heat.
7. Add the diced veggies and sauté for 2-3 minutes or until they are slightly softened.
8. Stir in the diced vegan cheese, fresh herbs, salt and pepper to taste.
9. Serve.

Nutritional Value: Calories: 322 Protein: 18g Fat: 28g Carbohydrates: 36g Fiber: 12g Sugar: 9g

40. Vegan Breakfast Sandwich With Tempeh Bacon

Cooking Time: 15 minutes **Prep. Time:** 10 minutes **Servings:** 1
Ingredients:
- 2 slices of whole wheat bread
- 2 tbsp vegan mayonnaise
- 2 tbsp vegan cheese
- 2 slices of tomato
- 2 leaves of lettuce
- 4 slices of tempeh bacon
- 1 tbsp oil
- Salt and pepper to taste

Instructions:
1. Preheat a skillet on medium heat and add 1 tbsp oil.
2. Add the tempeh bacon slices, salt and pepper and cook for about 3-5 minutes on each side or until crispy.
3. Toast the bread slices.
4. Spread the vegan mayonnaise on one of the slices of toast.
5. Place the cheese, tomato, lettuce and tempeh bacon on the toast.
6. Place the second slice of toast on top.

7. Serve and enjoy.

Nutritional Value: Calories: 450 Protein: 20g Fat: 25g Carbohydrates: 40g Fiber: 5g

41. Vegan Breakfast Oatmeal Bake

Cooking Time: 30-35 minutes **Prep. Time:** 15 minutes **Servings:** 4
Ingredients:
- 2 cups rolled oats
- 2 cups unsweetened almond milk
- 1/2 cup maple syrup
- 1/4 cup diced apples
- 1/4 cup raisins
- 1/4 cup chopped pecans
- 1 teaspoon vanilla extract
- 1 teaspoon ground cinnamon
- 1/4 teaspoon salt
- Optional toppings: fresh berries, sliced banana, shredded coconut

Instructions:
1. Preheat the oven to 350°F (175°C).
2. In a large mixing bowl, combine the rolled oats, almond milk, maple syrup, diced apples, raisins, chopped pecans, vanilla extract, ground cinnamon, and salt.
3. Stir until well combined.
4. Pour the oatmeal mixture into a greased 8x8 inch baking dish.
5. Bake for 30-35 minutes, or until the top is golden brown and the oatmeal is cooked through.
6. Let it cool for a few minutes before serving.
7. Serve the oatmeal bake with fresh berries, sliced banana, shredded coconut or any toppings of your choice.

Nutritional Value: Calories: 361 Protein: 7g Fat: 14g Carbohydrates: 56g Fiber: 6g Sugar: 25g

42. Vegan Breakfast Chia Pudding

Prep. Time: 5 minutes + overnight refrigeration
Servings: 2
Ingredients:
- 1/2 cup chia seeds
- 1 1/2 cups unsweetened non-dairy milk
- 1/4 cup maple syrup or sweetener of your choice
- 1 tsp vanilla extract
- Fresh fruit, nuts, and seeds for topping

Instructions:
1. In a medium-sized mixing bowl, combine the chia seeds, non-dairy milk, maple syrup or sweetener, and vanilla extract.
2. Whisk the mixture until well combined.
3. Cover the bowl with plastic wrap and refrigerate overnight or for at least 4 hours.
4. The next day, give the pudding a good stir to break up any clumps that may have formed.
5. Divide the chia pudding into two bowls.
6. Top with your desired toppings such as fresh fruit, nuts, and seeds.
7. Serve and enjoy.

Nutritional Value: Calories: 300 Protein: 7g Fat: 17g Carbohydrates: 35g Fiber: 10g

43. Vegan Breakfast Bagel

Cooking Time: 15-20 minutes **Prep. Time:** 10 minutes **Servings:** 4
Ingredients:
- 4 vegan bagels
- 1/4 cup vegan cream cheese
- 1/4 cup diced tomatoes
- 1/4 cup diced avocado
- 1/4 cup sliced mushrooms
- 1/4 cup fresh baby spinach
- Salt and pepper, to taste
- Optional: vegan bacon or sausage

Instructions:
1. Preheat the oven to 350°F (175°C).
2. Cut the bagels in half and place them cut side up on a baking sheet.
3. Spread vegan cream cheese on the inside of each bagel half.
4. Add diced tomatoes, avocado, sliced mushrooms, and fresh baby spinach on top of the cream cheese.
5. Sprinkle with salt and pepper to taste.
6. Optional: Add vegan bacon or sausage if desired.
7. Bake in the preheated oven for 15-20 minutes, or until the bagels are crispy and the veggies are slightly softened.
8. Remove from the oven and let cool for a few minutes before serving.

Nutritional Value: Calories: 250 Protein: 7g Fat: 15g Carbohydrates: 24g Fiber: 4g Sugar: 2g

44. Vegan Breakfast Tofu Scramble Tacos

Cooking Time: 20 minutes **Prep. Time:** 10 minutes **Servings:** 4
Ingredients:
- 1 block of firm tofu, drained and crumbled
- 1 tbsp olive oil
- 1/2 small onion, diced
- 1/2 red bell pepper, diced
- 1/2 tsp ground cumin
- 1/4 tsp turmeric
- Salt and pepper, to taste
- 8 corn tortillas
- Salsa, avocado, fresh cilantro, or any other toppings of your choice

Instructions:
1. Heat the olive oil in a large skillet over medium heat. Add the onion and red bell pepper and sauté for about 5 minutes or until softened.
2. Crumble the tofu into the skillet and add the cumin, turmeric, salt, and pepper.

Cook for an additional 5-7 minutes or until the tofu is heated through.
3. While the tofu scramble is cooking, warm the tortillas in the oven or on a skillet.
4. Once everything is ready, assemble the tacos by placing some of the tofu scramble in each tortilla and adding your desired toppings such as salsa, avocado, cilantro, or any other you like.
5. Serve immediately and enjoy!

Nutritional Value per Serving: -Calories: 200 -Protein: 12g -Fat: 10g -Carbohydrates: 17g -Fiber: 3g

45. Vegan Breakfast Muffins With Zucchini And Carrot

Cooking Time: 25-30 minutes **Prep. Time:** 15 minutes **Servings:** 12
Ingredients:
- 1 and 1/2 cups all-purpose flour
- 1 teaspoon baking powder
- 1 teaspoon baking soda
- 1 teaspoon ground cinnamon
- 1/4 teaspoon salt
- 1 cup grated zucchini
- 1 cup grated carrots
- 3/4 cup unsweetened almond milk
- 1/2 cup maple syrup
- 1/4 cup coconut oil, melted
- 2 tablespoons ground flaxseed mixed with 6 tablespoons of water
- 1 teaspoon vanilla extract
- Optional toppings: chopped nuts, dried fruit, shredded coconut

Instructions:
1. Preheat the oven to 350°F (175°C) and line a muffin tin with paper liners.
2. In a large mixing bowl, combine the flour, baking powder, baking soda, ground cinnamon, and salt.
3. In another mixing bowl, combine the grated zucchini, grated carrots, almond milk, maple syrup, melted coconut oil, flaxseed mixture, and vanilla extract.
4. Add the wet ingredients to the dry ingredients and stir until just combined.
5. Fold in any desired toppings such as chopped nuts, dried fruit, or shredded coconut.
6. Fill the muffin cups 2/3 of the way full with the batter.
7. Bake for 25-30 minutes, or until a toothpick inserted into the center of a muffin comes out clean.
8. Remove from the oven and let cool for a few minutes before serving.

Nutritional Value: Calories: 150 Protein: 2g Fat: 6g Carbohydrates: 22g Fiber: 2g Sugar: 12g

46. Vegan Eggless French Toast

Cooking Time: 10 minutes **Prep. Time:** 10 minutes **Servings:** 2
Ingredients:
- 4 slices of whole wheat bread
- 1/2 cup unsweetened non-dairy milk
- 1 tbsp flour
- 1 tsp sugar
- 1 tsp vanilla extract
- 1/4 tsp ground cinnamon
- Vegan butter or oil for the skillet
- Maple syrup or powdered sugar for topping

Instructions:
1. In a shallow dish, mix together the non-dairy milk, flour, sugar, vanilla extract, and cinnamon.
2. Dip each slice of bread into the mixture, making sure both sides are well coated.
3. Heat a skillet over medium heat and add a small amount of vegan butter or oil.

4. Place the bread slices in the skillet and cook for 2-3 minutes on each side or until golden brown.
5. Serve with maple syrup or powdered sugar on top and enjoy!

Nutritional Value per Serving: -Calories: 250 -Protein: 6g -Fat: 8g -Carbohydrates: 37g -Fiber: 4g

47. Vegan Breakfast Omelets

Cooking Time: 10 minutes **Prep. Time:** 5 minutes **Servings:** 2

Ingredients:
- 1 cup firm tofu, crumbled
- 2 tablespoons nutritional yeast
- 1 teaspoon turmeric powder
- 1/4 teaspoon black salt (kala namak)
- 1/4 teaspoon garlic powder
- 1/4 teaspoon onion powder
- 2 tablespoons vegetable oil
- Optional fillings: diced vegetables, diced vegan cheese, diced vegan sausage or bacon

Instructions:
1. In a mixing bowl, combine crumbled tofu, nutritional yeast, turmeric powder, black salt, garlic powder and onion powder.
2. Mix well until the ingredients are well combined.
3. Heat a skillet over medium heat and add vegetable oil.
4. Add the tofu mixture to the skillet and spread it out evenly.
5. Add any desired fillings such as diced vegetables, diced vegan cheese, diced vegan sausage or bacon on top of the tofu mixture.
6. Cook for about 3-4 minutes, until the bottom is golden brown.
7. Carefully flip the omelets and cook for an additional 3-4 minutes, or until the other side is golden brown.
8. Remove from the heat and let it cool for a few minutes before serving.

Nutritional Value: Calories: 208 Protein: 11g Fat: 15g Carbohydrates: 9g Fiber: 2g Sugar: 2g

48. Vegan Breakfast Tofu Scramble With Turmeric

Cooking Time: 15 minutes **Prep. Time:** 5 minutes **Servings:** 2

Ingredients:
- 1 block of firm tofu, drained and crumbled
- 1 tbsp olive oil
- 1/2 small onion, diced
- 1/2 red bell pepper, diced
- 1/2 tsp ground cumin
- 1 tsp turmeric
- Salt and pepper, to taste
- Fresh herbs, such as parsley or cilantro, for garnish (optional)

Instructions:
1. In a skillet, heat the olive oil over medium heat.
2. Add the onion and red bell pepper, sauté for about 3-5 minutes or until softened.
3. Crumble the tofu into the skillet, add the cumin, turmeric, salt, and pepper.
4. Cook for an additional 5-7 minutes or until the tofu is heated through.
5. Garnish with fresh herbs, if desired and serve.

Nutritional Value: Calories: 200 Protein: 12g Fat: 12g Carbohydrates: 10g Fiber: 3g

49. Vegan Breakfast Hashbrowns

Cooking Time: 10 minutes **Prep. Time:** 5 minutes **Servings:** 2

Ingredients:

- 1 large russet potato, peeled and grated
- 1 small onion, finely diced
- 1 bell pepper, finely diced
- 1 tablespoon vegetable oil
- Salt and pepper, to taste
- Optional: diced vegan sausage or mushrooms

Instructions:
1. Heat the vegetable oil in a large skillet over medium heat.
2. Add the grated potato, onion, and bell pepper to the skillet. Season with salt and pepper.
3. Cook, stirring occasionally, for 10-15 minutes or until the potatoes are golden brown and crispy.
4. If desired, add diced vegan sausage or mushrooms and cook for an additional 5 minutes or until they are heated through.
5. Serve and enjoy!

Nutritional Value: Calories: 212 Protein: 12g Fat: 8g Carbohydrates: 29g Fiber: 9g Sugar: 1g

50. Vegan Breakfast Hashbrowns

Cooking Time: 10 minutes **Prep. Time:** 10 minutes **Servings:** 3

Ingredients:
- 2 cups grated potatoes
- 1/4 cup diced onion
- 1/4 cup diced bell pepper
- 1/4 cup diced mushrooms
- 1 tablespoon vegan butter or oil
- Salt and pepper, to taste

Optional: diced vegan sausage or diced firm tofu

Instructions:
1. Grate the potatoes and squeeze out any excess moisture.
2. In a pan, melt the vegan butter or heat the oil over medium heat.
3. Add the diced onion, bell pepper, and mushrooms, and sauté for a few minutes until they are softened.
4. Add the grated potatoes to the pan and stir to combine.
5. Press the mixture down into the pan with a spatula to create a flat surface.
6. Cook the hashbrowns for about 5 minutes, or until the bottom is golden brown.
7. Flip the hashbrowns and cook for an additional 5 minutes, or until the other side is golden brown.
8. Optional: add diced vegan sausage or firm tofu during step 3 or 4.
9. Season with salt and pepper to taste.
10. Serve hot and enjoy!

Nutritional Value: Calories: 344 Protein: 18g Fat: 13g Carbohydrates: 30g Fiber: 9g Sugar: 1g

Lunch

51. Grilled Vegetable Wrap

Cooking Time: 10 minutes **Prep. Time:** 5 minutes **Servings:** 2
Ingredients:
- 4 large flour tortillas
- 2 bell peppers, sliced
- 1 zucchini, sliced
- 1 red onion, sliced
- 1 cup sliced mushrooms
- 1 tbsp olive oil
- Salt and pepper, to taste
- 1 cup shredded cheese (cheddar or Monterey Jack)
- 1/4 cup chopped fresh herbs (basil, cilantro, parsley)

Instructions:
1. Preheat grill to medium-high heat.
2. In a large bowl, toss together the bell peppers, zucchini, onion, mushrooms, olive oil, salt, and pepper.
3. Grill vegetables for about 8-10 minutes, or until tender and slightly charred.
4. Lay the tortillas out on a work surface. Divide the cheese and vegetables among the tortillas, placing them in the center of each.
5. Sprinkle with herbs on top of the vegetables and cheese.
6. Fold the sides of the tortilla into the center, then roll up the tortilla to create a wrap.
7. Grill the wraps for 2-3 minutes on each side, or until the tortilla is golden brown and crispy.
8. Remove from grill and let cool for a couple of minutes.
9. Cut in half and serve warm.

Nutritional Value: Calories: 235 Protein: 18g Fat: 8g Carbohydrates: 35g Fiber: 4g Sugar: 2g

52. Black Bean And Sweet Potato Tacos

Cooking Time: 10 minutes **Prep. Time:** 20 minutes **Servings:** 4
Ingredients:
- 1 tablespoon olive oil
- 1 medium sweet potato, peeled and diced
- 1/2 teaspoon ground cumin
- Salt and pepper
- 1 can black beans, rinsed and drained
- 1/4 cup salsa
- 1/4 cup sour cream
- 8 corn tortillas
- 1/4 cup chopped fresh cilantro
- Lime wedges, for serving

Instructions:
1. Heat the olive oil in a large skillet over medium heat. Add the sweet potato and cumin and season with salt and pepper. Cook, stirring occasionally, until the sweet potato is tender, about 10 minutes.
2. Stir in the black beans and salsa and cook until heated through, about 2 minutes.
3. Meanwhile, warm the tortillas in the oven or on a gas stove, using tongs to hold them directly over the flame.
4. Serve the sweet potato and black bean mixture on the tortillas. Top with sour cream, cilantro, and lime wedges on the side. Enjoy!

Nutritional Value: Calories: 299 Protein: 12g Fat: 7g Carbohydrates: 38g Fiber: 4g Sugar: 4g

53. Spinach And Feta Stuffed Portobello Mushrooms

Cooking Time: 25 minutes **Prep. Time:** 15 minutes **Servings:** 4
Ingredients:
- 4 large portobello mushroom caps
- 1 tbsp olive oil
- 1 shallot, minced

- 2 cloves of garlic, minced
- 2 cups spinach leaves, chopped
- 1/2 cup crumbled feta cheese
- 1/4 cup breadcrumbs
- Salt and pepper, to taste

Instructions:
1. Preheat oven to 400 degrees F (200 degrees C).
2. Remove the stems from the mushrooms and scrape out the gills with a spoon.
3. Brush the mushroom caps with olive oil and season with salt and pepper.
4. In a pan, sauté shallot and garlic in olive oil until soft, about 3-5 minutes.
5. Add spinach leaves and cook until wilted.
6. Remove from heat and stir in feta cheese, breadcrumbs and season with salt and pepper.
7. Stuff the mixture into the mushroom caps and place them on a baking sheet.
8. Bake for 20-25 minutes, or until the mushrooms are tender and the filling is golden brown.
9. Remove from oven and let it cool for a couple of minutes.
10. Serve warm

Nutritional Value: Calories: 150 Fat: 12g Saturated Fat: 4g Cholesterol: 20mg Sodium: 380mg Carbohydrates: 7g Fiber: 2g Sugar: 2g Protein: 6g

54. Quinoa And Black Bean Salad

Cooking Time: 10 minutes **Prep. Time:** 20 minutes **Servings:** 4

Ingredients:
- 1 cup quinoa
- 2 cups water
- 1 teaspoon olive oil
- 1 teaspoon cumin
- 1/4 teaspoon salt
- 1 can black beans, rinsed and drained
- 1 red bell pepper, diced
- 1/2 red onion, diced
- 1/4 cup cilantro, chopped
- 1 lime, juiced
- 1/4 cup olive oil
- Salt and pepper to taste

Instructions:
1. Rinse the quinoa in a fine mesh strainer under running water for about 2 minutes.
2. In a medium saucepan, bring the quinoa, water, olive oil, cumin, and salt to a boil. Reduce heat to low, cover, and simmer for 15 minutes.
3. Remove the saucepan from the heat and let it sit, covered, for 5 minutes.
4. Fluff the quinoa with a fork and transfer it to a large bowl. Let it cool to room temperature.
5. Once the quinoa is cooled, add black beans, red bell pepper, red onion, cilantro, lime juice, olive oil and salt and pepper to taste. Toss to combine.
6. Serve chilled or at room temperature.

Nutritional Value: Calories: 300 Total Fat: 12g Carbohydrates: 40g Dietary Fiber: 7g Protein: 10g

55. Avocado And Tomato Toast

Cooking Time: 10 minutes **Prep. Time:** 5 minutes **Servings:** 2

Ingredients:
- 2 slices of bread (whole wheat, sourdough or any bread you prefer)
- 1 ripe avocado
- 1 medium tomato, diced
- Salt and pepper, to taste
- 1 tbsp olive oil
- 1 tbsp lemon juice
- Fresh herbs (basil, parsley or cilantro)

Instructions:
1. Preheat your oven or toaster to 200C/180C fan/gas 6.

2. Toast the bread until golden brown.
3. In a bowl, mash the avocado with a fork and mix in lemon juice, salt and pepper.
4. Spread the avocado mixture over the toast.
5. Top with diced tomatoes.
6. Drizzle olive oil over the tomatoes.
7. Sprinkle with fresh herbs.
8. Serve and enjoy.

Nutritional Value: Calories: 260 Fat: 18g Saturated Fat: 3g Cholesterol: 0mg Sodium: 200mg

Carbohydrates: 24g Fiber: 7g Sugar: 2g Protein: 5g

56. Lentil And Vegetable Curry

Cooking Time: 30 minutes **Prep. Time:** 15 minutes **Servings:** 4

Ingredients:
- 1 tablespoon vegetable oil
- 1 onion, diced
- 2 cloves garlic, minced
- 1 tablespoon grated ginger
- 1 tablespoon curry powder
- 1 teaspoon ground cumin
- 1 teaspoon ground turmeric
- Salt and pepper
- 1 cup red lentils, rinsed
- 2 cups vegetable broth
- 1 can diced tomatoes
- 1 cup frozen peas
- 1 cup diced carrots
- 1 cup diced potatoes
- 1/4 cup chopped fresh cilantro
- Lime wedges, for serving

Instructions:
1. Heat the oil in a large pot over medium heat. Add the onion, garlic, and ginger and cook until softened, about 5 minutes.
2. Stir in the curry powder, cumin, turmeric, and a pinch each of salt and pepper. Cook until fragrant, about 1 minute.
3. Add the lentils, broth, tomatoes, peas, carrots, and potatoes to the pot. Bring to a simmer, reduce heat and cover, and cook until the lentils are tender and the vegetables are cooked through, about 20 minutes.
4. Stir in the cilantro, and season with salt and pepper to taste.
5. Serve the curry over rice, and garnish with lime wedges on the side.

Nutritional Value: Calories: 187 Total Fat: 7g Carbohydrates: 37g Dietary Fiber: 8g Protein: 9g

57. Chickpea And Spinach Stew

Cooking Time: 30 minutes **Prep. Time:** 10 minutes **Servings:** 4

Ingredients:
- 1 tbsp olive oil
- 1 onion, diced
- 2 cloves of garlic, minced
- 1 tbsp ground cumin
- 1 tsp ground turmeric
- 1 tsp smoked paprika
- 1 can of chickpeas, drained and rinsed
- 1 cup vegetable broth
- 1 can diced tomatoes
- 2 cups fresh spinach leaves
- Salt and pepper, to taste
- Lemon juice, to taste
- Fresh herbs (basil, parsley or cilantro)

Instructions:
1. In a large pot or Dutch oven, heat the olive oil over medium heat.
2. Add the onion and garlic, and sauté until softened and lightly browned, about 5 minutes.
3. Add the cumin, turmeric and smoked paprika, and cook for another minute.

4. Add the chickpeas, vegetable broth, diced tomatoes, and bring to a boil.
5. Reduce the heat and simmer for 15-20 minutes, or until the stew thickens.
6. Stir in the spinach leaves and cook until wilted, about 2-3 minutes.
7. Season with salt, pepper and lemon juice to taste.
8. Garnish with fresh herbs and serve.

Nutritional Value: Calories: 150 Fat: 6g Saturated Fat: 1g Cholesterol: 0mg Sodium: 380mg Carbohydrates: 19g Fiber: 6g Sugar: 4g Protein: 6g

58. Vegetable And Tofu Stir Fry

Cooking Time: 15 minutes **Prep. Time:** 15 minutes **Servings:** 4
Ingredients:
- 1 block of firm tofu, pressed and diced
- 2 tablespoons oil (peanut, canola, or vegetable)
- 2 cloves garlic, minced
- 1 tablespoon grated ginger
- 2 cups mixed vegetables (such as bell peppers, broccoli, carrots, snow peas, bok choy, etc.)
- 2 tablespoons soy sauce
- 2 tablespoons rice vinegar
- 1 tablespoon cornstarch
- 1 teaspoon sesame oil
- Salt and pepper
- Sesame seeds and green onions, for garnish

Instructions:
1. Press the tofu for about 15-20 minutes. Cut it into cubes and season with a pinch of salt and pepper.
2. In a large skillet or wok, heat the oil over high heat. Add the tofu and cook, stirring occasionally, until golden brown, about 5 minutes.
3. Remove the tofu from the pan and set it aside.
4. In the same pan, add garlic and ginger, stir fry for a minute.
5. Add mixed vegetables and stir fry for 2-3 minutes or until vegetables are crisp-tender.
6. In a small bowl, whisk together soy sauce, rice vinegar, cornstarch, and sesame oil. Pour the mixture into the pan and stir to coat the vegetables.
7. Add the tofu back into the pan and stir fry everything together for a minute.
8. Serve the stir-fry over rice or noodles, garnish with sesame seeds and green onions.

Nutritional Value: Calories: 190 Fat: 3g Carbohydrates: 19g Fiber: 6g Sugar: 4g Protein: 36g

59. Cucumber And Hummus Sandwich

Cooking Time: 10 minutes **Prep. Time:** 55 minutes **Servings:** 1
Ingredients:
- 2 slices of bread (whole wheat, sourdough or any bread you prefer)
- 1/4 cup hummus
- 1/2 cucumber, thinly sliced
- 1/4 cup shredded lettuce or baby spinach
- Salt and pepper, to taste
- 1 tbsp olive oil
- 1 tbsp lemon juice

Instructions:
1. Toast or grill the bread until golden brown.
2. Spread hummus on one slice of bread.
3. Arrange the cucumber slices over the hummus.
4. Add shredded lettuce or spinach leaves on top of the cucumber.

5. Season with salt, pepper, olive oil, and lemon juice.
6. Put the other slice of bread on top of the sandwich.
7. Cut in half and serve.

Nutritional Value: Calories: 250 Fat: 12g Saturated Fat: 2g Cholesterol: 0mg Sodium: 380mg

Carbohydrates: 28g Fiber: 5g Sugar: 4g Protein: 8g

60. Broccoli And Cheddar Soup

Cooking Time: 15 minutes **Prep. Time:** 15 minutes **Servings:** 3

Ingredients:
- 1 tbsp butter
- 1 onion, diced
- 2 cloves garlic, minced
- 1 head broccoli, chopped into florets
- 4 cups chicken or vegetable broth
- 1 cup heavy cream
- 1 cup shredded cheddar cheese
- Salt and pepper to taste

Instructions:
1. In a large pot or Dutch oven, melt butter over medium heat. Add diced onion and minced garlic, and sauté until softened, about 5 minutes.
2. Add chopped broccoli and broth to the pot. Bring the mixture to a boil, then reduce heat and let simmer for 10-15 minutes, or until the broccoli is tender.
3. Remove pot from heat and use an immersion blender to puree the soup until smooth.
4. Stir in heavy cream and shredded cheddar cheese until the cheese is fully melted and incorporated.
5. Season with salt and pepper to taste.
6. Serve hot and enjoy!

Nutritional Value: Calories: 120 Fat: 14g Carbohydrates: 24g Fiber: 16g Sugar: 2g Protein: 32g

61. Grilled Eggplant And Zucchini Sandwich

Cooking Time: 20 minutes **Prep. Time:** 10 minutes **Servings:** 2

Ingredients:
- 2 slices of bread (whole wheat, sourdough or any bread you prefer)
- 1 eggplant, sliced lengthwise
- 1 zucchini, sliced lengthwise
- 1 tbsp olive oil
- Salt and pepper, to taste
- 1/4 cup hummus
- 1/4 cup chopped fresh herbs (basil, cilantro, parsley)
- 1/4 cup crumbled feta cheese
- 1/4 cup shredded lettuce or baby spinach

Instructions:
1. Preheat grill or grill pan to medium-high heat.
2. In a large bowl, toss together the eggplant, zucchini, olive oil, salt, and pepper.
3. Grill vegetables for about 8-10 minutes, or until tender and slightly charred.
4. Toast the bread until golden brown.
5. Spread hummus on one slice of bread.
6. Place the grilled vegetables on top of the hummus.
7. Sprinkle with herbs and feta cheese.
8. Add shredded lettuce or spinach leaves on top of the cheese.
9. Put the other slice of bread on top of the sandwich.
10. Cut in half and serve.

Nutritional Value: Calories: 310 Fat: 14g Saturated Fat: 3g Cholesterol: 10mg Sodium: 380mg

Carbohydrates: 35g Fiber: 8g Sugar: 10g Protein: 10g

62. Pasta Primavera

Cooking Time: 15 minutes **Prep. Time:** 15 minutes **Servings:** 2

Ingredients:
- 8 oz. of your choice of pasta (such as spaghetti or fettuccine)
- 2 tbsp olive oil
- 1 onion, diced
- 2 cloves garlic, minced
- 1 red bell pepper, sliced
- 1 yellow bell pepper, sliced
- 1 cup sliced mushrooms
- 1 cup cherry tomatoes, halved
- 1/2 cup heavy cream
- 1/4 cup grated Parmesan cheese
- Salt and pepper to taste
- Fresh basil leaves, chopped (optional)

Instructions:
1. Cook pasta according to package **Instructions:** until al dente. Drain and set aside.
2. In a large skillet, heat olive oil over medium heat. Add diced onion and minced garlic, and sauté until softened, about 5 minutes.
3. Add sliced bell peppers, mushrooms and cherry tomatoes to skillet. Cook for additional 5 minutes or until vegetables are tender.
4. Stir in heavy cream and grated Parmesan cheese, and cook until cheese is melted and sauce is heated through.
5. Season with salt and pepper to taste.
6. Add the cooked pasta to skillet, and toss to coat with the sauce.
7. Serve hot and enjoy! Optional: Garnish with fresh basil leaves.

Nutritional Value: Calories: 442 Fat: 12g Saturated Fat: 3g Cholesterol: 0mg Sodium: 380mg

Carbohydrates: 48g Fiber: 5g Sugar: 4g Protein: 8g

63. Roasted Vegetable And Feta Quiche

Cooking Time: 45 minutes **Prep. Time:** 20 minutes **Servings:** 5

Ingredients:
- 1 pie crust, store-bought or homemade
- 1/2 cup diced onion
- 1/2 cup diced bell pepper
- 1/2 cup diced zucchini
- 1/2 cup diced mushrooms
- 1 tbsp olive oil
- Salt and pepper, to taste
- 4 large eggs
- 1 cup heavy cream
- 1/2 cup crumbled feta cheese
- 1/4 cup grated Parmesan cheese
- 1/4 teaspoon ground nutmeg
- Chopped fresh herbs (basil, parsley or cilantro)

Instructions:
1. Preheat the oven to 375F (190C).
2. Roll out the pie crust and press it into a 9-inch pie dish.
3. In a large bowl, toss together the onion, bell pepper, zucchini, mushrooms, olive oil, salt, and pepper.
4. Spread the vegetables on a baking sheet and roast for about 20-25 minutes, or until tender and slightly charred.
5. In a separate bowl, whisk together the eggs, cream, feta cheese, Parmesan cheese, nutmeg, salt, and pepper.
6. Spread the vegetables over the bottom of the pie crust.
7. Pour the egg mixture over the vegetables.

8. Bake for 25-30 minutes, or until the quiche is set and golden brown on top.
9. Remove from the oven and let it cool for a couple of minutes.
10. Garnish with fresh herbs.

Nutritional Value: Calories: 320 Fat: 26g Saturated Fat: 13g Cholesterol: 160mg Sodium: 380mg
Carbohydrates: 16g Fiber: 2g Sugar: 2g Protein: 8g

64. Spicy Black Bean And Sweet Potato

Cooking Time: 30 minutes **Prep. Time:** 15 minutes **Servings:** 4
Ingredients:
- 1 medium sweet potato, peeled and diced
- 1 can (15 oz) black beans, rinsed and drained
- 1/2 cup diced onion
- 1/2 cup diced bell pepper
- 2 cloves garlic, minced
- 1 tbsp chili powder
- 1 tsp ground cumin
- 1/4 tsp cayenne pepper (optional)
- Salt and pepper to taste
- 8 corn tortillas
- 1 cup enchilada sauce
- 1 cup shredded Monterey Jack cheese
- Fresh cilantro, chopped (optional)

Instructions:
1. Preheat oven to 375 degrees F (190 degrees C).
2. In a saucepan, bring sweet potatoes to a boil. Reduce heat and simmer for 10 minutes or until tender. Drain and mash sweet potatoes.
3. In a skillet over medium heat, sauté onion, bell pepper and garlic until softened. Add in the black beans, chili powder, cumin, cayenne pepper, salt and pepper. Cook for an additional 5 minutes.
4. To assemble the enchiladas, spread a spoonful of mashed sweet potatoes on each tortilla. Then add some of the black bean mixture on top. Roll up the tortillas and place them seam side down in a baking dish.
5. Pour the enchilada sauce over the top of the tortillas and sprinkle with shredded cheese.
6. Bake for 20-25 minutes or until cheese is melted and bubbly.
7. Serve hot and enjoy! Optional: Garnish with fresh cilantro.

Nutritional Value: Calories: 312 Fat: 12g Saturated Fat: 6g Cholesterol: 23mg Sodium: 526mg Carbohydrates: 42g Fiber: 8g Sugar: 4g Protein: 12g

65. Vegetable And Lentil Shepherd's Pie

Cooking Time: 60 minutes **Prep. Time:** 20 minutes **Servings:** 6-8
Ingredients:
- 1 tbsp olive oil
- 1 onion, diced
- 2 cloves of garlic, minced
- 1 cup diced carrots
- 1 cup diced celery
- 1 cup diced potatoes
- 1 cup cooked green or brown lentils
- 1 can diced tomatoes
- 1 cup vegetable broth
- 1 tsp dried thyme
- Salt and pepper, to taste
- 1 cup frozen peas
- 1 cup shredded cheddar cheese

Instructions:
1. Preheat oven to 375F (190C).

2. In a large pot or Dutch oven, heat the olive oil over medium heat.
3. Add the onion and garlic, and sauté until softened and lightly browned, about 5 minutes.
4. Add the carrots, celery, and potatoes, and cook for another 5 minutes.
5. Add the lentils, diced tomatoes, vegetable broth, thyme, salt, and pepper.
6. Bring to a boil, then reduce the heat and simmer for 15-20 minutes, or until the vegetables are tender.
7. Stir in the frozen peas and cook for another 2 minutes.
8. Transfer the mixture to a large baking dish.
9. Sprinkle shredded cheese on top of the mixture.
10. Bake for 20-25 minutes, or until the cheese is melted and bubbly.
11. Remove from the oven and let it cool for a couple of minutes.
12. Serve and enjoy

Nutritional Value: Calories: 250 Fat: 9g Saturated Fat: 4g Cholesterol: 20mg Sodium: 380mg Carbohydrates: 30g Fiber: 8g Sugar: 5g Protein: 12g

66. Creamy Tomato And Basil Soup

Cooking Time: 20 minutes **Prep. Time:** 10 minutes **Servings:** 4
Ingredients:
- 2 tbsp olive oil
- 1 onion, diced
- 2 cloves garlic, minced
- 2 cans (28 oz) of diced tomatoes
- 2 cups vegetable or chicken broth
- 1/2 cup heavy cream
- 1/4 cup fresh basil leaves, chopped
- Salt and pepper to taste

Instructions:

1. In a large pot or Dutch oven, heat olive oil over medium heat. Add diced onion and minced garlic, and sauté until softened, about 5 minutes.
2. Add diced tomatoes and broth to the pot. Bring the mixture to a boil, then reduce heat and let simmer for 10-15 minutes.
3. Remove pot from heat and use an immersion blender to puree the soup until smooth.
4. Stir in heavy cream and chopped basil leaves. Cook for an additional 2-3 minutes or until heated through.
5. Season with salt and pepper to taste.
6. Serve hot and enjoy!

Nutritional Value: Calories: 207 Fat: 18g Saturated Fat: 11g Cholesterol: 56mg Sodium: 746mg Carbohydrates: 12g Fiber: 3g Sugar: 7g Protein: 3g

67. Grilled Vegetable And Mozzarella Panini

Cooking Time: 20 minutes **Prep. Time:** 10 minutes **Servings:** 4
Ingredients:
- 4 ciabatta rolls or focaccia bread
- 4 slices of mozzarella cheese
- 1 red bell pepper, sliced
- 1 zucchini, sliced
- 1 red onion, sliced
- 1 eggplant, sliced
- 2 tbsp olive oil
- Salt and pepper, to taste
- 1/4 cup chopped fresh basil leaves
- 1/4 cup balsamic glaze

Instructions:

1. Preheat grill or grill pan to medium-high heat.
2. In a large bowl, toss together the bell pepper, zucchini, onion, eggplant, olive oil, salt and pepper.

3. Grill vegetables for about 8-10 minutes, or until tender and slightly charred.
4. Cut the ciabatta rolls or focaccia bread in half and spread balsamic glaze over the inside of each roll.
5. Lay the slices of mozzarella cheese over the bottom half of each roll, then top with the grilled vegetables.
6. Sprinkle with fresh basil leaves.
7. Put the top half of the roll on top of the sandwich.
8. Grill the panini for 2-3 minutes on each side, or until the bread is golden brown and crispy and the cheese is melted.
9. Remove from grill and let cool for a couple of minutes.
10. Cut in half and serve.

Nutritional Value: Calories: 400 Fat: 20g Saturated Fat: 8g Cholesterol: 35mg Sodium: 600mg Carbohydrates: 42g Fiber: 3g Sugar: 8g Protein: 15g

68. Chickpea And Vegetable Curry

Cooking Time: 10 minutes **Prep. Time:** 5 minutes **Servings:** 4

Ingredients:
- 2 tbsp vegetable oil
- 1 onion, diced
- 2 cloves garlic, minced
- 1 tbsp ginger, minced
- 2 tbsp curry powder
- 1 tsp ground cumin
- 1 tsp ground coriander
- 1 tsp turmeric
- 1 tsp ground cinnamon
- 1 tsp cayenne pepper (optional)
- 1 can (14 oz) diced tomatoes
- 1 can (14 oz) chickpeas, rinsed and drained
- 1 cup diced vegetables of your choice (such as carrots, bell peppers, and potatoes)
- 1 cup coconut milk
- Salt and pepper to taste
- Fresh cilantro, chopped (optional)

Instructions:
1. In a large pot or Dutch oven, heat oil over medium heat. Add diced onion and sauté until softened, about 5 minutes.
2. Add garlic and ginger and sauté for an additional 2 minutes.
3. Add curry powder, cumin, coriander, turmeric, cinnamon, and cayenne pepper (if using) and cook for 1-2 minutes or until fragrant.
4. Add diced tomatoes, chickpeas, diced vegetables, and coconut milk. Bring the mixture to a boil, then reduce heat and let simmer for 10-15 minutes or until vegetables are tender.
5. Season with salt and pepper to taste.
6. Serve hot and enjoy! Optional: Garnish with fresh cilantro.

Nutritional Value: Calories: 314 Fat: 24g Saturated Fat: 17g Cholesterol: 0mg Sodium: 466mg Carbohydrates: 22g Fiber: 6g Sugar: 8g Protein: 7g

69. Vegetable And White Bean Chili

Cooking Time: 45 minutes **Prep. Time:** 15 minutes **Servings:** 4-6

Ingredients:
- 1 tbsp olive oil
- 1 onion, diced
- 2 cloves of garlic, minced
- 1 cup diced carrots
- 1 cup diced celery
- 1 cup diced zucchini
- 1 can diced tomatoes
- 1 can white beans, drained and rinsed
- 1 cup vegetable broth
- 2 tsp chili powder
- 1 tsp ground cumin
- Salt and pepper, to taste

- 1 cup frozen corn
- 1 cup shredded cheddar cheese
- Chopped fresh cilantro or parsley (optional)

Instructions:
1. In a large pot or Dutch oven, heat the olive oil over medium heat.
2. Add the onion and garlic, and sauté until softened and lightly browned, about 5 minutes.
3. Add the carrots, celery, zucchini, diced tomatoes, white beans, vegetable broth, chili powder, cumin, salt, and pepper.
4. Bring to a boil, then reduce the heat and simmer for 25-30 minutes, or until the vegetables are tender.
5. Stir in the frozen corn and cook for another 2 minutes.
6. Serve the chili in bowls and top each serving with shredded cheese and cilantro or parsley.

Nutritional Value: Calories: 250 Fat: 9g Saturated Fat: 4g Cholesterol: 20mg

70. Vegetable And Pesto Pizza

Cooking Time: 15-20 minutes **Prep. Time:** 10 minutes **Servings:** 3

Ingredients:
- 1 pre-made pizza crust
- 1/4 cup pesto sauce
- 1/2 cup diced bell pepper
- 1/2 cup diced onion
- 1/2 cup diced zucchini
- 1/2 cup sliced mushrooms
- 1/2 cup cherry tomatoes, halved
- 1 cup shredded mozzarella cheese
- Salt and pepper, to taste
- Fresh basil leaves (optional)

Instructions:
1. Preheat the oven to 425F (220C).
2. Spread the pesto sauce over the pizza crust.
3. Arrange the vegetables over the pesto sauce.
4. Season with salt and pepper.
5. Sprinkle shredded mozzarella cheese over the vegetables.
6. Place the pizza on a baking sheet or pizza stone and bake for 15-20 minutes, or until the crust is golden brown and the cheese is melted.
7. Remove from the oven and let it cool for a couple of minutes.
8. Garnish with fresh basil leaves, if desired.
9. Cut in wedges and serve.

Nutritional Value: Calories: 300 Fat: 20g Saturated Fat: 8g Cholesterol: 35mg

71. Grilled Vegetable And Feta Skewers

Cooking Time: 15 minutes **Prep. Time:** 10 minutes **Servings:** 4

Ingredients:
- 2 bell peppers, cut into chunks
- 1 onion, cut into chunks
- 1 zucchini, cut into chunks
- 1 yellow squash, cut into chunks
- 1/2 cup crumbled feta cheese
- 2 tbsp olive oil
- 2 cloves garlic, minced
- 1 tsp dried oregano
- Salt and pepper to taste
- Wooden skewers, soaked in water for 30 minutes

Instructions:
1. Preheat grill to medium-high heat.
2. In a large bowl, combine bell peppers, onion, zucchini, yellow squash, feta cheese, olive oil, garlic, oregano, salt and pepper.
3. Thread the vegetables and feta cheese onto skewers, alternating the vegetables and cheese.

4. Lightly oil the grill grates and place the skewers on the grill.
5. Grill for 10-12 minutes or until the vegetables are tender and slightly charred, turning occasionally.
6. Serve hot and enjoy!

Nutritional Value: Calories: 127 Fat: 9g Saturated Fat: 3g Cholesterol: 12mg Sodium: 222mg Carbohydrates: 9g Fiber: 2g Sugar: 4g Protein: 4g

72. Vegetable And Bean Burritos

Cooking Time: 20 minutes **Prep. Time:** 10 minutes **Servings:** 4

Ingredients:
- 4 large flour tortillas
- 1 tbsp olive oil
- 1 onion, diced
- 2 cloves of garlic, minced
- 1 cup diced bell pepper
- 1 cup diced zucchini
- 1 can black beans, drained and rinsed
- 1 tsp chili powder
- 1 tsp ground cumin
- Salt and pepper, to taste
- 1 cup shredded cheddar cheese
- 1/2 cup salsa
- 1/2 cup sour cream (optional)
- Chopped fresh cilantro or parsley (optional)

Instructions:
1. In a large skillet or saucepan, heat the olive oil over medium heat.
2. Add the onion and garlic, and sauté until softened and lightly browned, about 5 minutes.
3. Add the bell pepper and zucchini, and cook for another 5 minutes.
4. Stir in the black beans, chili powder, cumin, salt, and pepper.
5. Cook for another 5 minutes, or until the vegetables are tender.
6. Warm up the tortillas in the microwave for 30 seconds or in a dry pan for a few seconds.
7. Place 1/4 of the bean and vegetable mixture on each tortilla, add shredded cheese and salsa, and roll up the tortilla tightly around the filling.
8. Place the burritos on a baking sheet and bake for 15-20 minutes or until the cheese is melted and the burritos are heated through.

Nutritional Value: Calories: 388 Fat: 12g Saturated Fat: 1g Cholesterol: 2mg Sodium: 637mg Carbohydrates: 45g Fiber: 3g Sugar: 1g

73. Vegetable And Tofu Pad Thai

Cooking Time: 30 minutes **Prep. Time:** 15 minutes **Servings:** 4

Ingredients:
- 8 oz. rice noodles
- 2 tbsp vegetable oil
- 1 onion, sliced
- 2 cloves garlic, minced
- 1 red bell pepper, sliced
- 1 cup sliced mushrooms
- 1 cup sliced carrots
- 1 cup bean sprouts
- 1 cup firm tofu, diced
- 1/4 cup soy sauce
- 2 tbsp brown sugar
- 2 tbsp rice vinegar
- 1 tbsp fish sauce (optional)
- 1 tsp red pepper flakes (optional)
- 2 eggs, lightly beaten
- 1/4 cup chopped peanuts
- 1/4 cup chopped fresh cilantro
- Lime wedges (optional)

Instructions:
1. Cook rice noodles according to package **Instructions:** until al dente. Drain and set aside.

2. In a large skillet or wok, heat oil over medium-high heat. Add onion and garlic, and sauté for 1-2 minutes.
3. Add red bell pepper, mushrooms, carrots and bean sprouts, and sauté for an additional 3-5 minutes or until vegetables are tender.
4. Push vegetables to the side of the skillet and add tofu, soy sauce, brown sugar, rice vinegar, fish sauce (if using) and red pepper flakes (if using). Cook for an additional 2-3 minutes or until tofu is heated through.
5. Add beaten eggs and stir until scrambled.
6. Add cooked noodles and toss to combine with the vegetables and tofu mixture.
7. Sprinkle with chopped peanuts and cilantro.
8. Serve hot and enjoy! Optional: Serve with lime wedges.

Nutritional Value: Calories: 437 Fat: 18g Saturated Fat: 3g Cholesterol: 82mg Sodium: 1291mg Carbohydrates: 56g Fiber: 4g Sugar: 11g Protein: 14g

74. Caprese Salad With Grilled Eggplant

Cooking Time: 15 minutes **Prep. Time:** 10 minutes **Servings:** 4
Ingredients:
- 1 large eggplant, sliced lengthwise
- 2 tbsp olive oil
- Salt and pepper, to taste
- 1 pint cherry tomatoes, halved
- 1/2 cup fresh basil leaves
- 8 oz fresh mozzarella cheese, sliced or torn
- Balsamic glaze, for drizzling

Instructions:
1. Preheat grill or grill pan to medium-high heat.
2. Brush the eggplant slices with olive oil and season with salt and pepper.
3. Grill the eggplant for about 8-10 minutes, or until tender and slightly charred, flipping halfway through.
4. Remove from the grill and let cool for a few minutes.
5. On a large serving platter, arrange the eggplant slices, cherry tomatoes, basil leaves, and mozzarella cheese.
6. Drizzle with balsamic glaze and season with additional salt and pepper, if desired.
7. Serve and enjoy.

Nutritional Value: Calories: 220 Fat: 17g Saturated Fat: 8g Cholesterol: 35mg Sodium: 360mg Carbohydrates: 8g Fiber: 3g Sugar: 6g Protein: 11g

75. Creamy Mushroom And Wild Rice Soup

Cooking Time: 25 minutes **Prep. Time:** 15 minutes **Servings:** 4
Ingredients:
- 1 tbsp butter
- 1 onion, diced
- 2 cloves garlic, minced
- 1 cup sliced mushrooms
- 1/4 cup all-purpose flour
- 4 cups chicken broth
- 1 cup cooked wild rice
- 1 cup heavy cream
- 1/2 cup grated Parmesan cheese
- Salt and pepper to taste
- Fresh parsley, chopped (optional)

Instructions:
1. In a large pot or Dutch oven, melt butter over medium heat. Add diced onion and minced garlic, and sauté until softened, about 5 minutes.
2. Add sliced mushrooms and sauté for an additional 2-3 minutes or until softened.

3. Sprinkle flour over the vegetables and stir to combine. Cook for 1-2 minutes or until the flour is lightly toasted.
4. Slowly add chicken broth, stirring constantly to prevent lumps from forming. Bring the mixture to a boil, then reduce heat and let simmer for 10-15 minutes.
5. Stir in cooked wild rice, heavy cream, and grated Parmesan cheese. Cook for an additional 2-3 minutes or until cheese is melted and the soup is heated through.
6. Season with salt and pepper to taste.
7. Serve hot and enjoy! Optional: Garnish with fresh parsley.

Nutritional Value: Calories: 391 Fat: 31g Saturated Fat: 19g Cholesterol: 101mg Sodium: 924mg Carbohydrates: 19g Fiber: 2g Sugar: 3g Protein: 10g

76. Spicy Sweet Potato And Black Bean Burrito Bowl

Cooking Time: 30 minutes **Prep. Time:** 10 minutes **Servings:** 4

Ingredients:
- 2 tbsp olive oil
- 1 large sweet potato, peeled and diced
- 1 tsp ground cumin
- 1 tsp smoked paprika
- 1/2 tsp cayenne pepper
- Salt and pepper, to taste
- 1 onion, diced
- 2 cloves of garlic, minced
- 1 can black beans, drained and rinsed
- 1 cup corn kernels, fresh or frozen
- 1 cup salsa
- 1/4 cup chopped fresh cilantro
- 4 cups cooked rice or quinoa
- 1 avocado, diced (optional)
- 1/4 cup sour cream (optional)
- 1/4 cup shredded cheddar cheese (optional)

Instructions:
1. In a large skillet or saucepan, heat the olive oil over medium heat.
2. Add the sweet potato and spices (cumin, paprika, cayenne, salt and pepper). Cook for 8-10 minutes or until the sweet potato is tender.
3. Add the onion and garlic, and sauté until softened and lightly browned, about 5 minutes.
4. Stir in the black beans, corn, salsa and cilantro. Cook for another 5 minutes, or until the vegetables are tender.
5. Serve the mixture over cooked rice or quinoa.
6. Top with diced avocado, sour cream, and shredded cheddar cheese if desired.

Nutritional Value Calories: 470 Fat: 12g Saturated Fat: 2.5g Cholesterol: 0mg Sodium: 830mg
Carbohydrates: 80g Fiber: 12g Sugar: 12g Protein: 12g

77. Vegetable And Chickpea Tagine

Cooking Time: 25 minutes **Prep. Time:** 10 minutes **Servings:** 5

Ingredients:
- 2 tbsp olive oil
- 1 onion, diced
- 2 cloves garlic, minced
- 1 tsp ground ginger
- 1 tsp ground cumin
- 1 tsp ground coriander
- 1 tsp ground cinnamon
- 1/4 tsp cayenne pepper (optional)
- 1 can (14 oz) diced tomatoes
- 1 cup diced carrots
- 1 cup diced potatoes
- 1 cup diced bell peppers

- 1 can (14 oz) chickpeas, drained and rinsed
- 1 cup vegetable broth
- 1/4 cup chopped fresh cilantro
- Salt and pepper to taste
- Cooked couscous or quinoa, for serving

Instructions:
1. In a large pot or Dutch oven, heat olive oil over medium heat. Add diced onion and minced garlic, and sauté until softened, about 5 minutes.
2. Add ginger, cumin, coriander, cinnamon, and cayenne pepper (if using) and cook for 1-2 minutes or until fragrant.
3. Add diced tomatoes, diced carrots, diced potatoes, diced bell peppers, chickpeas, and vegetable broth. Bring the mixture to a boil, then reduce heat and let simmer for 20-25 minutes or until vegetables are tender.
4. Stir in chopped cilantro, and season with salt and pepper to taste.
5. Serve hot over cooked couscous or quinoa, and enjoy!

Nutritional Value: Calories: 300 Fat: 9g Saturated Fat: 1g Carbohydrates: 24g Protein: 14g

78. Grilled Vegetable And Pesto Panini

Cooking Time: 20 minutes **Prep. Time:** 10 minutes **Servings:** 4
Ingredients:
- 4 ciabatta rolls or focaccia bread
- 1/4 cup pesto sauce
- 1 red bell pepper, sliced
- 1 zucchini, sliced
- 1 red onion, sliced
- 1 eggplant, sliced
- 2 tbsp olive oil
- Salt and pepper, to taste
- 1 cup shredded mozzarella cheese

Instructions:
1. Preheat grill or grill pan to medium-high heat.
2. In a large bowl, toss together the bell pepper, zucchini, onion, eggplant, olive oil, salt and pepper.
3. Grill vegetables for about 8-10 minutes, or until tender and slightly charred.
4. Cut the ciabatta rolls or focaccia bread in half and spread pesto sauce over the inside of each roll.
5. Lay the slices of mozzarella cheese over the bottom half of each roll, then top with the grilled vegetables.
6. Put the top half of the roll on top of the sandwich.
7. Grill the panini for 2-3 minutes on each side, or until the bread is golden brown and crispy and the cheese is melted.
8. Remove from grill and let cool for a couple of minutes.
9. Cut in half and serve.

Nutritional Value: Calories: 420 Fat: 24g Saturated Fat: 10g Cholesterol: 45mg Sodium: 700mg Carbohydrates: 36g Fiber: 3g Sugar: 6g Protein: 16g

79. Vegetable And Tofu Korma

Cooking Time: 30 minutes **Prep. Time:** 10 minutes **Servings:** 4
Ingredients:
- 2 tbsp vegetable oil
- 1 onion, diced
- 2 cloves of garlic, minced
- 2 tsp ginger paste
- 1 tsp cumin powder
- 1 tsp coriander powder
- 1 tsp garam masala
- 1/4 tsp turmeric powder
- 1/4 tsp red chili powder (optional)
- Salt and pepper, to taste

- 1 can diced tomatoes
- 1 cup water or vegetable broth
- 1 cup diced carrots
- 1 cup diced bell pepper
- 1 cup diced zucchini
- 1 cup diced potatoes
- 1 cup diced tofu
- 1/4 cup heavy cream or coconut milk (optional)
- 1/4 cup chopped fresh cilantro

Instructions:
1. In a large pot or Dutch oven, heat the oil over medium heat.
2. Add the onion and sauté until softened and lightly browned, about 5 minutes.
3. Add the garlic and ginger paste and sauté for another 2 minutes.
4. Add the cumin, coriander, garam masala, turmeric, red chili powder, salt and pepper and stir to combine.
5. Add the diced tomatoes, water or vegetable broth, and bring to a boil.
6. Add the diced vegetables and tofu, and reduce the heat to a simmer.
7. Cover and cook for 20-25 minutes or until the vegetables are tender.
8. Stir in the cream or coconut milk and cilantro.
9. Cook for 2-3 minutes to heat through.
10. Serve over rice or quinoa.

Nutritional Value: Calories: 250 Fat: 15g Saturated Fat: 5g Cholesterol: 0mg Sodium: 260mg Carbohydrates: 20g Fiber: 4g Sugar: 6g Protein: 10g

80. Tomato And Basil Pasta Salad

Cooking Time: 10 minutes **Prep. Time:** 10 minutes **Servings:** 4
Ingredients:
- 12 oz. pasta of your choice
- 2 cups cherry tomatoes, halved
- 1/2 cup fresh basil leaves, chopped
- 1/4 cup olive oil
- 2 cloves garlic, minced
- 2 tbsp red wine vinegar
- 1 tbsp Dijon mustard
- Salt and pepper to taste
- 1/2 cup grated Parmesan cheese (optional)

Instructions:
1. Cook pasta according to package **Instructions:** until al dente. Drain and rinse with cold water.
2. In a large bowl, combine cooked pasta, cherry tomatoes, and basil leaves.
3. In a small bowl, whisk together olive oil, garlic, red wine vinegar, Dijon mustard, salt, and pepper.
4. Pour the dressing over the pasta mixture, and toss to combine.
5. Refrigerate for at least 1 hour to allow the flavors to meld.
6. Serve cold and enjoy! Optional: garnish with grated Parmesan cheese.

Nutritional Value: Calories: 408 Fat: 17g Saturated Fat: 3g Cholesterol: 3mg Sodium: 84mg Carbohydrates: 56g Fiber: 2g Sugar: 3g Protein: 12g

81. Grilled Vegetable And Hummus Wrap

Cooking Time: 20 minutes **Prep. Time:** 10 minutes **Servings:** 4
Ingredients:
- 4 large flour tortillas
- 1/2 cup hummus
- 1 red bell pepper, sliced
- 1 zucchini, sliced
- 1 red onion, sliced
- 1 eggplant, sliced
- 2 tbsp olive oil
- Salt and pepper, to taste
- 1 cup arugula or mixed greens

- 1/4 cup chopped fresh parsley or cilantro

Instructions:
1. Preheat grill or grill pan to medium-high heat.
2. In a large bowl, toss together the bell pepper, zucchini, onion, eggplant, olive oil, salt and pepper.
3. Grill vegetables for about 8-10 minutes, or until tender and slightly charred.
4. Spread hummus on each tortilla.
5. Place the arugula or mixed greens and grilled vegetables on top of the hummus.
6. Sprinkle with fresh parsley or cilantro.
7. Roll up the tortilla tightly around the filling.
8. Grill the wrap for 2-3 minutes on each side, or until the bread is golden brown and crispy.
9. Remove from grill and let cool for a couple of minutes.
10. Cut in half and serve.

Nutritional Value: Calories: 300 Fat: 18g Saturated Fat: 3g Cholesterol: 0mg Sodium: 400mg Carbohydrates: 27g Fiber: 6g Sugar: 7g Protein: 8g

82. Vegetable And Lentil Shepherd's

Cooking Time: 60 minutes **Prep. Time:** 20 minutes **Servings:** 6

Ingredients:
- 1 cup green or brown lentils
- 2 cups vegetable broth
- 1 onion, diced
- 2 cloves garlic, minced
- 2 carrots, peeled and diced
- 2 cups diced mushrooms
- 1 cup frozen peas
- 2 tbsp tomato paste
- 1 tsp dried thyme
- 1 tsp dried rosemary
- Salt and pepper to taste
- 4 cups mashed potatoes
- 1/4 cup grated cheddar cheese (optional)

Instructions:
1. Preheat oven to 375°F (190°C)
2. In a large pot, bring lentils and vegetable broth to a boil. Reduce heat and let simmer for 20-25 minutes or until lentils are tender. Drain any excess liquid and set aside.
3. In a large skillet, heat oil over medium heat. Add diced onion, garlic, and diced carrots. Cook for 5-7 minutes or until vegetables are softened.
4. Add diced mushrooms, frozen peas, tomato paste, thyme, rosemary, salt, and pepper. Cook for an additional 5 minutes or until vegetables are tender.
5. Mix in the cooked lentils.
6. Transfer the vegetable and lentil mixture to a baking dish.
7. Spread the mashed potatoes over the top of the vegetable mixture, and smooth the surface with a spatula.
8. Sprinkle with grated cheddar cheese (if using).
9. Bake for 25-30 minutes or until the top is golden brown and the filling is heated through.
10. Serve hot and enjoy!

Nutritional Value: Calories: 446 Fat: 8g Saturated Fat: 3g Cholesterol: 11mg Sodium: 748mg Carbohydrates: 71g Fiber: 22g Sugar: 6g Protein: 21g

83. Lentil And Vegetable Stew

Cooking Time: 30 minutes **Prep. Time:** 10 minutes **Servings:** 4

Ingredients:
- 1 tbsp olive oil
- 1 onion, diced
- 2 cloves of garlic, minced
- 1 cup diced carrots
- 1 cup diced celery

- 1 cup diced potatoes
- 1 cup cooked green or brown lentils
- 1 can diced tomatoes
- 2 cups vegetable broth
- 1 tsp dried thyme
- 1 tsp dried rosemary
- Salt and pepper, to taste
- 1 cup frozen peas
- 1 cup chopped kale or spinach
- 1/4 cup grated Parmesan cheese (optional)

Instructions:
1. In a large pot or Dutch oven, heat the olive oil over medium heat.
2. Add the onion and garlic, and sauté until softened and lightly browned, about 5 minutes.
3. Add the carrots, celery, and potatoes, and cook for another 5 minutes.
4. Add the lentils, diced tomatoes, vegetable broth, thyme, rosemary, salt, and pepper.
5. Bring to a boil, then reduce the heat and simmer for 25-30 minutes, or until the vegetables are tender.
6. Stir in the frozen peas and kale or spinach and cook for another 5 minutes.
7. Serve the stew in bowls and top each serving with grated Parmesan cheese, if desired.

Nutritional Value: Calories: 260 Fat: 5g Saturated Fat: 1g Cholesterol: 0mg Sodium: 540mg Carbohydrates: 42g Fiber: 14g Sugar: 8g Protein: 14g

84. Vegetable And Quinoa Fried Rice

Cooking Time: 30 minutes **Prep. Time:** 15 minutes **Servings:** 3

Ingredients:
- 1 cup quinoa
- 2 cups vegetable broth
- 2 tbsp vegetable oil
- 1 onion, diced
- 2 cloves garlic, minced
- 1 cup diced carrots
- 1 cup diced bell peppers
- 1 cup frozen peas
- 2 eggs, lightly beaten
- 2 tbsp soy sauce
- 1 tbsp rice vinegar
- 1 tsp sesame oil
- Salt and pepper to taste
- Green onions, sliced (optional)
- Sesame seeds (optional)

Instructions:
1. Rinse quinoa in a fine mesh strainer and place it in a saucepan with the vegetable broth. Bring the mixture to a boil, then reduce heat and let simmer for 15-20 minutes or until the quinoa is tender and the liquid is absorbed.
2. In a large skillet or wok, heat vegetable oil over medium-high heat. Add diced onion, minced garlic, diced carrots, diced bell peppers, and frozen peas. Stir-fry for 5-7 minutes or until vegetables are tender.
3. Push the vegetables to the side of the skillet, and add beaten eggs. Scramble the eggs until cooked through.
4. Stir in cooked quinoa, soy sauce, rice vinegar, sesame oil, salt and pepper. Cook for an additional 2-3 minutes or until heated through.
5. Serve hot and enjoy! Optional: Garnish with sliced green onions and sesame seeds.

Nutritional Value: Calories: 449 Fat: 11g Saturated Fat: 2g Cholesterol: 0mg Sodium: 414mg Carbohydrates: 35g Fiber: 13g Sugar: 2g Protein: 24g

85. Vegetable And Ricotta Calzones

Cooking Time: 20 minutes **Prep. Time:** 15 minutes **Servings:** 4

Ingredients:
- 2 cups all-purpose flour
- 1/2 tsp salt
- 1/2 tsp sugar
- 1/2 tsp active dry yeast
- 1/2 cup warm water
- 1/4 cup olive oil
- 1 cup diced onion
- 1 cup diced bell pepper
- 1 cup diced mushrooms
- 1/2 tsp dried oregano
- 1/2 tsp dried basil
- Salt and pepper, to taste
- 1 cup ricotta cheese
- 1 cup shredded mozzarella cheese
- 1 egg, beaten (for egg wash)

Instructions:
1. In a large bowl, mix the flour, salt, sugar, and yeast. Slowly pour in the warm water and olive oil, stirring until the dough comes together.
2. Knead the dough for about 5 minutes on a floured surface, then place it back in the bowl and cover with a damp cloth. Let it rest for about 10 minutes.
3. Preheat the oven to 425F (220C).
4. In a large skillet, heat the olive oil over medium heat. Add the onions, bell pepper, mushrooms, oregano, basil, salt, and pepper. Cook until the vegetables are softened, about 5-7 minutes.
5. Roll out the dough on a floured surface to about 1/4 inch thickness.
6. Divide the dough into 4 equal parts.
7. Spread 1/4 cup of ricotta cheese on one half of each dough circle, leaving a 1/2 inch border around the edge.
8. Add 1/4 cup of the vegetable mixture and 1/4 cup of mozzarella cheese on top of the ricotta cheese.
9. Brush the edges of the dough with the beaten egg.
10. Fold the other half of the dough over the filling, press the edges together to seal.
11. Place the calzones on a baking sheet lined with parchment paper.
12. Brush the top of the calzones with the remaining beaten egg.
13. Bake for 20-25 minutes or until the calzones are golden brown.
14. Let it cool for a couple of minutes before serving.

Nutritional Value: Calories: 480 Fat: 24g Saturated Fat: 8g Cholesterol: 55mg Sodium: 600mg
Carbohydrates: 49g Fiber: 2g Sugar: 2g Protein: 17g

86. Vegetable And Cheese Strata

Cooking Time: 45 minutes **Prep. Time:** 20 minutes **Servings:** 6

Ingredients:
- 1 loaf of bread, cubed
- 1 cup diced vegetables (such as bell peppers, mushrooms, onions, or spinach)
- 6 eggs
- 2 cups milk
- 1 tsp dried basil
- 1 tsp dried oregano
- Salt and pepper to taste
- 2 cups shredded cheese (such as cheddar or mozzarella)

Instructions:
1. Grease a 9x13 inch baking dish.
2. Spread half of the bread cubes in the bottom of the dish.
3. Top the bread with diced vegetables and half of the shredded cheese.
4. Repeat layering with the remaining bread, vegetables and cheese.
5. In a medium bowl, whisk together eggs, milk, basil, oregano, salt and pepper.
6. Pour the egg mixture over the bread and vegetables.

7. Cover the dish with foil and refrigerate overnight.
8. Preheat the oven to 350°F (175°C)
9. Remove the foil from the dish and bake for 40-45 minutes or until the strata is set and the top is golden brown.
10. Let it cool for a few minutes before serving.

Nutritional Value: Calories: 335 Fat: 22g Saturated Fat: 12g Cholesterol: 218mg Sodium: 667mg Carbohydrates: 18g Fiber: 2g Sugar: 5g Protein: 17g

87. Vegetable And Tofu Teriyaki

Cooking Time: 30 minutes **Prep. Time:** 10 minutes **Servings:** 4
Ingredients:
- 1 block of firm tofu
- 1 tbsp corn starch
- 1 tbsp vegetable oil
- 1 onion, diced
- 2 cloves of garlic, minced
- 1 cup diced bell pepper
- 1 cup diced carrots
- 1 cup diced mushrooms
- 1 cup broccoli florets
- 1/2 cup vegetable broth
- 1/4 cup soy sauce
- 2 tbsp honey
- 2 tbsp rice vinegar
- 1 tbsp sesame oil
- 1 tsp cornstarch
- 2 tbsp water
- 1 green onion, thinly sliced (optional)
- Sesame seeds (optional)

Instructions:
1. Drain the tofu and press it between paper towels to remove excess water. Cut the tofu into cubes.
2. In a shallow dish, toss the tofu with corn starch.
3. In a large skillet, heat the vegetable oil over medium-high heat.
4. Add the tofu cubes and cook until they are golden brown on all sides. Remove from skillet and set aside.
5. In the same skillet, add the onion, garlic, bell pepper, carrots, mushrooms, and broccoli and sauté for about 5 minutes or until softened.
6. In a small bowl, mix together the broth, soy sauce, honey, rice vinegar, sesame oil, cornstarch and water.
7. Add the tofu and the teriyaki sauce to the skillet and stir until everything is well coated.
8. Let simmer for 2-3 minutes, or until the sauce has thickened and the vegetables are cooked to your liking.
9. Serve the stir fry over rice and garnish with green onions and sesame seeds, if desired.

Nutritional Value: Calories: 270 Fat: 14g Saturated Fat: 2g Cholesterol: 0mg Sodium: 830mg Carbohydrates: 24g Fiber: 3g Sugar: 16g Protein: 14g

88. Vegetable And Cashew Stir Fry

Cooking Time: 30 minutes **Prep. Time:** 10 minutes **Servings:** 4
Ingredients:
- 1 cup raw cashews
- 2 tablespoons vegetable oil
- 2 cloves of garlic, minced
- 1 tablespoon grated ginger
- 1 red bell pepper, sliced
- 1 yellow onion, sliced
- 1 cup sliced mushrooms
- 1 cup sliced carrots
- 1 cup sliced bok choy
- 1/4 cup soy sauce
- 1 tablespoon rice vinegar
- 1 tablespoon honey

- 1 teaspoon cornstarch
- 2 tablespoons water
- Salt and pepper, to taste
- Sesame seeds (optional)
- Green onions, thinly sliced (optional)

Instructions:
1. In a pan, toast the cashews over medium heat until golden and fragrant, about 3-5 minutes. Remove from pan and set aside.
2. In the same pan, heat the vegetable oil over medium-high heat.
3. Add garlic and ginger and sauté for about 30 seconds.
4. Add the bell pepper, onion, mushrooms, carrots, and bok choy. Season with salt and pepper, to taste.
5. Stir fry for about 5-7 minutes or until the vegetables are tender.
6. In a small bowl, mix together the soy sauce, rice vinegar, honey, cornstarch and water.
7. Add the sauce to the pan and stir to coat the vegetables.
8. Let simmer for 2-3 minutes, or until the sauce has thickened.
9. Stir in the toasted cashews.
10. Serve the stir fry over rice and garnish with sesame seeds and green onions, if desired.

Nutritional Value: Calories: 430 Fat: 27g Saturated Fat: 5g Cholesterol: 0mg Sodium: 930mg Carbohydrates: 34g Fiber: 4g Sugar: 15g Protein: 12g

89. Vegetable And Black Bean Enchiladas

Cooking Time: 35 minutes **Prep. Time:** 10 minutes **Servings:** 5
Ingredients:
- 1 tbsp vegetable oil
- 1 onion, diced
- 2 cloves garlic, minced
- 1 red bell pepper, diced
- 1 cup sliced mushrooms
- 1 cup corn kernels
- 1 can (14 oz) black beans, drained and rinsed
- 1/4 cup chopped fresh cilantro
- 1 tsp ground cumin
- Salt and pepper to taste
- 8 corn tortillas
- 2 cups enchilada sauce
- 1 cup shredded cheddar cheese

Instructions:
1. Preheat oven to 375°F (190°C).
2. In a large skillet, heat vegetable oil over medium-high heat. Add diced onion, minced garlic, diced red bell pepper and sliced mushrooms. Cook for 5-7 minutes or until vegetables are softened.
3. Stir in corn kernels, black beans, cilantro, cumin, salt and pepper. Cook for an additional 2-3 minutes or until heated through.
4. Spread a spoonful of enchilada sauce on each tortilla.
5. Place a spoonful of the vegetable mixture on the center of each tortilla. Roll up the tortillas and place them seam-side down in a baking dish.
6. Pour the remaining enchilada sauce over the top of the enchiladas.
7. Sprinkle shredded cheddar cheese on top of the enchiladas.
8. Bake for 20-25 minutes or until the cheese is melted and the enchiladas are heated through.
9. Serve hot and enjoy!

Nutritional Value: Calories: 394 Fat: 18g Saturated Fat: 8g Cholesterol: 30mg Sodium: 947mg Carbohydrates: 44g

90. Vegetable And White Bean Soup

Cooking Time: 30 minutes **Prep. Time:** 10 minutes **Servings:** 4

Ingredients:
- 1 tbsp olive oil
- 1 onion, diced
- 2 cloves garlic, minced
- 2 carrots, peeled and diced
- 2 celery stalks, diced
- 4 cups vegetable broth
- 1 can (15 oz) white beans, drained and rinsed
- 1 tsp dried thyme
- 1 tsp dried rosemary
- Salt and pepper to taste
- 1/4 cup chopped fresh parsley or basil (optional)

Instructions:
1. In a large pot or Dutch oven, heat olive oil over medium heat. Add diced onion, minced garlic, diced carrots, and diced celery. Sauté for 5-7 minutes or until vegetables are softened.
2. Add vegetable broth, white beans, thyme, rosemary, salt and pepper. Bring the mixture to a boil, then reduce heat and let simmer for 20-25 minutes or until vegetables are tender.
3. Use an immersion blender to puree the soup until it reaches your desired consistency.
4. Stir in chopped parsley or basil (if using)
5. Serve hot and enjoy!

Nutritional Value: Calories: 199 Fat: 4g Saturated Fat: 0.5g Cholesterol: 0mg Sodium: 572mg Carbohydrates: 30g Fiber: 8g Sugar: 3g Protein: 10g

91. Vegetable And Tofu Lettuce Wraps

Cooking Time: 10 minutes **Prep. Time:** 55 minutes **Servings:** 2

Ingredients:
- 1 tbsp vegetable oil
- 1 onion, diced
- 2 cloves garlic, minced
- 1 red bell pepper, diced
- 1 cup sliced mushrooms
- 1 cup diced carrots
- 1 cup diced water chestnuts
- 1 block (14 oz) firm tofu, drained and crumbled
- 2 tbsp soy sauce
- 1 tbsp hoisin sauce
- 1 tbsp rice vinegar
- 1 tsp sesame oil
- Salt and pepper to taste
- Lettuce leaves (such as butter lettuce or bibb lettuce) for wrapping
- Sesame seeds and green onions for garnish

Instructions:
1. In a large skillet, heat vegetable oil over medium-high heat. Add diced onion, minced garlic, diced red bell pepper, sliced mushrooms, diced carrots, and diced water chestnuts. Cook for 5-7 minutes or until vegetables are softened.
2. Add crumbled tofu, soy sauce, hoisin sauce, rice vinegar, sesame oil, salt and pepper. Cook for an additional 2-3 minutes or until heated through.
3. To serve, spoon a small amount of the tofu and vegetable mixture onto a lettuce leaf. Garnish with sesame seeds and green onions.
4. Fold the lettuce leaf around the filling and enjoy!

Nutritional Value: Calories: 106 Fat: 7g Saturated Fat: 1g Cholesterol: 0mg Sodium: 468mg Carbohydrates: 8g Fiber: 2g Sugar: 4g Protein: 5g

92. Vegetable And Feta Frittata

Cooking Time: 30 minutes **Prep. Time:** 1 minutes **Servings:** 4

Ingredients:
- 8 eggs
- 1/4 cup milk
- Salt and pepper, to taste
- 2 tablespoons olive oil
- 1 onion, diced
- 2 cloves of garlic, minced
- 1 red bell pepper, diced
- 1 cup sliced mushrooms
- 1 cup spinach
- 1/4 cup crumbled feta cheese

Instructions:
1. In a large bowl, whisk together the eggs, milk, salt, and pepper.
2. Heat the olive oil in a 10-inch skillet over medium-high heat.
3. Add the onion, garlic, bell pepper, mushrooms and sauté until softened, about 5 minutes.
4. Add the spinach and sauté until wilted, about 2 minutes.
5. Reduce the heat to medium-low.
6. Pour the egg mixture over the vegetables and stir gently to combine.
7. Sprinkle the feta cheese over the top.
8. Cook the frittata, without stirring, until the eggs are set on the bottom and the top is just set, about 10-15 minutes.
9. Place the skillet under the broiler and broil for 2-3 minutes or until the top is lightly golden and the eggs are fully set.
10. Remove from the oven and let it cool for a couple of minutes before slicing and serving.

Nutritional Value: Calories: 240 Fat: 19g Saturated Fat: 5g Cholesterol: 370mg Sodium: 390mg Carbohydrates: 5g Fiber: 1g

93. Vegetable And Chickpea Curry

Cooking Time: 35 minutes **Prep. Time:** 15 minutes **Servings:** 4

Ingredients:
- 1 tbsp vegetable oil
- 1 onion, diced
- 2 cloves garlic, minced
- 2 tbsp curry powder
- 1 tsp ground ginger
- 1 tsp ground cumin
- 1 tsp ground coriander
- 1/2 tsp ground turmeric
- 1 can (14 oz) diced tomatoes
- 1 can (15 oz) chickpeas, drained and rinsed
- 1 cup diced vegetables (such as bell peppers, carrots, and cauliflower)
- 1 cup coconut milk
- Salt and pepper to taste
- Fresh cilantro, chopped (optional)

Instructions:
1. In a large pot or Dutch oven, heat vegetable oil over medium heat. Add diced onion and minced garlic. Cook for 5-7 minutes or until softened.
2. Stir in curry powder, ginger, cumin, coriander, and turmeric. Cook for 1-2 minutes or until fragrant.
3. Add diced tomatoes, chickpeas, diced vegetables, coconut milk, salt, and pepper. Bring the mixture to a boil, then reduce heat and let simmer for 20-25 minutes or until vegetables are tender.
4. Serve hot and enjoy! Optional: Garnish with fresh cilantro

Nutritional Value: Calories: 185 Fat: 12g Saturated Fat: 8g Cholesterol: 0mg Sodium:

517mg Carbohydrates: 16g Fiber: 4g Sugar: 5g Protein: 5g

94. Vegetable And Pesto Linguine

Cooking Time: 20 minutes **Prep. Time:** 10 minutes **Servings:** 4
Ingredients:
- 8 oz linguine pasta
- 1 tbsp olive oil
- 1 onion, diced
- 2 cloves of garlic, minced
- 1 cup diced bell pepper
- 1 cup sliced mushrooms
- 1 cup cherry tomatoes, halved
- 1/4 cup prepared basil pesto
- Salt and pepper, to taste
- 1/4 cup grated Parmesan cheese
- Chopped fresh basil or parsley (optional)

Instructions:
1. Bring a large pot of salted water to a boil. Add the linguine and cook according to package **Instructions:** until al dente.
2. Drain the pasta and set aside.
3. In a large skillet, heat the olive oil over medium heat.
4. Add the onion, garlic, bell pepper, mushrooms, and cherry tomatoes. Season with salt and pepper, to taste.
5. Sauté for about 5-7 minutes or until the vegetables are tender.
6. Stir in the pesto.
7. Add the cooked and drained pasta to the skillet and toss to coat with the vegetable and pesto mixture.
8. Serve in bowls and top each serving with grated Parmesan cheese and chopped fresh basil or parsley, if desired.

Nutritional Value: Calories: 380 Fat: 17g Saturated Fat: 4g Cholesterol: 10mg Sodium: 480mg Carbohydrates: 45g Fiber: 3g Sugar: 3g Protein: 12g

95. Vegetable And Chickpea Shawarma

Cooking Time: 30 minutes **Prep. Time:** 15 minutes **Servings:** 4
Ingredients:
- 1 can (15 oz) chickpeas, drained and rinsed
- 2 tbsp olive oil
- 1 tsp ground cumin
- 1 tsp ground coriander
- 1 tsp smoked paprika
- 1 tsp garlic powder
- 1/2 tsp ground cinnamon
- Salt and pepper to taste
- 1 onion, sliced
- 1 bell pepper, sliced
- 1 zucchini, sliced
- Pita bread, warmed
- Tzatziki sauce or hummus, for serving

Instructions:
1. Preheat oven to 425°F (220°C).
2. In a large bowl, combine chickpeas, olive oil, cumin, coriander, paprika, garlic powder, cinnamon, salt, and pepper. Toss to coat.
3. Spread the chickpea mixture on a baking sheet and bake for 25-30 minutes or until crispy and golden brown.
4. In a separate pan, sauté onions, bell peppers, and zucchini until softened.
5. To serve, fill pita bread with the chickpea mixture, sautéed vegetables, and tzatziki sauce or hummus.
6. Roll up the pita bread and enjoy!

Nutritional Value: Calories: 449 Fat: 18g Saturated Fat: 2g Cholesterol: 0mg Sodium: 637mg Carbohydrates: 59g Fiber: 8g Sugar: 7g

Main Recipes

96. Lentil Soup

Cooking Time: 40 minutes **Prep. Time:** 10 minutes **Servings:** 4

- 1 tbsp olive oil
- 1 onion, diced
- 2 cloves garlic, minced
- 2 carrots, peeled and diced
- 2 celery stalks, diced
- 1 tsp ground cumin
- 1 tsp ground coriander
- 1 tsp smoked paprika
- 1 tsp ground ginger
- 1/2 tsp ground turmeric
- 1 can (14 oz) diced tomatoes
- 1 cup dried lentils, rinsed and picked over
- 4 cups vegetable broth
- Salt and pepper to taste
- Fresh cilantro, chopped (optional)

Instructions:
1. In a large pot or Dutch oven, heat olive oil over medium heat. Add diced onion, minced garlic, diced carrots, diced celery, cumin, coriander, paprika, ginger, and turmeric. Cook for 5-7 minutes or until vegetables are softened.
2. Stir in diced tomatoes, lentils, and vegetable broth. Bring the mixture to a boil, then reduce heat and let simmer for 30-40 minutes or until lentils are tender.
3. Season with salt and pepper to taste.
4. Use an immersion blender to puree the soup until it reaches your desired consistency.
5. Stir in chopped cilantro (if using)
6. Serve hot and enjoy!

Nutritional Value: Calories: 210 Fat: 4g Saturated Fat: 0.5g Cholesterol: 0mg Sodium: 526mg Carbohydrates: 29g Fiber: 11g Sugar: 6g Protein: 12g

97. Vegetable Curry

Cooking Time: 30 minutes **Prep. Time:** 15 minutes **Servings:** 4

Ingredients:
- 1 onion, diced
- 2 cloves of garlic, minced
- 1 tablespoon of ginger, grated
- 2 tablespoons of vegetable oil
- 1 tablespoon of curry powder
- 1 teaspoon of cumin powder
- 1 teaspoon of coriander powder
- 1/2 teaspoon of turmeric powder
- 1/4 teaspoon of cayenne pepper (optional)
- 1 can of diced tomatoes
- 1 cup of coconut milk
- 1 cup of water
- 1 cup of mixed vegetables (such as carrots, bell peppers, potatoes, and peas)
- 1/4 cup of chopped cilantro for garnish
- Salt and pepper to taste

Instructions:
1. Heat the oil in a large pan over medium heat.
2. Add the onion and sauté for about 5 minutes, until softened.
3. Add the garlic and ginger and sauté for another minute.
4. Add the curry powder, cumin powder, coriander powder, turmeric powder, and cayenne pepper (if using) and stir for about 30 seconds.
5. Add the diced tomatoes, coconut milk, and water. Stir to combine.
6. Add the mixed vegetables and bring the mixture to a simmer.
7. Reduce the heat to low and let the curry simmer for about 15-20 minutes, or until the vegetables are tender.
8. Season with salt and pepper to taste.

9. Serve over rice or with naan bread, garnished with cilantro.

Nutritional Value: Calories: 227 kcal Fat: 18.5g Protein: 4.5g Carbs: 13.9g Fiber: 4.5g Sugar: 5.5g

98. Spaghetti With Marinara Sauce

Cooking Time: 10 minutes **Prep. Time:** 5 minutes **Servings:** 4

Ingredients:
- 1 lb spaghetti
- 1 tbsp olive oil
- 1 onion, diced
- 2 cloves garlic, minced
- 1 can (28 oz) crushed tomatoes
- 1 tsp dried basil
- 1 tsp dried oregano
- Salt and pepper to taste
- Parmesan cheese, grated (optional)
- Fresh basil, chopped (optional)

Instructions:
1. Bring a large pot of salted water to a boil. Add the spaghetti and cook according to package Instructions or until al dente. Drain the pasta and reserve 1 cup of the pasta cooking water.
2. In a large saucepan, heat olive oil over medium heat. Add diced onion and minced garlic. Cook for 5-7 minutes or until softened.
3. Stir in crushed tomatoes, basil, oregano, salt, and pepper. Bring the mixture to a simmer and let cook for 15-20 minutes.
4. If the sauce is too thick, add a little of the reserved pasta cooking water to thin it out.
5. Toss the cooked spaghetti with the marinara sauce.
6. Serve hot, with grated Parmesan cheese and chopped fresh basil (if using)

Nutritional Value: Calories: 380 Fat: 6g Saturated Fat: 1g Cholesterol: 0mg Sodium: 437mg Carbohydrates: 68g Fiber: 6g Sugar: 12g Protein: 13g

99. Grilled Portobello Mushrooms

Cooking Time: 10 minutes **Prep. Time:** 15 minutes **Servings:** 4

Ingredients:
- 4 large Portobello mushrooms
- 1/4 cup of olive oil
- 2 cloves of garlic, minced
- 2 tablespoons of balsamic vinegar
- 1 tablespoon of soy sauce
- 1 teaspoon of dried basil
- Salt and pepper to taste
- Lemon wedges for garnish

Instructions:
1. Clean the mushrooms by gently wiping them with a damp cloth.
2. Remove the stem and scrape out the gills with a spoon.
3. In a small bowl, mix together the olive oil, garlic, balsamic vinegar, soy sauce, dried basil, salt and pepper.
4. Brush the mushrooms with the marinade, making sure to coat both sides.
5. Heat the grill to medium-high heat.
6. Grill the mushrooms for about 5 minutes per side, or until tender.
7. Serve the mushrooms hot with lemon wedges as garnish.

Nutritional Value Calories: 78 kcal Fat: 7.7g Protein: 2.1g Carbs: 3.7g Fiber: 1.1g Sugar: 1.7g

100. Ratatouille

Cooking Time: 30 minutes **Prep. Time:** 10 minutes **Servings:** 4

Ingredients:
- 2 tbsp olive oil
- 1 onion, diced
- 2 cloves garlic, minced
- 1 eggplant, diced

- 2 bell peppers (one red, one yellow), diced
- 2 zucchinis, diced
- 2 cups diced tomatoes
- 1 tsp dried thyme
- 1 tsp dried basil
- Salt and pepper to taste
- Fresh basil, chopped (optional)

Instructions:
1. In a large skillet or Dutch oven, heat olive oil over medium heat. Add diced onion and minced garlic. Cook for 5-7 minutes or until softened.
2. Add the diced eggplant, bell peppers, and zucchinis. Cook for 10-15 minutes, stirring occasionally, or until the vegetables are softened.
3. Stir in diced tomatoes, thyme, basil, salt, and pepper. Bring the mixture to a simmer and let cook for an additional 10-15 minutes.
4. If the mixture becomes too thick, add a little water to thin it out.
5. Serve hot as a side dish, or over pasta, rice, or crusty bread. Garnish with chopped fresh basil (if using)

Nutritional Value: Calories: 131 Fat: 7g Saturated Fat: 1g Cholesterol: 0mg Sodium: 338mg Carbohydrates: 17g Fiber: 6g Sugar: 8g Protein: 3g

101. Vegetable Stir-Fry

Cooking Time: 15 minutes **Prep. Time:** 10 minutes **Servings:** 3

Ingredients:
- 1 tbsp vegetable oil
- 1 onion, sliced
- 2 cloves garlic, minced
- 2 cups sliced vegetables (such as bell peppers, carrots, broccoli, and mushrooms)
- 2 tbsp soy sauce
- 1 tbsp rice vinegar
- 1 tsp brown sugar
- 1 tsp cornstarch
- Salt and pepper to taste
- Cooked rice or noodles, for serving

Instructions:
1. In a large skillet or wok, heat vegetable oil over high heat. Add sliced onion and minced garlic. Cook for 2-3 minutes or until softened.
2. Add the sliced vegetables and stir-fry for 5-7 minutes or until they are tender but still crisp.
3. In a small bowl, mix together soy sauce, rice vinegar, brown sugar, cornstarch, salt and pepper.
4. Pour the sauce over the vegetables and stir-fry for an additional 1-2 minutes or until the sauce has thickened.
5. Serve the stir-fry over cooked rice or noodles.

Nutritional Value: Calories: 210 Fat: 8g Saturated Fat: 1g Cholesterol: 0mg Sodium: 865mg Carbohydrates: 26g Fiber: 3g Sugar: 7g Protein: 4g

102. Spinach And Feta Stuffed Shells

Cooking Time: 30 minutes **Prep. Time:** 15 minutes **Servings:** 4

Ingredients:
- 1 box of jumbo pasta shells
- 1 tablespoon of olive oil
- 1 onion, diced
- 2 cloves of garlic, minced
- 1 (10 ounce) package of frozen spinach, thawed and squeezed dry
- 1 cup of crumbled feta cheese
- 1/4 cup of grated Parmesan cheese
- 1/4 cup of chopped fresh parsley
- 1/2 cup of ricotta cheese

- Salt and pepper to taste
- 1 (24 ounce) jar of marinara sauce

Instructions:
1. Preheat the oven to 375°F (190°C)
2. Cook the pasta shells according to the package instructions
3. Drain and rinse the shells with cold water to cool them down.
4. Heat the olive oil in a skillet over medium heat.
5. Add the onion and sauté for about 5 minutes, or until softened.
6. Add the garlic and sauté for another minute.
7. In a large bowl, mix together the spinach, feta cheese, Parmesan cheese, parsley, ricotta cheese, salt, and pepper.
8. Stuff the mixture into the cooled pasta shells.
9. Spread 1/4 cup of marinara sauce on the bottom of a baking dish.
10. Arrange the stuffed shells on top of the sauce.
11. Pour the remaining marinara sauce over the shells.
12. Cover the dish with foil and bake for 20-25 minutes, or until heated through.
13. Remove the foil and bake for an additional 5-10 minutes, or until the top is lightly browned.

Nutritional Value Calories: 607 kcal Fat: 22.9g Protein: 27.6g Carbs: 70.6g Fiber: 5.6g Sugar: 10.3g

103.   Black Bean Tacos

Cooking Time: 15 minutes **Prep. Time:** 10 minutes **Servings:** 2
Ingredients:
- 1 tbsp vegetable oil
- 1 onion, diced
- 2 cloves garlic, minced
- 1 can (15 oz) black beans, drained and rinsed
- 1 tsp ground cumin
- 1 tsp chili powder
- Salt and pepper to taste
- 8-12 corn tortillas
- Toppings of your choice (such as diced tomatoes, shredded lettuce, cheese, sour cream, avocado, etc)

Instructions:
1. In a large skillet, heat vegetable oil over medium heat. Add diced onion and minced garlic. Cook for 5-7 minutes or until softened.
2. Stir in black beans, cumin, chili powder, salt, and pepper. Cook for an additional 5-7 minutes or until heated through.
3. Mash the black bean mixture with a fork or potato masher, leaving some beans whole for texture.
4. Heat the tortillas in a dry skillet or on a griddle over medium heat, until warm and pliable.
5. Assemble the tacos by spooning the black bean mixture onto the tortillas and adding toppings of your choice.
6. Serve and enjoy!

Nutritional Value: Calories: 212 Fat: 5g Saturated Fat: 1g Cholesterol: 0mg Sodium: 481mg Carbohydrates: 34g Fiber: 8g Sugar: 2g Protein: 9g

104.   Falafel

Cooking Time: 10 minutes **Prep. Time:** 10 minutes **Servings:** 3
Ingredients:
- 1 cup dried chickpeas, soaked overnight
- 1 onion, chopped
- 2 cloves garlic, minced
- 1/4 cup fresh parsley, chopped
- 1/4 cup fresh cilantro, chopped
- 2 tbsp flour

- 1 tsp ground cumin
- 1 tsp ground coriander
- 1/2 tsp baking powder
- Salt and pepper to taste
- Vegetable oil, for frying
- Pita bread, lettuce, tomatoes, and tahini sauce, for serving.

Instructions:
1. Drain the soaked chickpeas and place them in a food processor. Pulse until coarsely ground.
2. In a large mixing bowl, combine the ground chickpeas, chopped onion, minced garlic, chopped parsley, chopped cilantro, flour, cumin, coriander, baking powder, salt and pepper. Mix until well combined.
3. Use your hands to shape the mixture into small balls or patties.
4. Heat the oil in a deep pan or pot over medium-high heat. Fry the falafel balls in batches for 3-4 minutes per side or until golden brown. Drain on paper towels.
5. Serve the falafel in pita bread with lettuce, tomatoes and tahini sauce.

Nutritional Value: Calories: 255 Fat: 15g Saturated Fat: 1.5g Cholesterol: 0mg Sodium: 657mg Carbohydrates: 25g Fiber: 5g Sugar: 3g Protein: 7g

105. Vegetable Lasagna

Cooking Time: 45 minutes **Prep. Time:** 30 minutes **Servings:** 8

Ingredients:
- 1 tablespoon of olive oil
- 1 onion, diced
- 2 cloves of garlic, minced
- 1 zucchini, diced
- 1 bell pepper, diced
- 1 eggplant, diced
- 1 cup of sliced mushrooms
- 2 cups of spinach, chopped
- 1 teaspoon of dried basil
- 1 teaspoon of dried oregano
- Salt and pepper to taste
- 1 (15 ounce) container of ricotta cheese
- 1 egg
- 1/4 cup of grated Parmesan cheese
- 1/4 cup of chopped fresh parsley
- 1 (24 ounce) jar of marinara sauce
- 12 lasagna noodles, cooked according to package instructions
- 2 cups of shredded mozzarella cheese

Instructions:
1. Preheat the oven to 375°F (190°C).
2. Heat the olive oil in a skillet over medium heat.
3. Add the onion and sauté for about 5 minutes, or until softened.
4. Add the garlic, zucchini, bell pepper, eggplant, mushrooms, spinach, basil, oregano, salt, and pepper. Cook for 10-15 minutes or until the vegetables are tender.
5. In a medium bowl, mix together the ricotta cheese, egg, Parmesan cheese, parsley, and 1/2 teaspoon each of salt and pepper.
6. Spread 1/4 cup of marinara sauce on the bottom of a 9x13 inch baking dish.
7. Place 3 lasagna noodles on top of the sauce.
8. Spread 1/3 of the ricotta mixture over the noodles.
9. Spread 1/3 of the vegetable mixture over the ricotta.
10. Sprinkle 1/3 of the mozzarella cheese over the vegetables.
11. Repeat the layers twice more, ending with a layer of mozzarella cheese.
12. Cover the dish with foil and bake for 25 minutes.
13. Remove the foil and bake for an additional 20-25 minutes or until the cheese is golden brown and bubbly.

14. Let it cool for a few minutes before slicing and serving.

Nutritional Value: Calories: 368 kcal Fat: 17.8g Protein: 21.1g Carbs: 28.8g Fiber: 4.1g Sugar: 7.8g

106. Vegetable Paella

Cooking Time: 35 minutes **Prep. Time:** 15 minutes **Servings:** 2

Ingredients:
- 2 tbsp olive oil
- 1 onion, diced
- 2 cloves garlic, minced
- 1 red bell pepper, diced
- 1 cup diced tomatoes
- 1 tsp smoked paprika
- 1/2 tsp saffron threads
- 1 cup short-grain rice
- 2 cups vegetable broth
- 1 cup green beans, trimmed
- 1 cup peas
- Salt and pepper to taste
- Lemon wedges, for serving
- Fresh parsley, chopped (optional)

Instructions:
1. In a large paella pan or wide skillet, heat olive oil over medium heat. Add diced onion, minced garlic, and diced red bell pepper. Cook for 5-7 minutes or until softened.
2. Stir in diced tomatoes, smoked paprika, saffron threads, rice, and vegetable broth. Bring the mixture to a simmer and let cook for 10-15 minutes, or until the rice is almost tender.
3. Stir in green beans and peas, and season with salt and pepper to taste. Cover the pan and let cook for an additional 5-7 minutes or until the rice is tender and the vegetables are cooked through.
4. Remove the pan from the heat and let stand for 5 minutes before serving.
5. Serve with lemon wedges and garnish with chopped parsley (if using)

Nutritional Value: Calories: 260 Fat: 6g Saturated Fat: 1g Cholesterol: 0mg Sodium: 816mg Carbohydrates: 44g Fiber: 4g Sugar: 5g Protein: 7g

107. Eggplant Parmesan

Cooking Time: 40 minutes **Prep. Time:** 20 minutes **Servings:** 4

Ingredients:
- 2 medium eggplants, sliced into 1/4 inch rounds
- Salt
- 1 cup of all-purpose flour
- 2 eggs, beaten
- 1 cup of breadcrumbs
- 1/4 cup of grated Parmesan cheese
- 1 teaspoon of dried basil
- 1 teaspoon of dried oregano
- Salt and pepper to taste
- 1 cup of marinara sauce
- 1 cup of shredded mozzarella cheese
- 1/4 cup of chopped fresh basil for garnish

Instructions:
1. Preheat the oven to 375°F (190°C)
2. Place the eggplant slices in a single layer on a baking sheet and sprinkle with salt. Let them sit for about 15 minutes to release some of their moisture.
3. Rinse the eggplant slices and pat them dry with paper towels.
4. Place the flour, eggs, breadcrumbs, Parmesan cheese, basil, oregano, salt and pepper in three separate shallow dishes.
5. Dredge each eggplant slice in flour, shaking off any excess. Dip into the beaten eggs, then coat with breadcrumb mixture.
6. Heat a large skillet over medium heat and add enough oil to coat the bottom of the pan.

7. Add the eggplant slices and cook until golden brown on both sides, about 3-4 minutes per side.
8. Spread a thin layer of marinara sauce on the bottom of a 9x13 inch baking dish.
9. Place the fried eggplant slices on top of the sauce.
10. Spread the remaining marinara sauce over the eggplant slices.
11. Sprinkle the mozzarella cheese over the sauce.
12. Bake for 15-20 minutes, or until the cheese is melted and bubbly.
13. Garnish with fresh basil before serving.

Nutritional Value Calories: 468 kcal Fat: 21.7g Protein: 20.1g Carbs: 49.6g Fiber: 9.6g Sugar: 12.2g

108. Vegan Shepherd's Pie

Cooking Time: 50 minutes **Prep. Time:** 20 minutes **Servings:** 2
Ingredients:
- 2 tbsp olive oil
- 1 onion, diced
- 2 cloves garlic, minced
- 2 carrots, peeled and diced
- 2 celery stalks, diced
- 2 cups diced mushrooms
- 1 cup frozen peas
- 1 can (14 oz) diced tomatoes
- 1 tsp dried thyme
- 1 tsp dried rosemary
- Salt and pepper to taste
- 3 cups mashed potatoes (made with non-dairy milk)

Instructions:
1. Preheat the oven to 375F.
2. In a large pot or Dutch oven, heat olive oil over medium heat. Add diced onion, minced garlic, diced carrots, diced celery, and mushrooms. Cook for 5-7 minutes or until vegetables are softened.
3. Stir in frozen peas, diced tomatoes, thyme, rosemary, salt and pepper. Bring the mixture to a simmer and let cook for an additional 10-15 minutes or until the vegetables are tender.
4. Transfer the vegetable mixture to a baking dish.
5. Spread the mashed potatoes over the vegetable mixture, making sure to spread it evenly.
6. Bake for 20-25 minutes or until the potatoes are golden brown.
7. Serve hot and enjoy!

Nutritional Value: Calories: 276 Fat: 8g Saturated Fat: 1g Cholesterol: 0mg Sodium: 526mg Carbohydrates: 42g Fiber: 7g Sugar: 8g Protein: 7g

109. Vegetable Paella

Cooking Time: 30 minutes **Prep. Time:** 20 minutes **Servings:** 4
Ingredients:
- 1 tablespoon of olive oil
- 1 onion, diced
- 2 cloves of garlic, minced
- 1 red bell pepper, diced
- 1 cup of sliced mushrooms
- 1 cup of sliced zucchini
- 1 cup of frozen peas
- 1 teaspoon of paprika
- 1 teaspoon of turmeric
- 1 teaspoon of cumin
- Salt and pepper to taste
- 1 cup of Arborio rice
- 2 cups of vegetable broth
- 1 cup of diced tomatoes
- 1/4 cup of chopped fresh parsley for garnish
- Lemon wedges for garnish

Instructions:

1. Heat the olive oil in a large paella pan or a wide skillet over medium heat.
2. Add the onion and sauté for about 5 minutes, or until softened.
3. Add the garlic, bell pepper, mushrooms, zucchini, peas, paprika, turmeric, cumin, salt, and pepper. Sauté for another 5 minutes or until the vegetables are tender.
4. Stir in the rice and cook for 1-2 minutes.
5. Add the vegetable broth and diced tomatoes, bring to a simmer.
6. Reduce the heat to low, cover the pan and simmer for 20-25 minutes, or until the rice is tender and most of the liquid has been absorbed.
7. Remove the pan from heat and let it sit for a few minutes before fluffing the rice with a fork.
8. Garnish with parsley and serve with lemon wedges.

Nutritional Value: Calories: 334 kcal Fat: 6.2g Protein: 7.5g Carbs: 63.5g Fiber: 4.3g Sugar: 4.6g

110.   Vegetable Pad Thai

Cooking Time: 10 minutes **Prep. Time:** 20 minutes **Servings:** 4
Ingredients:
- 8 oz rice noodles
- 2 tbsp vegetable oil
- 2 cloves garlic, minced
- 1 onion, sliced
- 1 red bell pepper, sliced
- 1 cup sliced mushrooms
- 1 cup bean sprouts
- 2 eggs, lightly beaten (omit for vegan option)
- 2 tbsp soy sauce
- 2 tbsp rice vinegar
- 2 tbsp brown sugar
- 1 tsp chili flakes (optional)
- Salt and pepper to taste
- 2 green onions, thinly sliced
- 1/4 cup chopped peanuts
- Lime wedges, for serving
- Cilantro, chopped (optional)

Instructions:
1. Soak the rice noodles in warm water for 15-20 minutes or until softened. Drain and set aside.
2. Heat the oil in a large skillet or wok over medium-high heat. Add garlic and onion and cook for 2-3 minutes or until softened.
3. Add the red bell pepper, mushrooms, and bean sprouts. Stir-fry for an additional 2-3 minutes or until the vegetables are tender.
4. Push the vegetables to one side of the pan, and add the beaten eggs to the other side. Scramble the eggs until cooked through, then stir the eggs into the vegetables.
5. In a small bowl, mix together soy sauce, rice vinegar, brown sugar, chili flakes, salt, and pepper.
6. Add the sauce to the skillet along with the softened noodles. Stir-fry for an additional 2-3 minutes or until the noodles are coated in the sauce.
7. Remove skillet from heat, stir in green onions, chopped peanuts, and cilantro (if using).
8. Serve with lime wedges on the side and enjoy!

Nutritional Value: Calories: 431 Fat: 17g Saturated Fat: 2g Cholesterol: 97mg Sodium: 1235mg Carbohydrates: 59g Fiber: 4g Sugar: 12g Protein: 11g

111.   Vegetable Biryani

Cooking Time: 40 minutes **Prep. Time:** 20 minutes **Servings:** 4
Ingredients:

- 1 tablespoon of ghee or oil
- 1 onion, diced
- 2 cloves of garlic, minced
- 1 tablespoon of ginger, grated
- 1 cup of diced carrots
- 1 cup of diced potatoes
- 1 cup of frozen peas
- 1 cup of diced bell peppers
- 1 teaspoon of cumin powder
- 1 teaspoon of coriander powder
- 1 teaspoon of turmeric powder
- 1 teaspoon of garam masala
- Salt and pepper to taste
- 2 cups of basmati rice, rinsed and drained
- 2 cups of vegetable broth
- 1/4 cup of chopped fresh cilantro for garnish
- 1/4 cup of raisins (optional)
- 1/4 cup of cashews (optional)

Instructions:
1. Heat the ghee or oil in a large pot over medium heat.
2. Add the onion and sauté for about 5 minutes, or until softened.
3. Add the garlic and ginger and sauté for another minute.
4. Add the carrots, potatoes, peas, bell peppers, cumin powder, coriander powder, turmeric powder, garam masala, salt, and pepper. Sauté for 5 minutes or until the vegetables are tender.
5. Stir in the rice and cook for 2 minutes.
6. Add the vegetable broth, bring to a simmer.
7. Reduce the heat to low, cover the pot and simmer for 18-20 minutes, or until the rice is tender and most of the liquid has been absorbed.
8. Remove the pot from heat and let it sit for a few minutes before fluffing the rice with a fork.
9. Garnish with cilantro, raisins, and cashews if using.

Nutritional Value: Calories: 441 kcal Fat: 8.2g Protein: 8.2g Carbs: 80.9g Fiber: 5.4g Sugar: 4.2g

112. Grilled Eggplant Salad

Cooking Time: 5 minutes **Prep. Time:** 15 minutes **Servings:** 3

Ingredients:
- 2 large eggplants, sliced into 1/2-inch rounds
- 2 tbsp olive oil
- Salt and pepper to taste
- 2 cloves garlic, minced
- 2 tbsp red wine vinegar
- 1 tbsp honey
- 1/4 cup chopped fresh basil
- 1/4 cup chopped fresh parsley
- 1/4 cup chopped fresh mint
- 1/4 cup chopped fresh dill
- 1/4 cup chopped fresh cilantro
- Feta cheese, crumbled (optional)

Instructions:
1. Preheat grill to high heat.
2. Brush eggplant slices with olive oil and season with salt and pepper.
3. Grill the eggplant slices for 3-4 minutes per side or until tender and grill marks appear.
4. Remove from grill and let cool.
5. In a small bowl, mix together minced garlic, red wine vinegar, honey, and a pinch of salt and pepper.
6. In a large bowl, combine the grilled eggplant slices, the dressing, and all the chopped herbs. Toss to combine.
7. Let the salad sit for at least 10 minutes to allow the flavors to meld together.
8. Before serving, add crumbled feta cheese (if using) and toss to combine.

9. Serve as a side dish or as a main dish with some pita bread.

Nutritional Value: Calories: 108 Fat: 7g Saturated Fat: 1g Cholesterol: 0mg Sodium: 160mg Carbohydrates: 11g Fiber: 4g Sugar: 6g Protein: 2g

113. Vegetable And Tofu Fried Rice

Cooking Time: 20 minutes **Prep. Time:** 15 minutes **Servings:** 4

Ingredients:
- 1 tablespoon of oil
- 1 onion, diced
- 2 cloves of garlic, minced
- 1 tablespoon of ginger, grated
- 1 cup of diced carrots
- 1 cup of frozen peas
- 1 cup of diced bell peppers
- 1 teaspoon of soy sauce
- 1 teaspoon of rice vinegar
- 1 teaspoon of sesame oil
- Salt and pepper to taste
- 2 cups of cooked white rice, cooled and fluffed
- 1 (14 ounce) package of firm tofu, drained and diced
- 2 tablespoons of chopped fresh cilantro or green onions for garnish

Instructions:
1. Heat the oil in a large pan over medium heat.
2. Add the onion and sauté for about 5 minutes, or until softened.
3. Add the garlic and ginger and sauté for another minute.
4. Add the carrots, peas, bell peppers, soy sauce, rice vinegar, sesame oil, salt and pepper. Sauté for 5 minutes or until the vegetables are tender.
5. Add the tofu and cook for an additional 3-5 minutes, or until the tofu is heated through and lightly browned.
6. Stir in the cooked rice and cook for an additional 2-3 minutes, or until the rice is heated through.
7. Garnish with cilantro or green onions before serving.

Nutritional Value: Calories: 264 kcal Fat: 10.4g Protein: 12.5g Carbs: 32.3g Fiber: 3.8g Sugar: 3.5g

114. Vegetable And Quinoa Salad

Cooking Time: 20 minutes **Prep. Time:** 5 minutes **Servings:** 5

Ingredients:
- 1 cup quinoa
- 2 cups vegetable broth
- 1 tbsp olive oil
- 1 red bell pepper, diced
- 1 yellow bell pepper, diced
- 1 zucchini, diced
- 1 cup cherry tomatoes, halved
- 1/4 cup red onion, diced
- 1/4 cup chopped fresh parsley
- 1/4 cup chopped fresh mint
- 1/4 cup chopped fresh cilantro
- 2 tbsp red wine vinegar
- 2 tbsp lemon juice
- 1 tsp honey
- Salt and pepper to taste

Instructions:
1. Rinse the quinoa thoroughly in a fine-mesh strainer.
2. In a medium saucepan, bring the vegetable broth to a boil. Add the quinoa, reduce the heat to low, cover, and simmer for 18-20 minutes or until the liquid is absorbed and the quinoa is tender.

3. Remove from heat, fluff the quinoa with a fork, and let it cool to room temperature.
4. In a large bowl, combine the cooled quinoa, diced red and yellow bell peppers, diced zucchini, halved cherry tomatoes, diced red onion, chopped parsley, mint, and cilantro.
5. In a small bowl, whisk together olive oil, red wine vinegar, lemon juice, honey, and salt and pepper.
6. Pour the dressing over the quinoa mixture and toss to combine.
7. Let the salad sit for at least 10 minutes to allow the flavors to meld together.
8. Taste and adjust the seasoning as needed.
9. Serve as a side dish or as a main dish.

Nutritional Value: Calories: 236 Fat: 6g Saturated Fat: 0.8g Cholesterol: 0mg Sodium: 314mg Carbohydrates: 39g Fiber: 5g Sugar: 7g Protein: 7g

115. Vegetable Korma

Cooking Time: 30 minutes **Prep. Time:** 20 minutes **Servings:** 4

Ingredients:
- 1 tablespoon of oil or ghee
- 1 onion, finely diced
- 2 cloves of garlic, minced
- 1 tablespoon of ginger, grated
- 2 tablespoons of korma curry powder
- 1 teaspoon of ground cumin
- 1 teaspoon of ground coriander
- 1/2 teaspoon of ground turmeric
- 1/2 teaspoon of ground cinnamon
- Salt and pepper to taste
- 1 can of diced tomatoes
- 1 cup of coconut milk
- 1 cup of vegetable broth
- 2 cups of mixed vegetables (such as bell peppers, carrots, cauliflower, and peas)
- 1/4 cup of chopped fresh cilantro for garnish
- Cooked rice or naan bread for serving

Instructions:
1. Heat the oil or ghee in a large pot over medium heat.
2. Add the onion and sauté for about 5 minutes, or until softened.
3. Add the garlic and ginger and sauté for another minute.
4. Add the korma curry powder, cumin, coriander, turmeric, cinnamon, salt and pepper, and stir for about 1 minute until fragrant.
5. Add the diced tomatoes, coconut milk, and vegetable broth. Bring to a simmer.
6. Add the mixed vegetables and stir to combine.
7. Reduce the heat to low and let the curry simmer for 20-25 minutes or until the vegetables are tender and the sauce has thickened.
8. Garnish with cilantro before serving.

Nutritional Value: Calories: 348 kcal Fat: 26g Protein: 7g Carbs: 25g Fiber: 5g Sugar: 7g

116. Vegetable Risotto

Cooking Time: 25 minutes **Prep. Time:** 15 minutes **Servings:** 4

Ingredients:
- 2 tbsp olive oil
- 1 onion, diced
- 2 cloves garlic, minced
- 1 cup Arborio rice
- 1/2 cup white wine
- 4 cups vegetable broth
- 1 cup diced asparagus
- 1 cup diced mushrooms
- 1 cup frozen peas
- 1/4 cup grated Parmesan cheese (omit for vegan option)
- Salt and pepper to taste
- Fresh parsley, chopped (optional)

Instructions:

1. In a large pot or Dutch oven, heat olive oil over medium heat. Add diced onion and minced garlic and cook for 2-3 minutes or until softened.
2. Add the Arborio rice and stir to coat with the oil. Cook for 1-2 minutes or until the rice is lightly toasted.
3. Pour in the white wine and stir until the wine is absorbed.
4. Gradually add the vegetable broth, 1 cup at a time, stirring constantly and allowing each cup of broth to be absorbed before adding the next.
5. Once all the broth has been added, stir in the diced asparagus, diced mushrooms, frozen peas, and grated Parmesan cheese (if using).
6. Cook until the vegetables are tender and the rice is creamy, about 15-20 minutes.
7. Remove from heat and season with salt and pepper to taste.
8. Let the risotto sit for a few minutes before serving.
9. Garnish with chopped parsley (if using)

Nutritional Value: Calories: 358 Fat: 11g Saturated Fat: 3g Cholesterol: 8mg Sodium: 717mg Carbohydrates: 49g Fiber: 3g Sugar: 4g Protein: 11g

117. Vegetable Pot Pie

Cooking Time: 45 minutes **Prep. Time:** 20 minutes **Servings:** 4

Ingredients:
- 1 tablespoon of oil
- 1 onion, diced
- 2 cloves of garlic, minced
- 1 cup of diced carrots
- 1 cup of diced potatoes
- 1 cup of frozen peas
- 1 cup of diced bell peppers
- 1 teaspoon of dried thyme
- 1 teaspoon of dried rosemary
- 1/4 cup of all-purpose flour
- 1 cup of vegetable broth
- 1 cup of milk or cream
- Salt and pepper to taste
- 1 sheet of puff pastry, thawed
- 1 egg, beaten for egg wash

Instructions:
1. Preheat the oven to 425°F (220°C).
2. Heat the oil in a large pot over medium heat.
3. Add the onion and sauté for about 5 minutes, or until softened.
4. Add the garlic, carrots, potatoes, peas, bell peppers, thyme, rosemary, salt and pepper. Sauté for 5 minutes or until the vegetables are tender.
5. Sprinkle the flour over the vegetables and stir to combine.
6. Slowly pour in the vegetable broth and milk or cream, stirring constantly.
7. Bring the mixture to a simmer, and cook for 2-3 minutes, or until the sauce thickens.
8. Remove the pot from heat and let it cool for a few minutes.
9. Roll out the puff pastry sheet on a lightly floured surface.
10. Spoon the vegetable filling into a 9-inch pie dish or four individual ramekins.
11. Cut the puff pastry sheet to fit the top of the dish or ramekins.
12. Brush the puff pastry with the beaten egg.
13. Serve and enjoy

Nutritional Value: Calories: 322 Fat: 9g Saturated Fat: 2g Cholesterol: 15mg Sodium: 454mg Carbohydrates: 36g Fiber: 13g Sugar: 2g Protein: 9g

118. Roasted Cauliflower Soup

Cooking Time: 45 minutes **Prep. Time:** 15 minutes **Servings:** 6

Ingredients:

- 1 head cauliflower, chopped
- 2 tbsp olive oil
- Salt and pepper to taste
- 1 onion, diced
- 2 cloves garlic, minced
- 4 cups vegetable broth
- 1 cup milk or cream (omit for vegan option)
- 1/4 cup grated Parmesan cheese (omit for vegan option)
- Fresh parsley, chopped (optional)

Instructions:
1. Preheat the oven to 375°F.
2. Spread the chopped cauliflower on a baking sheet. Drizzle with olive oil and season with salt and pepper. Roast for 25-30 minutes or until golden brown.
3. In a large pot or Dutch oven, sauté diced onion and minced garlic in olive oil over medium heat for 2-3 minutes or until softened.
4. Add the roasted cauliflower, vegetable broth, milk or cream (if using) and bring to a simmer.
5. Reduce heat and let simmer for 10-15 minutes or until the cauliflower is very tender.
6. Remove from heat and let cool for a few minutes.
7. Using an immersion blender, blend the soup until smooth.
8. Return the pot to the heat, stir in grated Parmesan cheese (if using) and cook for an additional 2-3 minutes or until cheese is melted.
9. Season with salt and pepper to taste.
10. Serve in bowls and garnish with chopped parsley (if using)

Nutritional Value: Calories: 156 Fat: 12g Saturated Fat: 3g Cholesterol: 12mg Sodium: 814mg Carbohydrates: 10g Fiber: 3g Sugar: 4g Protein: 6g

119.　　Vegan Chili

Cooking Time: 1 hour **Prep. Time:** 15 minutes
Servings: 4
Ingredients:
- 1 tablespoon of oil
- 1 onion, diced
- 2 cloves of garlic, minced
- 1 cup of diced carrots
- 1 cup of diced bell peppers
- 2 cups of diced tomatoes
- 1 cup of vegetable broth
- 1 can of kidney beans, drained and rinsed
- 1 can of black beans, drained and rinsed
- 1 tablespoon of chili powder
- 1 teaspoon of cumin
- 1/2 teaspoon of smoked paprika
- Salt and pepper to taste
- 1/4 cup of chopped fresh cilantro for garnish
- Vegan sour cream or shredded vegan cheese for garnish
- Cooked rice or quinoa for serving

Instructions:
1. Heat the oil in a large pot over medium heat.
2. Add the onion and sauté for about 5 minutes, or until softened.
3. Add the garlic, carrots, bell peppers, chili powder, cumin, smoked paprika, salt, and pepper. Sauté for 5 minutes or until the vegetables are tender.
4. Stir in the diced tomatoes and vegetable broth. Bring to a simmer.
5. Add the kidney beans, black beans, and bring to a simmer.
6. Reduce the heat to low and let the chili simmer for 30-40 minutes, or until the vegetables are tender and the sauce has thickened.
7. Garnish with cilantro, vegan sour cream or shredded vegan cheese before serving.

8. Serve over cooked rice or quinoa.

Nutritional Value: Calories: 365 kcal Fat: 7g Protein: 18g Carbs: 61g Fiber: 18g Sugar: 12g

120. Vegetable Enchiladas

Cooking Time: 35 minutes **Prep. Time:** 10 minutes **Servings:** 5

Ingredients:
- 1 tbsp vegetable oil
- 1 onion, diced
- 2 cloves garlic, minced
- 1 cup diced bell peppers
- 1 cup diced zucchini
- 1 cup corn kernels
- 1 can black beans, drained and rinsed
- 1 cup diced tomatoes
- 1 tsp cumin powder
- 1 tsp chili powder
- Salt and pepper to taste
- 8-10 corn tortillas
- 1 cup grated cheddar cheese or vegan cheese
- 1 cup enchilada sauce
- Fresh cilantro, chopped (optional)

Instructions:
1. Preheat oven to 375°F.
2. In a large skillet, heat vegetable oil over medium heat. Add diced onion, minced garlic, diced bell peppers and diced zucchini. Cook for about 5-7 minutes or until softened.
3. Add corn kernels, black beans, diced tomatoes, cumin powder, chili powder, salt and pepper. Cook for an additional 2-3 minutes.
4. Spread a thin layer of enchilada sauce on the bottom of a baking dish.
5. Take each tortilla and fill it with the vegetable mixture, roll it up and place it seam side down in the baking dish.
6. Once all the tortillas are filled and placed in the baking dish, pour the remaining enchilada sauce over the top.
7. Sprinkle grated cheese over the top.
8. Bake in the oven for 20-25 minutes or until cheese is melted and bubbly.
9. Remove from the oven and let cool for a few minutes.
10. Garnish with chopped cilantro (if using) before serving.

Nutritional Value: Calories: 312 Fat: 14g Saturated Fat: 6g Cholesterol: 26mg Sodium: 708mg Carbohydrates: 36g Fiber: 7g Sugar: 5g Protein: 13g

121. Grilled Vegetable Skewers

Cooking Time: 20 minutes **Prep. Time:** 15 minutes **Servings:** 4

Ingredients:
- 2 bell peppers, cut into 1-inch squares
- 2 zucchinis, cut into 1-inch slices
- 1 red onion, cut into wedges
- 1 pint of cherry tomatoes
- 1/4 cup of olive oil
- 2 cloves of garlic, minced
- 2 tablespoons of balsamic vinegar
- 2 teaspoons of dried oregano
- Salt and pepper to taste
- Skewers (soak wooden skewers in water for 30 minutes before using)

Instructions:
1. Preheat grill to medium-high heat.
2. In a small bowl, mix together olive oil, garlic, balsamic vinegar, oregano, salt and pepper.
3. Thread vegetables onto skewers, alternating between each vegetable.
4. Brush skewers with marinade, reserving some for basting later.
5. Grill skewers for 10-15 minutes, turning occasionally and brushing with marinade,

or until vegetables are tender and slightly charred.
6. Remove skewers from grill and serve immediately.

Nutritional Value: Calories: 168 kcal Fat: 14g Protein: 2g Carbs: 11g Fiber: 3g Sugar: 7g

122. Roasted Vegetable And Hummus Wrap

Cooking Time: 35 minutes **Prep. Time:** 15 minutes **Servings:** 4
Ingredients:
- 1 red bell pepper, diced
- 1 yellow bell pepper, diced
- 1 small eggplant, diced
- 1 small zucchini, diced
- 1 tbsp olive oil
- Salt and pepper to taste
- 4 large whole wheat tortillas
- 1 cup hummus
- 1/2 cup crumbled feta cheese (omit for vegan option)
- 1/4 cup chopped fresh parsley

Instructions:
1. Preheat the oven to 425°F.
2. Spread the diced red bell pepper, diced yellow bell pepper, diced eggplant, and diced zucchini on a baking sheet. Drizzle with olive oil and season with salt and pepper. Roast for 25-30 minutes or until golden brown.
3. Remove from the oven and let cool.
4. Lay out the whole wheat tortillas on a flat surface. Spread hummus on each tortilla.
5. Add the roasted vegetables on top of the hummus.
6. Sprinkle crumbled feta cheese (if using) and chopped parsley on top of the vegetables.
7. Tightly roll up the tortilla to form a wrap.
8. Heat a large skillet over medium heat and cook the wraps for 2-3 minutes per side or until golden brown.
9. Slice in half and serve warm.

Nutritional Value: Calories: 335 Fat: 16g Saturated Fat: 3g Cholesterol: 10mg Sodium: 537mg Carbohydrates: 38g Fiber: 8g Sugar: 6g Protein: 13g

123. Vegetable And Bean Enchiladas

Cooking Time: 30 minutes **Prep. Time:** 15 minutes **Servings:** 4
Ingredients:
- 1 tablespoon of oil
- 1 onion, diced
- 2 cloves of garlic, minced
- 1 cup of diced bell peppers
- 1 cup of diced zucchini
- 1 can of black beans, drained and rinsed
- 1 cup of frozen corn
- 1 cup of enchilada sauce
- 8 corn tortillas
- 1 cup of shredded vegan cheese (optional)
- 1/4 cup of chopped fresh cilantro for garnish

Instructions:
1. Preheat the oven to 375°F (190°C).
2. Heat the oil in a large skillet over medium heat.
3. Add the onion and sauté for about 5 minutes, or until softened.
4. Add the garlic, bell peppers, zucchini, black beans, and corn. Sauté for 5 minutes or until the vegetables are tender.
5. Stir in 1/2 cup of enchilada sauce.
6. Spread 1/4 cup of enchilada sauce on the bottom of a 9x13 inch baking dish.
7. Spoon about 1/4 cup of the vegetable mixture onto each tortilla and roll up.
8. Arrange the enchiladas seam-side down in the baking dish.

9. Pour the remaining enchilada sauce over the top of the enchiladas and sprinkle with cheese, if using.
10. Bake for 15-20 minutes, or until the cheese is melted and the enchiladas are heated through.
11. Garnish with cilantro before serving.

Nutritional Value: Calories: 421 kcal Fat: 19g Protein: 16g Carbs: 52g Fiber: 13g Sugar: 6g

124. Vegetable And Cashew Cream Pasta

Cooking Time: 20 minutes **Prep. Time:** 5 minutes **Servings:** 2

Ingredients:
- 8 oz. spaghetti or any pasta of your choice
- 1 tbsp olive oil
- 1 onion, diced
- 2 cloves garlic, minced
- 1 cup diced mushrooms
- 1 cup diced bell peppers
- 1 cup diced zucchini
- 1 tsp dried thyme
- Salt and pepper to taste
- 1/2 cup raw cashews, soaked in water for at least 2 hours (or overnight)
- 1/2 cup water
- 1/4 cup grated Parmesan cheese (omit for vegan option)
- Fresh parsley, chopped (optional)

Instructions:
1. Cook pasta according to package instructions Drain and set aside.
2. In a large skillet, heat olive oil over medium heat. Add diced onion, minced garlic, diced mushrooms, diced bell peppers, diced zucchini, dried thyme, salt and pepper. Cook for about 5-7 minutes or until softened.
3. While the vegetables are cooking, drain the soaked cashews and add them to a blender along with 1/2 cup water. Blend until smooth and creamy.
4. Add the cashew cream to the skillet with the vegetables and stir until heated through.
5. Add the cooked pasta to the skillet and toss to coat with the sauce.
6. Stir in grated Parmesan cheese (if using) and cook for an additional 2-3 minutes or until cheese is melted.
7. Serve in bowls and garnish with chopped parsley (if using)

Nutritional Value: Calories: 513 Fat: 26g Saturated Fat: 5g Cholesterol: 8mg Sodium: 124mg Carbohydrates: 57g Fiber: 7g Sugar: 7g Protein: 17g

125. Vegetable And Black Bean Burger

Cooking Time: 10 minutes **Prep. Time:** 10 minutes **Servings:** 4

Ingredients:
- 1 cup cooked black beans
- 1 cup cooked brown rice
- 1/2 cup diced onion
- 1/2 cup diced bell pepper
- 1/2 cup grated carrots
- 1/4 cup bread crumbs
- 2 tbsp flaxseed meal
- 2 tbsp chopped cilantro
- 1 tsp ground cumin
- Salt and pepper to taste
- 1 tbsp vegetable oil
- Whole wheat buns or lettuce wraps for serving
- Optional toppings: avocado, cheese, lettuce, tomato, ketchup, mustard, mayo

Instructions:

1. In a large mixing bowl, mash the black beans with a fork or potato masher.
2. Add the cooked brown rice, diced onion, diced bell pepper, grated carrots, bread crumbs, flaxseed meal, chopped cilantro, ground cumin, salt, and pepper. Mix well until everything is evenly distributed.
3. Divide the mixture into 4-6 portions and shape each portion into a patty.
4. Heat a large skillet over medium-high heat and add the vegetable oil. Cook the patties for about 3-4 minutes per side or until golden brown.
5. Serve the burgers on whole wheat buns or lettuce wraps with your choice of toppings.

Nutritional Value: Calories: 280 Fat: 6g Saturated Fat: 1g Cholesterol: 0mg Sodium: 270mg Carbohydrates: 48g Fiber: 8g Sugar: 3g Protein: 10g

126. Vegetable And Lentil Dahl

Cooking Time: 30 minutes **Prep. Time:** 15 minutes **Servings:** 4
Ingredients:
- 1 tablespoon of oil
- 1 onion, finely diced
- 2 cloves of garlic, minced
- 1 tablespoon of ginger, grated
- 2 tablespoons of curry powder
- 1 teaspoon of ground cumin
- 1 teaspoon of ground coriander
- 1/2 teaspoon of ground turmeric
- 1/2 teaspoon of ground cinnamon
- Salt and pepper to taste
- 1 can of diced tomatoes
- 1 cup of red lentils, rinsed and drained
- 2 cups of vegetable broth
- 1 cup of mixed vegetables (such as bell peppers, carrots, and peas)
- 1/4 cup of chopped fresh cilantro for garnish
- Cooked rice or naan bread for serving

Instructions:
1. Heat the oil in a large pot over medium heat.
2. Add the onion and sauté for about 5 minutes, or until softened.
3. Add the garlic and ginger and sauté for another minute.
4. Add the curry powder, cumin, coriander, turmeric, cinnamon, salt and pepper. Stir for about 1 minute until fragrant.
5. Add the diced tomatoes, lentils, vegetable broth, and mixed vegetables. Bring to a simmer.
6. Reduce the heat to low and let the Dahl simmer for 20-25 minutes or until the lentils and vegetables are tender and the sauce has thickened.
7. Garnish with cilantro before serving.

Nutritional Value: Calories: 324 kcal Fat: 6g Protein: 16g Carbs: 52g Fiber: 16g Sugar: 12g

127. Vegetable And Tofu Korma

Cooking Time: 20 minutes **Prep. Time:** 20 minutes **Servings:** 4
Ingredients:
- 1 tbsp vegetable oil
- 1 onion, diced
- 2 cloves garlic, minced
- 1 tbsp ginger, grated
- 1 tsp ground cumin
- 1 tsp ground coriander
- 1 tsp ground turmeric
- 1 tsp garam masala
- 1/2 tsp ground cinnamon
- Salt and pepper to taste
- 1 cup diced tomatoes
- 1 cup coconut milk
- 1 cup diced vegetables (such as carrots, bell peppers, and potatoes)
- 1 block firm tofu, diced

- 1/4 cup cashews, soaked in water for at least 2 hours (or overnight)
- Fresh cilantro, chopped (optional)
- Cooked rice or naan bread for serving

Instructions:
1. In a large pot or Dutch oven, heat vegetable oil over medium heat. Add diced onion, minced garlic, and grated ginger. Cook until softened, about 3-4 minutes.
2. Add ground cumin, ground coriander, ground turmeric, garam masala, ground cinnamon, salt and pepper. Cook for an additional 2 minutes.
3. Add diced tomatoes, coconut milk, diced vegetables, diced tofu, and soaked cashews. Stir to combine.
4. Bring the mixture to a simmer and let cook for 10-15minutes or until the vegetables are tender.
5. Remove from heat and stir in chopped cilantro (if using)
6. Serve over cooked rice or with naan bread.

Nutritional Value: Calories: 365 Fat: 22g Saturated Fat: 11g Cholesterol: 0mg Sodium: 205mg Carbohydrates: 30g Fiber: 6g Sugar: 8g Protein: 13g

128. Vegetable And Tofu Scramble

Cooking Time: 15 minutes **Prep. Time:** 10 minutes **Servings:** 4

Ingredients:
- 1 tablespoon of oil
- 1 onion, diced
- 2 cloves of garlic, minced
- 1 cup of diced bell peppers
- 1 cup of diced mushrooms
- 1 cup of diced tomatoes
- 1 block of firm tofu, crumbled
- 1 teaspoon of turmeric powder
- Salt and pepper to taste
- 1/4 cup of chopped fresh cilantro for garnish
- Served with toast or tortillas

Instructions:
1. Heat the oil in a large skillet over medium heat.
2. Add the onion and sauté for about 5 minutes, or until softened.
3. Add the garlic, bell peppers, mushrooms, tomatoes, and sauté for another 5 minutes or until the vegetables are tender.
4. Add the crumbled tofu, turmeric powder, salt, and pepper. Stir until the tofu is evenly coated with the spices.
5. Cook for another 5 minutes or until the tofu is heated through.
6. Garnish with cilantro before serving.

Nutritional Value: Calories: 123 kcal Fat: 8g Protein: 8g Carbs: 9g Fiber: 2g Sugar: 4g

129. Vegetable And Lentil Shepherd's Pie

Cooking Time: 45 minutes **Prep. Time:** 15 minutes **Servings:** 4

Ingredients:
- 1 tbsp vegetable oil
- 1 onion, diced
- 2 cloves garlic, minced
- 1 cup diced carrots
- 1 cup diced celery
- 1 cup frozen peas
- 1 cup cooked green or brown lentils
- 1 cup vegetable broth
- 1 tsp dried thyme
- 1 tsp dried rosemary
- Salt and pepper to taste
- 3 cups mashed potatoes
- 1/4 cup grated Parmesan cheese (omit for vegan option)

Instructions:

1. Preheat the oven to 375°F.
2. In a large skillet, heat vegetable oil over medium heat. Add diced onion, minced garlic, diced carrots, diced celery, and frozen peas. Cook for about 5-7 minutes or until softened.
3. Add cooked lentils, vegetable broth, dried thyme, dried rosemary, salt, and pepper. Bring to a simmer and let cook for an additional 5 minutes.
4. Transfer the vegetable and lentil mixture to a baking dish.
5. Spread the mashed potatoes over the top of the mixture and smooth out with a fork.
6. Sprinkle grated Parmesan cheese over the top of the mashed potatoes (if using).
7. Bake in the oven for 25-30 minutes or until the top is golden brown and bubbly.
8. Let cool for a few minutes before serving.

Nutritional Value: Calories: 297 Fat: 8g Saturated Fat: 2g Cholesterol: 8mg Sodium: 177mg Carbohydrates: 44g Fiber: 8g Sugar: 6g Protein: 12g

130. Vegetable And Pesto Quiche

Cooking Time: 45 minutes **Prep. Time:** 20 minutes **Servings:** 4

Ingredients:
- 1 pre-made 9-inch pie crust
- 1/4 cup of pesto
- 1/2 cup of diced bell peppers
- 1/2 cup of diced tomatoes
- 1/2 cup of diced mushrooms
- 1/2 cup of diced onion
- 3 eggs
- 1 cup of milk
- 1 cup of shredded cheese (cheddar or mozzarella)
- Salt and pepper to taste
- 1/4 cup of chopped fresh basil for garnish

Instructions:
1. Preheat the oven to 375°F (190°C).
2. Spread the pesto on the bottom of the pre-made pie crust.
3. Sprinkle the diced bell peppers, tomatoes, mushrooms, and onion on top of the pesto.
4. In a mixing bowl, beat the eggs, milk, salt, and pepper. Pour the mixture over the vegetables.
5. Sprinkle the shredded cheese on top of the quiche.
6. Bake for 30-35 minutes or until the quiche is set and the crust is golden brown.
7. Garnish with fresh basil before serving.

Nutritional Value: Calories: 456 kcal Fat: 33g Protein: 14g Carbs: 27g Fiber: 2g Sugar: 5g

131. Vegetable And Tofu Broccoli Stir Fry-

Cooking Time: 20 minutes **Prep. Time:** 15 minutes **Servings:** 4

Ingredients:
- 1 tablespoon of oil
- 1 onion, thinly sliced
- 2 cloves of garlic, minced
- 1 cup of broccoli florets
- 1 cup of sliced bell peppers
- 1 block of firm tofu, cut into small cubes
- 2 tablespoons of soy sauce
- 2 tablespoons of hoisin sauce
- 1 teaspoon of sesame oil
- 1 teaspoon of cornstarch
- Salt and pepper to taste
- 1/4 cup of chopped fresh cilantro for garnish
- Served with rice or quinoa

Instructions:
1. Heat the oil in a large skillet or wok over high heat.

2. Add the onion and sauté for about 2 minutes, or until softened.
3. Add the garlic and sauté for another 30 seconds.
4. Add the broccoli, bell peppers, and tofu, and stir-fry for 3-5 minutes or until the vegetables are tender and the tofu is slightly golden brown.
5. In a small bowl, mix together soy sauce, hoisin sauce, sesame oil, cornstarch, salt and pepper.
6. Pour the sauce over the stir-fry and cook for another 2-3 minutes or until the sauce is thickened.
7. Garnish with cilantro before serving.

Nutritional Value: Calories: 181 kcal Fat: 11g Protein: 11g Carbs: 11g Fiber: 3g Sugar: 4g

132. Vegetable And Ricotta Stuffed Shells

Cooking Time: 25 minutes **Prep. Time:** 10 minutes **Servings:** 2

Ingredients:
- 12 jumbo pasta shells
- 1 tbsp olive oil
- 1 onion, diced
- 2 cloves garlic, minced
- 1 cup diced mushrooms
- 1 cup diced bell peppers
- 1 cup frozen spinach, thawed and squeezed dry
- 1 cup ricotta cheese
- 1 cup shredded mozzarella cheese
- 1/4 cup grated Parmesan cheese
- 1 egg
- Salt and pepper to taste
- 2 cups marinara sauce

Instructions:
1. Preheat the oven to 375°F.
2. Cook the pasta shells according to the package instructions until al dente. Drain and set aside.
3. In a large skillet, heat olive oil over medium heat. Add diced onion, minced garlic, diced mushrooms, diced bell peppers, frozen spinach, salt and pepper. Cook for about 5-7 minutes or until softened.
4. In a mixing bowl, combine ricotta cheese, shredded mozzarella cheese, grated Parmesan cheese, egg, and a pinch of salt and pepper. Mix well.
5. Stuff each pasta shell with the cheese mixture and place them in a baking dish.
6. Pour marinara sauce over the shells.
7. Cover with foil and bake for 20-25 minutes or until the cheese is melted and bubbly.
8. Remove from the oven and let cool for a few minutes before serving.

Nutritional Value: Calories: 330 Fat: 17g Saturated Fat: 9g Cholesterol: 63mg Sodium: 679mg Carbohydrates: 24g Fiber: 3g Sugar: 6g Protein: 17g

133. Vegetable And Black Bean Quesadilla

Cooking Time: 15 minutes **Prep. Time:** 10 minutes **Servings:** 4

Ingredients:
- 4 large flour tortillas
- 1 cup of shredded cheese (cheddar or Monterey jack)
- 1 can of black beans, drained and rinsed
- 1 cup of diced bell peppers
- 1 cup of diced onions
- 1 cup of diced tomatoes
- 1/4 cup of chopped fresh cilantro
- Sour cream or salsa for garnish

Instructions:
1. Heat a large skillet over medium heat.

2. Place one tortilla in the skillet and sprinkle 1/4 cup of cheese, 1/4 cup of black beans, 1/4 cup of bell peppers, 1/4 cup of onions, and 1/4 cup of tomatoes over one half of the tortilla.
3. Fold the other half of the tortilla over the filling, press down gently with a spatula.
4. Cook for 2-3 minutes per side or until the tortilla is golden brown and the cheese is melted.
5. Repeat with the remaining tortillas and filling.
6. Cut into wedges, garnish with cilantro, and serve with sour cream or salsa.

Nutritional Value: Calories: 356 kcal Fat: 12g Protein: 16g Carbs: 46g Fiber: 8g Sugar: 4g

134. Vegetable And Tofu Fried Rice

Cooking Time: 20 minutes **Prep. Time:** 15 minutes **Servings:** 4
Ingredients:
- 1 tablespoon of oil
- 1 onion, diced
- 2 cloves of garlic, minced
- 1 cup of diced carrots
- 1 cup of diced bell peppers
- 2 cups of cooked white or brown rice
- 1 block of firm tofu, cut into small cubes
- 2 tablespoons of soy sauce
- 2 tablespoons of oyster sauce
- 1 teaspoon of sesame oil
- 1 teaspoon of sugar
- Salt and pepper to taste
- 1/4 cup of chopped green onions for garnish
- 1/4 cup of chopped cilantro for garnish

Instructions:
1. Heat the oil in a large skillet or wok over high heat.
2. Add the onion and sauté for about 2 minutes, or until softened.
3. Add the garlic and sauté for another 30 seconds.
4. Add the carrots, bell peppers, and tofu and stir-fry for 3-5 minutes or until the vegetables are tender and the tofu is slightly golden brown.
5. Add the cooked rice and stir-fry for another 2-3 minutes or until the rice is heated through.
6. In a small bowl, mix together soy sauce, oyster sauce, sesame oil, sugar, salt and pepper.
7. Pour the sauce over the stir-fry and cook for another 2-3 minutes or until the sauce is thickened and evenly mixed with the rice.
8. Garnish with green onions and cilantro before serving.

Nutritional Value: Calories: 314 kcal Fat: 12g Protein: 11g Carbs: 42g Fiber: 3g Sugar: 5g

135. Vegetable And Tofu Curry

Cooking Time: 30 minutes **Prep. Time:** 15 minutes **Servings:** 4
Ingredients:
- 2 tablespoons of oil
- 1 onion, diced
- 2 cloves of garlic, minced
- 2 tablespoons of curry powder
- 1 teaspoon of ground cumin
- 1 teaspoon of ground coriander
- 1/2 teaspoon of ground turmeric
- 1/2 teaspoon of ground cinnamon
- Salt and pepper to taste
- 1 can of diced tomatoes
- 1 cup of coconut milk
- 1 cup of diced carrots
- 1 cup of diced bell peppers
- 1 block of firm tofu, cut into small cubes

- 1/4 cup of chopped fresh cilantro for garnish
- Cooked rice or naan bread for serving

Instructions:
1. Heat the oil in a large pot over medium heat.
2. Add the onion and sauté for about 5 minutes, or until softened.
3. Add the garlic, curry powder, cumin, coriander, turmeric, cinnamon, salt and pepper. Stir for about 1 minute until fragrant.
4. Add the diced tomatoes, coconut milk, carrots, bell peppers, and tofu. Bring to a simmer.
5. Reduce the heat to low and let the curry simmer for 20-25 minutes or until the vegetables are tender.
6. Garnish with cilantro before serving.

Nutritional Value: Calories: 303 kcal Fat: 24g Protein: 12g Carbs: 18g Fiber: 5g Sugar: 8g

136. Vegetable And Lentil Soup

Cooking Time: 15 minutes **Prep. Time:** 5 minutes **Servings:** 4

Ingredients:
- 1 tbsp olive oil
- 1 onion, diced
- 2 cloves garlic, minced
- 2 carrots, peeled and diced
- 2 celery stalks, diced
- 1 cup green or brown lentils, rinsed
- 4 cups vegetable broth
- 2 cups water
- 1 can diced tomatoes
- 1 tsp dried thyme
- 1 tsp dried oregano
- Salt and pepper to taste
- 1 cup chopped kale or spinach (optional)
- 1/4 cup chopped fresh parsley or cilantro (optional)

Instructions:
1. In a large pot or Dutch oven, heat olive oil over medium heat. Add diced onion, minced garlic, diced carrots, and diced celery. Cook for about 5-7 minutes or until softened.
2. Add rinsed lentils, vegetable broth, water, diced tomatoes, dried thyme, dried oregano, salt and pepper. Bring to a boil, then reduce the heat and let simmer for about 30 minutes or until the lentils are tender.
3. If desired, add chopped kale or spinach and let cook for an additional 5 minutes or until wilted.
4. Remove from heat and stir in chopped parsley or cilantro (if using)
5. Serve hot, garnished with additional fresh herbs or a drizzle of olive oil if desired.

Nutritional Value: Calories: 235 Fat: 4g Saturated Fat: 1g Cholesterol: 0mg Sodium: 898mg Carbohydrates: 37g Fiber: 14g Sugar: 6g Protein: 13g

137. Vegetable And Tofu Pad Thai

Cooking Time: 20 minutes **Prep. Time:** 15 minutes **Servings:** 4

Ingredients:
- 8 oz. of rice noodles
- 2 tablespoons of oil
- 2 cloves of garlic, minced
- 1/2 cup of diced onion
- 1 cup of sliced bell peppers
- 1 cup of sliced mushrooms
- 1 block of firm tofu, cut into small cubes
- 2 tablespoons of soy sauce
- 2 tablespoons of oyster sauce
- 1 tablespoon of brown sugar
- 1 teaspoon of chili flakes (optional)
- 2 eggs, lightly beaten

- 1/4 cup of chopped peanuts
- 1/4 cup of chopped cilantro
- Lime wedges for serving

Instructions:
1. Soak the rice noodles in warm water for 15 minutes or until softened. Drain and set aside.
2. Heat the oil in a large skillet or wok over high heat.
3. Add the garlic, onion, bell peppers, mushrooms, and tofu, and stir-fry for 3-5 minutes or until the vegetables are tender and the tofu is slightly golden brown.
4. Add the soy sauce, oyster sauce, brown sugar, and chili flakes (if using) and stir-fry for another 2-3 minutes or until the sauce is thickened.
5. Push the vegetables and tofu to one side of the skillet and pour the eggs into the other side. Scramble the eggs until cooked through.
6. Add the rice noodles and toss to combine with the vegetables and tofu.
7. Garnish with peanuts and cilantro before serving. Serve with lime wedges on the side.

Nutritional Value: Calories: 365 kcal Fat: 13g Protein: 24g Carbohydrates: 32g Fiber: 9g Sugar: 2g

138. Vegetable And Tofu Satay

Cooking Time: 10 minutes **Prep. Time:** 5 minutes **Servings:** 4

Ingredients:
- 1 block firm tofu, pressed and diced
- 1/4 cup soy sauce
- 2 tbsp brown sugar
- 2 tbsp rice vinegar
- 2 tbsp vegetable oil
- 2 cloves garlic, minced
- 1 tsp grated ginger
- 1/4 tsp red pepper flakes
- Salt and pepper to taste
- 1 red bell pepper, sliced
- 1 yellow bell pepper, sliced
- 1 onion, sliced
- 1 cup sliced mushrooms
- Skewers (if using wooden skewers, soak in water for at least 30 minutes before using)
- Peanut sauce for serving

Instructions:
1. In a shallow dish, mix together the soy sauce, brown sugar, rice vinegar, vegetable oil, minced garlic, grated ginger, red pepper flakes, salt, and pepper.
2. Add the diced tofu and toss to coat. Let marinate for at least 30 minutes.
3. Preheat grill or grill pan to medium-high heat.
4. Thread the marinated tofu, bell peppers, onion, and mushrooms onto skewers.
5. Grill the skewers for about 8-10 minutes, turning occasionally, or until the vegetables are tender and the tofu is slightly charred.
6. Serve with peanut sauce for dipping.

Nutritional Value: Calories: 245 Fat: 17g Saturated Fat: 2g Cholesterol: 0mg Sodium: 1044mg Carbohydrates: 15g Fiber: 2g Sugar: 10g Protein: 12g

139. Vegetable And Tofu Tikka Masala

Cooking Time: 30 minutes **Prep. Time:** 15 minutes **Servings:** 4

Ingredients:

2 tablespoons of oil
- 1 onion, finely diced
- 2 cloves of garlic, minced
- 1 tablespoon of ginger, grated
- 2 tablespoons of tikka masala powder
- 1 teaspoon of ground cumin

- 1 teaspoon of ground coriander
- 1/2 teaspoon of ground turmeric
- Salt and pepper to taste
- 1 can of diced tomatoes
- 1 cup of coconut milk
- 1 cup of diced carrots
- 1 cup of diced bell peppers
- 1 block of firm tofu, cut into small cubes
- 1/4 cup of chopped fresh cilantro for garnish
- Cooked rice or naan bread for serving

Instructions:
1. Heat the oil in a large pot over medium heat.
2. Add the onion and sauté for about 5 minutes, or until softened.
3. Add the garlic and ginger and sauté for another minute.
4. Add the tikka masala powder, cumin, coriander, turmeric, salt, and pepper. Stir for about 1 minute until fragrant.
5. Add the diced tomatoes, coconut milk, carrots, bell peppers, and tofu. Bring to a simmer.
6. Reduce the heat to low and let the curry simmer for 20-25 minutes or until the vegetables are tender.
7. Garnish with cilantro before serving.

Nutritional Value: Calories: 303 kcal Fat: 24g Protein: 12g Carbs: 18g Fiber: 5g Sugar: 8g

140. Vegetable And Tofu Enchiladas

Cooking Time: 30 minutes **Prep. Time:** 15 minutes **Servings:** 4

Ingredients:
- 8 corn tortillas
- 1 can of enchilada sauce
- 1 cup of diced bell peppers
- 1 cup of diced onions
- 1 cup of diced mushrooms
- 1 block of firm tofu, crumbled
- 1 cup of shredded cheese (cheddar or Monterey jack)
- 1/4 cup of chopped fresh cilantro for garnish
- Sour cream or salsa for garnish

Instructions:
1. Preheat the oven to 375°F (190°C).
2. Spread 1/4 cup of enchilada sauce on the bottom of a 9x13 inch baking dish.
3. In a mixing bowl, combine the bell peppers, onions, mushrooms, tofu, and 1/2 cup of cheese.
4. Place about 1/4 cup of the vegetable and tofu mixture in the center of each tortilla. Roll up the tortillas and place them seam-side down in the baking dish.
5. Pour the remaining enchilada sauce over the top of the tortillas and sprinkle with the remaining cheese.
6. Bake for 20-25 minutes or until the cheese is melted and the tortillas are crispy.
7. Garnish with cilantro and serve with sour cream or salsa.

Nutritional Value: Calories: 327 kcal Fat: 18g Protein: 16g Carbs: 25g Fiber: 5g Sugar: 5g

141. Vegetable And Tofu And Vegetable Pot Pie

Cooking Time: 40 minutes **Prep. Time:** 20 minutes **Servings:** 5

Ingredients:
- 1 tbsp vegetable oil
- 1 onion, diced
- 2 cloves garlic, minced
- 2 cups diced mixed vegetables (such as carrots, celery, and peas)
- 1 block firm tofu, pressed and diced
- 1/4 cup all-purpose flour
- 2 cups vegetable broth
- 1/2 cup milk (or non-dairy milk)

- 1 tsp dried thyme
- 1 tsp dried rosemary
- Salt and pepper to taste
- 1 sheet puff pastry, thawed
- 1 egg (or non-dairy milk), beaten (for brushing)

Instructions:
1. Preheat the oven to 400°F.
2. In a large pot or Dutch oven, heat vegetable oil over medium heat. Add diced onion, minced garlic, mixed vegetables and diced tofu. Cook for about 5-7 minutes or until softened.
3. Sprinkle flour over the vegetables and tofu and stir to combine. Cook for 2-3 minutes, stirring constantly.
4. Slowly add the vegetable broth, milk, dried thyme, dried rosemary, salt, and pepper to the pot. Bring to a simmer and let cook for an additional 5 minutes or until the sauce thickens.
5. Remove from heat.
6. Pour the vegetable and tofu mixture into a 9-inch pie dish.
7. Roll out the puff pastry to fit over the top of the pie dish, and press the edges to seal. Brush the beaten egg or non-dairy milk over the top of the pastry.
8. Bake the pot pie for 25-30 minutes or until the pastry is golden brown and puffed.
9. Let cool for a few minutes before serving.

Nutritional Value: Calories: 318 Fat: 21g Saturated Fat: 5g Cholesterol: 14mg Sodium: 519mg Carbohydrates: 26g Fiber: 3g Sugar: 4g Protein: 7g

142. Vegetable And Tofu And Vegetable Biryani

Cooking Time: 45 minutes **Prep. Time:** 20 minutes **Servings:** 4
Ingredients:

- 2 cups of basmati rice
- 1 tablespoon of oil
- 1 onion, diced
- 2 cloves of garlic, minced
- 1 tablespoon of ginger, grated
- 2 teaspoons of ground cumin
- 2 teaspoons of ground coriander
- 1 teaspoon of ground turmeric
- 1 teaspoon of garam masala
- Salt and pepper to taste
- 2 cups of diced vegetables (carrots, bell peppers, peas)
- 1 block of firm tofu, cut into small cubes
- 1/2 cup of cashews
- 1/4 cup of raisins
- 1/4 cup of chopped fresh cilantro for garnish
- 1/4 cup of chopped fresh mint for garnish

Instructions:
1. Rinse the rice in cold water and drain.
2. In a pot, bring 4 cups of water to a boil. Add the rice and stir. Reduce the heat to low, cover the pot and let it simmer for 18-20 minutes or until the rice is tender and the water is absorbed. Remove from heat and set aside.
3. In a pan, heat oil and sauté onions until translucent.
4. Add the garlic and ginger and sauté for another minute.
5. Add the cumin, coriander, turmeric, garam masala, salt and pepper. Stir for about 1 minute until fragrant.
6. Add the diced vegetables, tofu, cashews and raisins and sauté for about 5-7 minutes or until the vegetables are tender.
7. Add the sautéed vegetables and tofu mixture to the cooked rice and stir gently.
8. Garnish with cilantro and mint before serving.

Nutritional Value: Calories: 466 kcal Fat: 17g Protein: 14g Carbs: 68g Fiber: 4g Sugar: 7g

Salad

143. Greek Salad Recipe

Prep. Time: 5 minutes **Servings:** 2
Ingredients:
- 4 cups chopped romaine lettuce
- 1 cup chopped tomatoes
- 1 cup diced cucumber
- 1/2 cup sliced red onion
- 1/2 cup sliced kalamata olives
- 1/2 cup crumbled feta cheese
- 1/4 cup chopped fresh parsley
- 2 tbsp olive oil
- 2 tbsp red wine vinegar
- 1 clove of garlic, minced
- 1 tsp dried oregano
- Salt and pepper to taste

Instructions:
1. In a large mixing bowl, combine chopped romaine lettuce, chopped tomatoes, diced cucumber, sliced red onion, sliced kalamata olives, crumbled feta cheese, and chopped parsley.
2. In a small mixing bowl, whisk together olive oil, red wine vinegar, minced garlic, dried oregano, salt, and pepper.
3. Drizzle the dressing over the salad and toss to coat evenly.
4. Serve the Greek salad immediately or chilled.

Nutritional Value: Calories: 205 Fat: 17g Saturated Fat: 5g Cholesterol: 18mg Sodium: 528mg Carbohydrates: 10g Fiber: 3g Sugar: 3g Protein: 5g

144. Classic Caprese Salad

Prep. Time: 10 minutes **Servings:** 4
Ingredients:
- 2 cups of cherry tomatoes, halved
- 8 oz fresh mozzarella cheese, diced
- 1/4 cup fresh basil leaves, torn
- 2 tablespoons extra-virgin olive oil
- 1 tablespoon balsamic vinegar
- Salt and pepper, to taste

Instructions:
1. On a large platter or in a large bowl, combine the cherry tomatoes, mozzarella cheese, and basil leaves.
2. In a small bowl, whisk together the olive oil and balsamic vinegar.
3. Pour the dressing over the salad and season with salt and pepper to taste.
4. Toss everything together gently until well combined.
5. Let the salad sit for 5-10 minutes to allow the flavors to meld together.
6. Serve and enjoy!

Nutritional Value: Calories: 251 Fat: 21g Saturated Fat: 8g Cholesterol: 42mg Sodium: 327mg Carbohydrates: 5g Fiber: 1g Sugar: 3g Protein: 12g

145. Caesar Salad

Prep. Time: 10 minutes **Servings:** 2
Ingredients:
- 1 head of romaine lettuce, washed and chopped
- 1/2 cup croutons
- 1/2 cup grated Parmesan cheese
- 1/2 cup Caesar salad dressing
- 2 cloves of garlic, minced
- 2 anchovy fillets, minced (optional)
- 1 tbsp lemon juice
- 1 tsp Dijon mustard
- 1/4 tsp Worcestershire sauce
- Salt and pepper to taste
- 1/4 cup chopped fresh parsley

Instructions:
1. In a large mixing bowl, combine the chopped romaine lettuce, croutons, and grated Parmesan cheese.

2. In a small mixing bowl, whisk together the Caesar salad dressing, minced garlic, minced anchovy fillets (if using), lemon juice, Dijon mustard, Worcestershire sauce, salt, and pepper.
3. Drizzle the dressing over the salad and toss to coat evenly.
4. Sprinkle with chopped parsley before serving.

Nutritional Value : Calories: 213 Fat: 18g Saturated Fat: 4g Cholesterol: 14mg Sodium: 953mg Carbohydrates: 7g Fiber: 2g Sugar: 2g Protein: 7g

146. Arugula And Parmesan Salad

Prep. Time: 10 minutes **Servings:** 4
Ingredients:
- 6 cups fresh arugula
- 1/4 cup shaved Parmesan cheese
- 1/4 cup extra-virgin olive oil
- 2 tablespoons lemon juice
- 1 teaspoon Dijon mustard
- Salt and pepper, to taste

Instructions:
1. In a large bowl, combine the arugula and shaved Parmesan cheese.
2. In a small bowl, whisk together the olive oil, lemon juice, and Dijon mustard.
3. Pour the dressing over the salad and season with salt and pepper to taste.
4. Toss everything together gently until well combined.
5. Let the salad sit for 5-10 minutes to allow the flavors to meld together.
6. Serve and enjoy!

Nutritional Value: Calories: 140 Fat: 14g Saturated Fat: 2g Cholesterol: 3mg Sodium: 110mg Carbohydrates: 2g Fiber: 1g Sugar: 0g Protein: 3g

147. Spinach And Strawberry Salad

Prep. Time: 5 minutes **Servings:** 3
Ingredients:
- 6 cups fresh spinach leaves, washed and dried
- 1 cup fresh strawberries, hulled and sliced
- 1/4 cup sliced red onion
- 1/4 cup crumbled feta cheese
- 1/4 cup toasted pecans, chopped
- 2 tbsp olive oil
- 2 tbsp balsamic vinegar
- 1 tsp honey
- 1/4 tsp salt
- 1/8 tsp black pepper

Instructions:
1. In a large mixing bowl, combine the fresh spinach leaves, sliced strawberries, sliced red onion, crumbled feta cheese, and chopped pecans.
2. In a small mixing bowl, whisk together the olive oil, balsamic vinegar, honey, salt, and black pepper.
3. Drizzle the dressing over the salad and toss to coat evenly.
4. Serve the salad immediately.

Nutritional Value: Calories: 164 Fat: 13g Saturated Fat: 2g Cholesterol: 5mg Sodium: 196mg Carbohydrates: 10g Fiber: 2g Sugar: 7g Protein: 3g

148. Broccoli And Cheddar Salad

Prep. Time: 20 minutes **Cooking Time:** None **Servings:** 6
Ingredients:
- 6 cups broccoli florets
- 1 cup shredded cheddar cheese
- 1/2 cup mayonnaise
- 2 tablespoons Dijon mustard
- 2 tablespoons apple cider vinegar

- 1/4 cup sugar
- Salt and pepper, to taste

Instructions:
1. In a large bowl, combine the broccoli florets and shredded cheddar cheese.
2. In a small bowl, whisk together the mayonnaise, Dijon mustard, apple cider vinegar, and sugar.
3. Pour the dressing over the salad and season with salt and pepper to taste.
4. Toss everything together gently until well combined.
5. Let the salad sit in the refrigerator for at least 1 hour to allow the flavors to meld together.
6. Serve and enjoy!

Nutritional Value: Calories: 207 Fat: 18g Saturated Fat: 4g Cholesterol: 15mg Sodium: 260mg Carbohydrates: 8g Fiber: 2g Sugar: 6g Protein: 6g

149. Roasted Beet And Goat Cheese Salad

Prep. Time: 10 minutes **Servings:** 4
Ingredients:
- 4 medium beets, peeled and cubed
- 2 tbsp olive oil
- Salt and pepper to taste
- 6 cups mixed greens
- 1/4 cup crumbled goat cheese
- 2 tbsp balsamic vinaigrette
- 2 tbsp chopped fresh parsley or chives

Instructions:
1. Preheat the oven to 425°F (220°C). Line a baking sheet with parchment paper.
2. In a mixing bowl, toss the beets with olive oil, salt, and pepper. Spread the beets out in a single layer on the prepared baking sheet.
3. Roast the beets in the preheated oven for 20-25 minutes or until tender. Remove from the oven and let cool.
4. In a large mixing bowl, combine the mixed greens, crumbled goat cheese, and cooled beets.
5. Drizzle with the balsamic vinaigrette and toss to coat evenly.
6. Sprinkle with chopped parsley or chives before serving.

Nutritional Value: Calories: 156 Fat: 12g Saturated Fat: 3g Cholesterol: 6mg Sodium: 68mg Carbohydrates: 11g Fiber: 3g Sugar: 8g Protein: 4g

150. Kale And Quinoa Salad

Prep. Time: 20 minutes **Servings:** 4
Ingredients:
- 2 cups cooked quinoa
- 2 cups chopped kale
- 1/2 cup diced red onion
- 1/2 cup diced red bell pepper
- 1/2 cup crumbled feta cheese
- 1/4 cup fresh lemon juice
- 2 tablespoons extra-virgin olive oil
- 1 clove of garlic, minced
- Salt and pepper, to taste

Instructions:
1. In a large bowl, combine the cooked quinoa, chopped kale, red onion, red bell pepper, and crumbled feta cheese.
2. In a small bowl, whisk together the lemon juice, olive oil, minced garlic, salt, and pepper.
3. Pour the dressing over the salad and toss everything together gently until well combined.
4. Let the salad sit in the refrigerator for at least 30 minutes to allow the flavors to meld together.
5. Serve and enjoy!

Nutritional Value: Calories: 243 Fat: 11g Saturated Fat: 3g Cholesterol: 12mg Sodium: 178mg Carbohydrates: 27g Fiber: 3g Sugar: 2g Protein: 8g

151. Cucumber And Tomato Salad

Prep. Time: 5 minutes **Servings:** 4
Ingredients:
- 2 cups diced cucumber
- 2 cups diced tomatoes
- 1/4 cup diced red onion
- 2 tbsp chopped fresh parsley
- 2 tbsp olive oil
- 1 tbsp red wine vinegar
- 1 tsp honey
- 1/4 tsp salt
- 1/8 tsp black pepper

Instructions:
1. In a large mixing bowl, combine the diced cucumber, diced tomatoes, diced red onion, and chopped parsley.
2. In a small mixing bowl, whisk together the olive oil, red wine vinegar, honey, salt, and black pepper.
3. Drizzle the dressing over the salad and toss to coat evenly.
4. Serve the salad chilled or at room temperature.

Nutritional Value: Calories: 68 Fat: 6g Saturated Fat: 1g Cholesterol: 0mg Sodium: 120mg Carbohydrates: 5g Fiber: 1g Sugar: 3g Protein: 1g

152. Sweet Potato And Black Bean Salad

Prep. Time: 30 minutes **Cooking Time:** 30 minutes **Servings:** 4
Ingredients:
- 2 medium sweet potatoes, peeled and diced
- 1 can black beans, rinsed and drained
- 1/2 red onion, diced
- 1/2 red bell pepper, diced
- 1/4 cup chopped fresh cilantro
- 2 tablespoons olive oil
- 2 tablespoons lime juice
- 1 teaspoon ground cumin
- Salt and pepper, to taste

Instructions:
1. Preheat the oven to 400°F (200°C).
2. On a baking sheet, toss the diced sweet potatoes with 1 tablespoon of olive oil, salt, and pepper. Roast in the preheated oven for 25-30 minutes, or until tender and lightly golden brown.
3. In a large bowl, combine the roasted sweet potatoes, black beans, red onion, red bell pepper, and cilantro.
4. In a small bowl, whisk together the remaining 1 tablespoon of olive oil, lime juice, cumin, salt, and pepper.
5. Pour the dressing over the salad and toss everything together gently until well combined.
6. Let the salad sit in the refrigerator for at least 30 minutes to allow the flavors to meld together.
7. Serve and enjoy!

Nutritional Value: Calories: 242 Fat: 9g Saturated Fat: 1g Cholesterol: 0mg Sodium: 337mg Carbohydrates: 36g Fiber: 7g Sugar: 4g Protein: 7g

153. Potato Salad

Prep. Time: 20 minutes **Servings:** 4
Ingredients:
- 6 medium potatoes
- 2 eggs
- 1/2 cup mayonnaise
- 2 tablespoons dijon mustard
- 2 tablespoons apple cider vinegar
- 1/4 cup diced red onion
- 2 stalks celery, diced
- Salt and pepper, to taste
- Fresh parsley or chives, for garnish (optional)

Instructions:

1. Peel and chop the potatoes into bite-sized pieces. Boil in a pot of salted water until fork-tender, about 15-20 minutes.
2. While the potatoes are boiling, place the eggs in a separate pot and cover with water. Bring to a boil, then remove from heat and let sit for 10-12 minutes. Drain and rinse under cold water until cool enough to handle, then peel and chop.
3. Drain the potatoes and rinse under cold water until cooled.
4. In a large bowl, mix together the mayonnaise, dijon mustard, apple cider vinegar, red onion, and celery.
5. Add the cooled potatoes and eggs to the bowl and toss to coat with the dressing.
6. Season with salt and pepper to taste.
7. Cover and refrigerate for at least 30 minutes to allow the flavors to meld.
8. Before serving, garnish with fresh parsley or chives, if desired.

Nutritional Value: Calories: 200 Fat: 6g Saturated Fat: 2g Cholesterol: 0mg Sodium: 392mg Carbohydrates: 38g Fiber: 7g Sugar: 3g Protein: 6g

154. Carrot And Raisin Salad

Prep. Time: 10 minutes **Servings:** 3
Ingredients:
- 4 cups grated carrots
- 1/2 cup raisins
- 1/4 cup mayonnaise
- 2 tablespoons honey
- 1 tablespoon apple cider vinegar
- 1/4 teaspoon ground cinnamon
- Salt and pepper, to taste
- Chopped walnuts or pecans, for garnish (optional)

Instructions:
1. In a large bowl, mix together the grated carrots and raisins.
2. In a separate small bowl, mix together the mayonnaise, honey, apple cider vinegar, and cinnamon.
3. Pour the dressing over the carrots and raisins and toss to coat.
4. Season with salt and pepper to taste.
5. Cover and refrigerate for at least 30 minutes to allow the flavors to meld.
6. Before serving, garnish with chopped walnuts or pecans, if desired.

Nutritional Value: Calories: 198 Fat: 4g Saturated Fat: 0g Cholesterol: 0mg Sodium: 355mg Carbohydrates: 42g Fiber: 12g Sugar: 2g Protein: 8g

155. Avocado And Corn Salad

Prep. Time: 20 minutes **Servings:** 4
Ingredients:
- 2 ripe avocados, diced
- 2 cups fresh corn kernels (about 4 ears of corn)
- 1/2 red onion, diced
- 1/2 red bell pepper, diced
- 1/4 cup chopped fresh cilantro
- 2 tablespoons olive oil
- 2 tablespoons lime juice
- 1 teaspoon ground cumin
- Salt and pepper, to taste

Instructions:
1. In a large bowl, combine the diced avocado, corn kernels, red onion, red bell pepper, and cilantro.
2. In a small bowl, whisk together the olive oil, lime juice, cumin, salt, and pepper.
3. Pour the dressing over the salad and toss everything together gently until well combined.
4. Let the salad sit in the refrigerator for at least 30 minutes to allow the flavors to meld together.
5. Serve and enjoy!

Nutritional Value: Calories: 259 Fat: 21g Saturated Fat: 3g Cholesterol: 0mg Sodium: 121mg Carbohydrates: 19g Fiber: 6g Sugar: 4g Protein: 3g

156. Cabbage And Apple Salad

Prep. Time: 10 minutes **Servings:** 7
Ingredients:
- 6 cups thinly sliced green cabbage
- 2 cups diced Granny Smith apples
- 1/2 cup diced red onion
- 1/4 cup raisins
- 1/4 cup chopped walnuts or pecans
- 1/4 cup mayonnaise
- 2 tablespoons apple cider vinegar
- 1 tablespoon honey
- Salt and pepper, to taste

Instructions:
1. In a large bowl, mix together the sliced cabbage, diced apples, red onion, raisins, and chopped nuts.
2. In a separate small bowl, mix together the mayonnaise, apple cider vinegar, and honey.
3. Pour the dressing over the cabbage mixture and toss to coat.
4. Season with salt and pepper to taste.
5. Cover and refrigerate for at least 30 minutes to allow the flavors to meld.

Nutritional Value: Calories: 120 Fat: 9g Saturated Fat: 1g Cholesterol: 3mg Sodium: 105mg Carbohydrates: 10g Fiber: 2g Sugar: 7g Protein: 2g

157. Three Bean Salad

Prep. Time: 6 minutes **Servings:** 6
Ingredients:
- 1 can (15 oz) kidney beans, rinsed and drained
- 1 can (15 oz) chickpeas, rinsed and drained
- 1 can (15 oz) black-eyed peas, rinsed and drained
- 1/2 red onion, diced
- 1/2 red bell pepper, diced
- 1/4 cup chopped fresh parsley
- 1/4 cup red wine vinegar
- 2 tablespoons olive oil
- 1 clove of garlic, minced
- Salt and pepper, to taste

Instructions:
1. In a large bowl, combine the kidney beans, chickpeas, black-eyed peas, red onion, red bell pepper, and parsley.
2. In a small bowl, whisk together the red wine vinegar, olive oil, minced garlic, salt, and pepper.
3. Pour the dressing over the salad and toss everything together gently until well combined.
4. Let the salad sit in the refrigerator for at least 30 minutes to allow the flavors to meld together.
5. Serve and enjoy!

Nutritional Value: Calories: 198 Fat: 6g Saturated Fat: 1g Cholesterol: 0mg Sodium: 474mg Carbohydrates: 29g Fiber: 7g Sugar: 3g Protein: 8g

158. Chickpea And Cilantro Salad

Prep. Time: 10 minutes **Servings:** 2
Ingredients:
- 1 can chickpeas, drained and rinsed
- 1/4 cup diced red onion
- 1/4 cup chopped fresh cilantro
- 1/4 cup diced tomatoes
- 1/4 cup diced cucumber
- 2 tbsp lemon juice
- 1 tbsp olive oil
- Salt and pepper, to taste

Instructions:

1. In a large bowl, combine the chickpeas, red onion, cilantro, tomatoes, and cucumber.
2. In a separate small bowl, whisk together the lemon juice and olive oil. Season with salt and pepper to taste.
3. Pour the dressing over the chickpea mixture and toss to combine.
4. Serve chilled or at room temperature.

Nutritional Value Calories: 150 Total Fat: 7g Saturated Fat: 1g Cholesterol: 0mg Sodium: 380mg Total Carbohydrates: 19g Dietary Fiber: 5g Sugars: 3g Protein: 6g

159. Eggplant And Tomato Salad

Prep. Time: 5 minutes **Cooking Time:** 25 minutes **Servings:** 2
Ingredients:
- 1 medium eggplant, cut into 1/2-inch cubes
- 2 medium tomatoes, diced
- 1/4 cup diced red onion
- 2 cloves of garlic, minced
- 2 tbsp olive oil
- 1 tbsp red wine vinegar
- 1 tbsp chopped fresh basil
- Salt and pepper, to taste

Instructions:
1. Preheat oven to 425°F (220°C).
2. On a baking sheet, toss the eggplant with 1 tablespoon of olive oil, and season with salt and pepper. Roast for 20-25 minutes or until golden brown and tender.
3. In a large bowl, combine the roasted eggplant, tomatoes, red onion, and garlic.
4. In a small bowl, whisk together the remaining 1 tablespoon of olive oil, red wine vinegar, and basil. Season with salt and pepper to taste.
5. Pour the dressing over the eggplant mixture and toss to combine.
6. Serve chilled or at room temperature

Nutritional Value Calories: 150 Total Fat: 11g Saturated Fat: 1.5g Cholesterol: 0mg Sodium: 250mg Total Carbohydrates: 13g Dietary Fiber: 5g Sugars: 5g Protein: 2g

160. Zucchini And Olive Salad

Prep. Time: 20 minutes **Servings:** 4
Ingredients:
- 2 medium zucchinis, thinly sliced
- 1/2 cup sliced black olives
- 1/2 red onion, diced
- 1/4 cup chopped fresh parsley
- 2 tablespoons red wine vinegar
- 2 tablespoons olive oil
- 1 clove of garlic, minced
- Salt and pepper, to taste

Instructions:
- In a large bowl, combine the sliced zucchinis, black olives, red onion, and parsley.
- In a small bowl, whisk together the red wine vinegar, olive oil, minced garlic, salt, and pepper.
- Pour the dressing over the salad and toss everything together gently until well combined.
- Let the salad sit in the refrigerator for at least 30 minutes to allow the flavors to meld together.
- Serve and enjoy!

Nutritional Value: Calories: 120 Fat: 12g Saturated Fat: 2g Cholesterol: 0mg Sodium: 526mg Carbohydrates: 5g Fiber: 2g Sugar: 3g Protein: 2g

161. Artichoke And Parmesan Salad

Prep. Time: 20 minutes **Servings:** 4
Ingredients:

- 1 can (14 oz) artichoke hearts, drained and chopped
- 1/2 cup grated Parmesan cheese
- 1/4 cup chopped fresh parsley
- 2 tablespoons lemon juice
- 2 tablespoons olive oil
- 1 clove of garlic, minced
- Salt and pepper, to taste

Instructions:
1. In a large bowl, combine the chopped artichoke hearts, grated Parmesan cheese, and parsley.
2. In a small bowl, whisk together the lemon juice, olive oil, minced garlic, salt, and pepper.
3. Pour the dressing over the salad and toss everything together gently until well combined.
4. Let the salad sit in the refrigerator for at least 30 minutes to allow the flavors to meld together.
5. Serve and enjoy!

Nutritional Value: Calories: 159 Fat: 13g Saturated Fat: 3g Cholesterol: 8mg Sodium: 567mg Carbohydrates: 7g Fiber: 3g Sugar: 1g Protein: 6g

162. Green Bean And Almond Salad

Prep. Time: 20 minutes **Cooking Time:** 10 minutes **Servings:** 4

Ingredients:
- 1 lb fresh green beans, trimmed
- 1/2 cup slivered almonds
- 1/4 cup chopped fresh parsley
- 2 tablespoons lemon juice
- 2 tablespoons olive oil
- 1 clove of garlic, minced
- Salt and pepper, to taste

Instructions:
1. Bring a large pot of salted water to a boil. Add the green beans and cook for about 5-7 minutes or until tender but still crisp. Drain and rinse with cold water to stop the cooking process.
2. In a skillet over medium heat, toast the slivered almonds for about 2-3 minutes or until golden brown. Be careful not to burn them.
3. In a large bowl, combine the cooked green beans, toasted almonds, and parsley.
4. In a small bowl, whisk together the lemon juice, olive oil, minced garlic, salt, and pepper.
5. Pour the dressing over the salad and toss everything together gently until well combined.
6. Let the salad sit in the refrigerator for at least 30 minutes to allow the flavors to meld together.
7. Serve and enjoy!

Nutritional Value: Calories: 191 Fat: 16g Saturated Fat: 2g Cholesterol: 0mg Sodium: 16mg Carbohydrates: 11g Fiber: 4g Sugar: 3g Protein: 5g

163. Beet And Orange Salad

Prep. Time: 30 minutes **Cooking Time:** 1 hour **Servings:** 4

Ingredients:
- 3 medium beets, peeled and grated
- 2 oranges, segmented
- 1/4 cup chopped fresh parsley
- 2 tablespoons orange juice
- 2 tablespoons olive oil
- 1 tablespoon honey
- Salt and pepper, to taste

Instructions:
1. Preheat the oven to 400°F (200°C).
2. Place the whole beets in a baking dish and add enough water to come up about

1/4 inch of the sides. Cover the dish with foil and roast for 45 minutes to 1 hour or until tender when pierced with a fork.
3. Once the beets are cool enough to handle, peel and grate them.
4. In a large bowl, combine the grated beets, orange segments, and parsley.
5. In a small bowl, whisk together the orange juice, olive oil, honey, salt, and pepper.
6. Pour the dressing over the salad and toss everything together gently until well combined.
7. Let the salad sit in the refrigerator for at least 30 minutes to allow the flavors to meld together.
8. Serve and enjoy!

Nutritional Value: Calories: 152 Fat: 9g Saturated Fat: 1g Cholesterol: 0mg Sodium: 126mg Carbohydrates: 18g Fiber: 3g Sugar: 13g Protein: 2g

164. Squash And Feta Salad

Prep. Time: 5 minutes **Cooking Time:** 25 minutes **Servings:** 3
Ingredients:
- 2 cups diced butternut squash
- 1/4 cup crumbled feta cheese
- 2 tbsp chopped fresh parsley
- 1 tbsp olive oil
- 1 tbsp lemon juice
- 1 tsp honey
- Salt and pepper, to taste

Instructions:
- Preheat oven to 375°F (190°C).
- On a baking sheet, toss the squash with 1 tsp of olive oil, and season with salt and pepper. Roast for 20-25 minutes or until tender and golden brown.
- In a large bowl, combine the roasted squash, feta cheese, and parsley.
- In a small bowl, whisk together the remaining 2 tsp of olive oil, lemon juice and honey. Season with salt and pepper to taste.
- Pour the dressing over the squash mixture and toss to combine.
- Serve chilled or at room temperature

Nutritional Value: Calories: 110 Total Fat: 8g Saturated Fat: 3g Cholesterol: 15mg Sodium: 220mg Total Carbohydrates: 9g Dietary Fiber: 2g Sugars: 5g Protein: 2g

165. Cauliflower And Blue Cheese Salad

Prep. Time: 20 minutes **Servings:** 4
Ingredients:
- 1 head cauliflower, chopped into small florets
- 1/2 cup crumbled blue cheese
- 1/4 cup chopped fresh parsley
- 2 tablespoons lemon juice
- 2 tablespoons olive oil
- 1 clove of garlic, minced
- Salt and pepper, to taste

Instructions:
1. In a large bowl, combine the cauliflower florets, blue cheese, and parsley.
2. In a small bowl, whisk together the lemon juice, olive oil, minced garlic, salt, and pepper.
3. Pour the dressing over the salad and toss everything together gently until well combined.
4. Let the salad sit in the refrigerator for at least 30 minutes to allow the flavors to meld together.
5. Serve and enjoy!

Nutritional Value: Calories: 156 Fat: 13g Saturated Fat: 4g Cholesterol: 15mg Sodium: 303mg Carbohydrates: 7g Fiber: 2g

166. Radish And Cottage Cheese Salad

Prep. Time: 5 minutes **Servings:** 4
Ingredients:
- 1/2 cup thinly sliced radishes
- 1/2 cup small diced red onion
- 1/2 cup small diced cucumber
- 1/2 cup cottage cheese
- 1 tbsp chopped fresh dill
- 1 tbsp lemon juice
- 1 tsp honey
- Salt and pepper, to taste

Instructions:
1. In a large bowl, combine the radishes, red onion, cucumber and cottage cheese.
2. In a small bowl, whisk together the lemon juice, honey, and some salt and pepper.
3. Pour the dressing over the radish mixture and toss to combine.
4. Garnish with fresh dill and extra pepper before serving.

Nutritional Value: Calories: 60 Total Fat: 2g Saturated Fat: 1.5g Cholesterol: 5mg Sodium: 150mg Total Carbohydrates: 6g Dietary Fiber: 1g Sugars: 3g Protein: 4g

167. Pea And Mint Salad

Prep. Time: 15 minutes **Servings:** 4
Ingredients:
- 2 cups frozen peas, thawed
- 1/4 cup chopped fresh mint
- 1/4 cup chopped fresh parsley
- 2 tablespoons lemon juice
- 2 tablespoons olive oil
- 1 clove of garlic, minced
- Salt and pepper, to taste

Instructions:
1. In a large bowl, combine the thawed peas, mint, and parsley.
2. In a small bowl, whisk together the lemon juice, olive oil, minced garlic, salt, and pepper.
3. Pour the dressing over the salad and toss everything together gently until well combined.
4. Let the salad sit in the refrigerator for at least 30 minutes to allow the flavors to meld together.
5. Serve and enjoy!

Nutritional Value: Calories: 106 Fat: 8g Saturated Fat: 1g Cholesterol: 0mg Sodium: 68mg Carbohydrates: 7g Fiber: 2g Sugar: 3g Protein: 2g

168. Asparagus And Lemon Salad

Prep. Time: 5 minutes **Servings:** 6
Ingredients:
- 1 lb asparagus, trimmed and cut into 1-inch pieces
- 1/4 cup diced red onion
- 2 tbsp chopped fresh parsley
- 2 tbsp lemon juice
- 1 tbsp olive oil
- Salt and pepper, to taste

Instructions:
1. Bring a large pot of salted water to a boil.
2. Add the asparagus and cook for 2-3 minutes or until tender-crisp. Drain and immediately immerse in ice water to stop the cooking process. Drain again and pat dry.
3. In a large bowl, combine the blanched asparagus, red onion, and parsley.
4. In a small bowl, whisk together the lemon juice and olive oil. Season with salt and pepper to taste.
5. Pour the dressing over the asparagus mixture and toss to combine.
6. Serve chilled or at room temperature

Nutritional Value: Calories: 60 Total Fat: 4g Saturated Fat: 0.5g Cholesterol: 0mg Sodium: 10mg Total Carbohydrates: 5g Dietary Fiber: 2g Sugars: 2g Protein: 2g

169. Mushroom And Walnut Salad

Prep. Time: 10 minutes **Servings:** 2
Ingredients:
- 8 oz sliced mushrooms (shiitake, cremini, or button)
- 1/4 cup chopped walnuts
- 2 tbsp chopped fresh parsley
- 2 tbsp olive oil
- 1 tbsp balsamic vinegar
- Salt and pepper, to taste

Instructions:
1. In a large pan over medium heat, sauté the mushrooms in 1 tbsp of olive oil for about 5 minutes or until golden brown and tender.
2. In a large bowl, combine the sautéed mushrooms, chopped walnuts, and parsley.
3. In a small bowl, whisk together the remaining 1 tbsp of olive oil, balsamic vinegar and some salt and pepper.
4. Pour the dressing over the mushroom mixture and toss to combine.
5. Let the salad sit for 10-15 minutes to allow the flavors to meld together before serving.

Nutritional Value: Calories: 150 Total Fat: 14g Saturated Fat: 2g Cholesterol: 0mg Sodium: 50mg Total Carbohydrates: 6g Dietary Fiber: 2g Sugars: 3g Protein: 3g

170. Tomato And Mozzarella Salad

Prep. Time: 15 minutes **Servings:** 4
Ingredients:
- 4 large tomatoes, sliced
- 8 oz fresh mozzarella cheese, sliced
- 1/4 cup chopped fresh basil
- 2 tablespoons balsamic vinegar
- 2 tablespoons extra-virgin olive oil
- Salt and pepper, to taste

Instructions:
1. On a large serving platter, alternate the slices of tomatoes and mozzarella cheese.
2. Sprinkle the chopped basil over the top.
3. In a small bowl, whisk together the balsamic vinegar, olive oil, salt, and pepper.
4. Drizzle the dressing over the salad, and then season with additional salt and pepper to taste.
5. Let the salad sit in the refrigerator for at least 30 minutes to allow the flavors to meld together.
6. Serve and enjoy!

Nutritional Value: Calories: 275 Fat: 22g Saturated Fat: 10g Cholesterol: 49mg Sodium: 468mg Carbohydrates: 12g Fiber: 3g Sugar: 8g Protein: 12g

171. Cauliflower And Raisin Salad

Prep. Time: 15 minutes **Servings:** 5
Ingredients:
- 1 head cauliflower, cut into small florets
- 1/4 cup raisins
- 2 tbsp chopped fresh parsley
- 2 tbsp olive oil
- 1 tbsp apple cider vinegar
- 1 tsp Dijon mustard
- Salt and pepper, to taste

Instructions:
1. In a large pot of salted boiling water, add the cauliflower florets and cook for 3-5 minutes or until tender-crisp. Drain and immediately immerse in ice water to stop

the cooking process. Drain again and pat dry.
2. In a large bowl, combine the blanched cauliflower florets, raisins, and parsley.
3. In a small bowl, whisk together the olive oil, apple cider vinegar, Dijon mustard, and some salt and pepper.
4. Pour the dressing over the cauliflower mixture and toss to combine.
5. Let the salad sit for 10-15 minutes to allow the flavors to meld together before serving.

Nutritional Value: Calories: 120 Total Fat: 10g Saturated Fat: 1.5g Cholesterol: 0mg Sodium: 60mg Total Carbohydrates: 8g Dietary Fiber: 2g Sugars: 5g Protein: 2g

172. Watercress And Potato Salad

Prep. Time: 20 minutes **Cooking Time:** 20 minutes **Servings:** 4
Ingredients:
- 2 cups small new potatoes, quartered
- 1/2 cup chopped watercress
- 1/4 cup chopped fresh parsley
- 2 tablespoons Dijon mustard
- 2 tablespoons red wine vinegar
- 2 tablespoons olive oil
- 1 clove of garlic, minced
- Salt and pepper, to taste

Instructions:
1. Place the potatoes in a large pot and add enough water to cover. Bring to a boil and cook for about 15-20 minutes or until tender. Drain and rinse with cold water to stop the cooking process.
2. In a large bowl, combine the cooked potatoes, watercress, and parsley.
3. In a small bowl, whisk together the Dijon mustard, red wine vinegar, olive oil, minced garlic, salt, and pepper.
4. Pour the dressing over the salad and toss everything together gently until well combined.
5. Let the salad sit in the refrigerator for at least 30 minutes to allow the flavors to meld together.
6. Serve and enjoy!

Nutritional Value: Calories: 191 Fat: 10g Saturated Fat: 1g Cholesterol: 0mg Sodium: 158mg Carbohydrates: 21g Fiber: 3g Sugar: 2g Protein: 3g

173. Leek And Fennel Salad

Prep. Time: 20 minutes **Servings:** 4
Ingredients:
- 2 leeks, white and light green parts only, thinly sliced
- 1 fennel bulb, thinly sliced
- 1/4 cup chopped fresh parsley
- 2 tablespoons lemon juice
- 2 tablespoons olive oil
- 1 clove of garlic, minced
- Salt and pepper, to taste

Instructions:
1. In a large bowl, combine the sliced leeks, fennel, and parsley.
2. In a small bowl, whisk together the lemon juice, olive oil, minced garlic, salt, and pepper.
3. Pour the dressing over the salad and toss everything together gently until well combined.
4. Let the salad sit in the refrigerator for at least 30 minutes to allow the flavors to meld together.
5. Serve and enjoy!

Nutritional Value: Calories: 74 Fat: 7g Saturated Fat: 1g Cholesterol: 0mg Sodium: 37mg Carbohydrates: 5g Fiber: 2g Sugar: 2g Protein: 1g

174. Radicchio And Pear Salad

Prep. Time: 20 minutes **Servings:** 5
Ingredients:
- 1 head radicchio, thinly sliced
- 2 pears, cored and thinly sliced
- 1/4 cup chopped fresh parsley
- 2 tablespoons balsamic vinegar
- 2 tablespoons olive oil
- 1 clove of garlic, minced
- Salt and pepper, to taste

Instructions:
1. In a large bowl, combine the sliced radicchio, pears, and parsley.
2. In a small bowl, whisk together the balsamic vinegar, olive oil, minced garlic, salt, and pepper.
3. Pour the dressing over the salad and toss everything together gently until well combined.
4. Let the salad sit in the refrigerator for at least 30 minutes to allow the flavors to meld together.
5. Serve and enjoy!

Nutritional Value: Calories: 151 Fat: 11g Saturated Fat: 1g Cholesterol: 0mg Sodium: 25mg Carbohydrates: 13g Fiber: 3g Sugar: 8g Protein: 1g

175. Lentil And Spinach Salad

Prep. Time: 10 minutes **Cooking Time:** 30 minutes **Servings:** 4
Ingredients:
- 1 cup green lentils, rinsed and drained
- 2 cups spinach leaves, washed and dried
- 1/4 cup chopped fresh parsley
- 2 tablespoons red wine vinegar
- 2 tablespoons olive oil
- 1 clove of garlic, minced
- Salt and pepper, to taste

Instructions:
1. In a large pot, bring 4 cups of water to a boil. Add the lentils and reduce the heat to a simmer. Cook for about 20-25 minutes or until tender. Drain and rinse with cold water to stop the cooking process.
2. In a large bowl, combine the cooked lentils, spinach leaves, and parsley.
3. In a small bowl, whisk together the red wine vinegar, olive oil, minced garlic, salt, and pepper.
4. Pour the dressing over the salad and toss everything together gently until well combined.
5. Let the salad sit in the refrigerator for at least 30 minutes to allow the flavors to meld together.
6. Serve and enjoy!

Nutritional Value: Calories: 186 Fat: 7g Saturated Fat: 1g Cholesterol: 0mg Sodium: 23mg Carbohydrates: 22g Fiber: 8g Sugar: 2g Protein: 9g

176. Endive And Roquefort Salad

Prep. Time: 10 minutes **Cooking Time:** None **Servings:** 4
Ingredients:
- 2 heads of Belgian endive, thinly sliced
- 1/2 cup crumbled Roquefort cheese
- 1/4 cup chopped fresh parsley
- 2 tablespoons red wine vinegar
- 2 tablespoons olive oil
- 1 clove of garlic, minced
- Salt and pepper, to taste

Instructions:
1. In a large bowl, combine the sliced endive, crumbled Roquefort cheese, and parsley.
2. In a small bowl, whisk together the red wine vinegar, olive oil, minced garlic, salt, and pepper.

3. Pour the dressing over the salad and toss everything together gently until well combined.
4. Let the salad sit in the refrigerator for at least 30 minutes to allow the flavors to meld together.
5. Serve and enjoy!

Nutritional Value: Calories: 179 Fat: 16g Saturated Fat: 8g Cholesterol: 39mg Sodium: 463mg Carbohydrates: 5g Fiber: 2g Sugar: 3g Protein: 5g

177. Cucumber And Dill Salad

Prep. Time: 10 minutes **Cooking Time:** None
Servings: 4
Ingredients:
- 2 large cucumbers, thinly sliced
- 1/4 cup chopped fresh dill
- 2 tablespoons white wine vinegar
- 2 tablespoons olive oil
- 1 clove of garlic, minced
- Salt and pepper, to taste

Instructions:
1. In a large bowl, combine the sliced cucumbers, chopped dill.
2. In a small bowl, whisk together the white wine vinegar, olive oil, minced garlic, salt, and pepper.
3. Pour the dressing over the salad and toss everything together gently until well combined.
4. Let the salad sit in the refrigerator for at least 30 minutes to allow the flavors to meld together.
5. Serve and enjoy!

Nutritional Value: Calories: 111 Fat: 10g Saturated Fat: 1g Cholesterol: 0mg Sodium: 6mg Carbohydrates: 5g Fiber: 1g Sugar: 3g Protein: 1g

178. Pea And Pecorino Salad

Prep. Time: 10 minutes **Servings:** 4
Ingredients:
- 2 cups frozen peas, thawed
- 1/2 cup grated Pecorino cheese
- 1/4 cup chopped fresh parsley
- 2 tablespoons lemon juice
- 2 tablespoons olive oil
- 1 clove of garlic, minced
- Salt and pepper, to taste

Instructions:
1. In a large bowl, combine the thawed peas, grated Pecorino cheese, and parsley.
2. In a small bowl, whisk together the lemon juice, olive oil, minced garlic, salt, and pepper.
3. Pour the dressing over the salad and toss everything together gently until well combined.
4. Let the salad sit in the refrigerator for at least 30 minutes to allow the flavors to meld together.
5. Serve and enjoy!

Nutritional Value: Calories: 202 Fat: 13g Saturated Fat: 6g Cholesterol: 27mg Sodium: 367mg Carbohydrates: 12g Fiber: 3g Sugar: 4g Protein: 10g

179. Apple And Celery Salad

Apple and Celery Salad Total Time: 10 minutes
Prep. Time: 10 minutes
Ingredients:
- 2 cups of thinly sliced celery
- 2 cups of thinly sliced Granny Smith apples
- 1/4 cup of chopped parsley
- 1/4 cup of chopped toasted pecans
- 2 tablespoons of lemon juice
- 2 tablespoons of olive oil
- 1 tablespoon of honey
- Salt and pepper to taste

Instructions:
1. In a large mixing bowl, combine the celery, apples, parsley, and pecans.

2. In a small mixing bowl, whisk together the lemon juice, olive oil, honey, salt, and pepper to make the dressing.
3. Pour the dressing over the celery and apple mixture and toss to coat.
4. Serve the salad immediately or refrigerate until ready to serve.

Nutritional Value: Calories: 158 Fat: 13g Saturated Fat: 2g Cholesterol: 0mg Sodium: 34mg Carbohydrates: 12g Fiber: 2g Sugar: 9g Protein: 1g

180. Carrot And Cashew Salad

Prep. Time: 15 minutes **Servings:** 3
Ingredients:
- 3 cups grated carrots
- 1 cup roasted cashews
- 1/4 cup chopped cilantro
- 2 tbsp honey
- 2 tbsp olive oil
- 1 tbsp apple cider vinegar
- 1 tsp ground cumin
- Salt and pepper, to taste

Instructions:
1. In a large bowl, combine the grated carrots, roasted cashews, and chopped cilantro.
2. In a separate small bowl, whisk together the honey, olive oil, apple cider vinegar, cumin, salt, and pepper.
3. Pour the dressing over the carrot mixture and toss to coat evenly.
4. Chill in the refrigerator for at least 30 minutes before serving. Enjoy!

Nutritional Value: Calories: 177 Fat: 5g Saturated Fat: 0g Cholesterol: 0mg Sodium: 356mg Carbohydrates: 28g Fiber: 14g Sugar: 2g Protein: 8g

181. Zucchini And Basil Salad

Prep. Time: 5 minutes **Servings:** 2

Ingredients:
- 2 medium zucchinis, thinly sliced
- 1/4 cup chopped fresh basil
- 2 tbsp olive oil
- 1 tbsp lemon juice
- 1 tsp honey
- Salt and pepper, to taste

Instructions:
1. In a large bowl, combine the thinly sliced zucchinis and chopped basil.
2. In a small bowl, whisk together the olive oil, lemon juice, honey, salt, and pepper.
3. Pour the dressing over the zucchini mixture and toss to coat evenly.
4. Serve immediately or chill in the refrigerator for at least 30 minutes before serving. Enjoy!

Nutritional Value: Calories: 113 Fat: 11g Saturated Fat: 1.5g Carbohydrates: 6g Fiber: 2g Protein: 2g Sodium: 8mg

182. Cauliflower And Parmesan Salad

Prep. Time: 10 minutes **Cooking Time:** 10 minutes **Servings:** 5
Ingredients:
- 1 head of cauliflower, cut into small florets
- 1/4 cup of chopped parsley
- 1/4 cup of chopped toasted hazelnuts
- 1/4 cup of grated Parmesan cheese
- 2 tablespoons of lemon juice
- 2 tablespoons of olive oil
- 1 tablespoon of Dijon mustard
- Salt and pepper to taste

Instructions:
1. Bring a large pot of salted water to a boil. Add the cauliflower florets and cook for 5-7 minutes, or until tender but still firm. Drain and rinse the cauliflower under cold water to stop the cooking process.

2. In a large mixing bowl, combine the cooked cauliflower, parsley, hazelnuts and Parmesan cheese.
3. In a small mixing bowl, whisk together the lemon juice, olive oil, Dijon mustard, salt, and pepper to make the dressing.
4. Pour the dressing over the cauliflower mixture and toss to coat.
5. Serve the salad immediately or refrigerate until ready to serve.

Nutritional Value: Calories: 180 Fat: 16g Saturated Fat: 4g Cholesterol: 8mg Sodium: 191mg Carbohydrates: 7g Fiber: 2g Sugar: 2g Protein: 5g

183. Beet And Horseradish Salad

Prep. Time: 5 minutes **Servings:** 4
Ingredients:
- 4 medium beets, cooked and sliced
- 2 tbsp prepared horseradish
- 2 tbsp sour cream
- 2 tbsp mayonnaise
- 1 tbsp red wine vinegar
- Salt and pepper, to taste

Instructions:
1. In a large bowl, combine the cooked and sliced beets.
2. In a separate small bowl, whisk together the horseradish, sour cream, mayonnaise, red wine vinegar, salt, and pepper.
3. Pour the dressing over the beets and toss to coat evenly.
4. Chill in the refrigerator for at least 30 minutes before serving. Enjoy!

Nutritional Value: Calories: 185 Fat: 4g Saturated Fat: 0g Cholesterol: 0mg Sodium: 348mg Carbohydrates: 22g Fiber: 13g Sugar: 2g Protein: 10g

184. Eggplant And Walnut Salad

Prep. Time: 15 minutes **Cooking Time:** 30 minutes **Servings:** 3
Ingredients:
- 1 large eggplant
- 1/4 cup of chopped parsley
- 1/4 cup of chopped toasted walnuts
- 1/4 cup of crumbled feta cheese
- 2 tablespoons of red wine vinegar
- 2 tablespoons of olive oil
- 1 tablespoon of honey
- Salt and pepper to taste

Instructions:
1. Preheat the oven to 375°F (190°C). Line a baking sheet with parchment paper.
2. Cut the eggplant into 1/2-inch slices and place them on the prepared baking sheet. Brush the eggplant slices with olive oil and season with salt and pepper.
3. Roast the eggplant for 25-30 minutes, or until tender and golden brown. Remove from the oven and let it cool.
4. In a large mixing bowl, combine the cooked eggplant, parsley, walnuts, and feta cheese.
5. In a small mixing bowl, whisk together the red wine vinegar, olive oil, honey, salt, and pepper to make the dressing.
6. Pour the dressing over the eggplant mixture and toss to coat.
7. Serve the salad immediately or refrigerate until ready to serve.

Nutritional Value: Calories: 191 Fat: 16g Saturated Fat: 3g Cholesterol: 8mg Sodium: 195mg Carbohydrates: 10g Fiber: 3g Sugar: 6g Protein: 4g

185. Fennel And Orange Salad

Prep. Time: 15 minutes **Servings:** 6
Ingredients:

- 2 medium fennel bulbs, thinly sliced
- 2 oranges, peeled and segmented
- 1/4 cup chopped fresh parsley
- 2 tbsp olive oil
- 1 tbsp lemon juice
- 1 tsp honey
- Salt and pepper, to taste

Instructions:
1. In a large bowl, combine the thinly sliced fennel, orange segments, and chopped parsley.
2. In a small bowl, whisk together the olive oil, lemon juice, honey, salt, and pepper.
3. Pour the dressing over the fennel mixture and toss to coat evenly.
4. Serve immediately or chill in the refrigerator for at least 30 minutes before serving. Enjoy!

Nutritional Value: Calories: 201 Fat: 2g Saturated Fat: 0g Cholesterol: 0mg Sodium: 360mg Carbohydrates: 18g Fiber: 18g Sugar: 6g Protein: 9g

186. Cabbage And Cheddar Salad

Prep. Time: 15 minutes **Servings:** 4
Ingredients:
- 1/2 head of green cabbage, thinly sliced
- 1/2 cup of grated cheddar cheese
- 1/4 cup of chopped parsley
- 1/4 cup of chopped toasted sunflower seeds
- 2 tablespoons of apple cider vinegar
- 2 tablespoons of olive oil
- 1 tablespoon of Dijon mustard
- Salt and pepper to taste

Instructions:
1. In a large mixing bowl, combine the cabbage, cheddar cheese, parsley, and sunflower seeds.
2. In a small mixing bowl, whisk together the apple cider vinegar, olive oil, Dijon mustard, salt, and pepper to make the dressing.
3. Pour the dressing over the cabbage mixture and toss to coat.
4. Serve the salad immediately or refrigerate until ready to serve.

Nutritional Value: Calories: 156 Fat: 13g Saturated Fat: 3g Cholesterol: 12mg Sodium: 195mg Carbohydrates: 6g Fiber: 2g Sugar: 3g Protein: 6g

187. Carrot And Parsley Salad

Prep. Time: 10 minutes **Servings:** 3
Ingredients:
- 4 cups grated carrots
- 1/2 cup chopped fresh parsley
- 2 tbsp olive oil
- 1 tbsp lemon juice
- 1 tsp honey
- Salt and pepper, to taste

Instructions:
1. In a large bowl, combine the grated carrots and chopped parsley.
2. In a separate small bowl, whisk together the olive oil, lemon juice, honey, salt, and pepper.
3. Pour the dressing over the carrot mixture and toss to coat evenly.
4. Serve immediately or chill in the refrigerator for at least 30 minutes before serving. Enjoy!

Nutritional Value: Calories: 96 Fat: 7g Saturated Fat: 1g Carbohydrates: 8g Fiber: 3g Protein: 1g Sodium: 81mg

188. Radish And Mint Salad

Prep. Time: 10 minutes **Servings:** 3
Ingredients:
- 1 bunch of radishes, thinly sliced

- 1/4 cup of chopped mint
- 1/4 cup of chopped toasted pumpkin seeds
- 2 tablespoons of lemon juice
- 2 tablespoons of olive oil
- 1 tablespoon of honey
- Salt and pepper to taste

Instructions:
1. In a large mixing bowl, combine the radishes, mint, and pumpkin seeds.
2. In a small mixing bowl, whisk together the lemon juice, olive oil, honey, salt, and pepper to make the dressing.
3. Pour the dressing over the radish mixture and toss to coat.
4. Serve the salad immediately or refrigerate until ready to serve.

Nutritional Value: Calories: 87 Fat: 7g Saturated Fat: 1g Cholesterol: 0mg Sodium: 71mg Carbohydrates: 6g Fiber: 2g Sugar: 3g Protein: 2g

189. Spinach And Blue Cheese Salad

Prep. Time: 15 minutes **Servings:** 5
Ingredients:
- 6 cups fresh spinach leaves
- 1/2 cup crumbled blue cheese
- 1/2 cup chopped walnuts
- 2 tbsp olive oil
- 1 tbsp balsamic vinegar
- 1 tsp honey
- Salt and pepper, to taste

Instructions:
1. In a large bowl, combine the fresh spinach leaves, crumbled blue cheese, and chopped walnuts.
2. In a separate small bowl, whisk together the olive oil, balsamic vinegar, honey, salt, and pepper.
3. Pour the dressing over the spinach mixture and toss to coat evenly.
4. Serve immediately. Enjoy!

Nutritional Value: Calories: 266 Fat: 14g Saturated Fat: 3g Cholesterol: 21mg Sodium: 537mg Carbohydrates: 28g Fiber: 14g Sugar: 1g Protein: 20g

190. Potato And Leek Salad

Prep. Time: 10 minutes **Cooking Time:** 20 minutes **Servings:** 4
Ingredients:
- 2 large potatoes, peeled and diced
- 1 large leek, thinly sliced
- 1/4 cup of chopped parsley
- 1/4 cup of chopped toasted hazelnuts
- 2 tablespoons of red wine vinegar
- 2 tablespoons of olive oil
- 1 tablespoon of Dijon mustard
- Salt and pepper to taste

Instructions:
1. Bring a large pot of salted water to a boil. Add the potatoes and cook for 10-15 minutes, or until tender. Drain and rinse the potatoes under cold water to stop the cooking process.
2. In a large skillet, heat some oil over medium heat. Add the leeks and sauté until they are tender and golden brown, about 10 minutes.
3. In a large mixing bowl, combine the cooked potatoes, sautéed leeks, parsley, and hazelnuts.
4. In a small mixing bowl, whisk together the red wine vinegar, olive oil, Dijon mustard, salt, and pepper to make the dressing.
5. Pour the dressing over the potato mixture and toss to coat.
6. Serve the salad immediately or refrigerate until ready to serve.

Nutritional Value: Calories: 216 Fat: 16g Saturated Fat: 2g Cholesterol: 0mg Sodium: 96mg Carbohydrates: 17g Fiber: 3g Sugar: 2g Protein: 3g

191. Black Bean And Mango Salad

Prep. Time: 15 minutes **Servings:** 4
Ingredients:
- 1 can of black beans, rinsed and drained
- 1 ripe mango, peeled and diced
- 1/4 cup of chopped cilantro
- 1/4 cup of chopped toasted pumpkin seeds
- 2 tablespoons of lime juice
- 2 tablespoons of olive oil
- 1 tablespoon of honey
- Salt and pepper to taste

Instructions:
1. In a large mixing bowl, combine the black beans, mango, cilantro, and pumpkin seeds.
2. In a small mixing bowl, whisk together the lime juice, olive oil, honey, salt, and pepper to make the dressing.
3. Pour the dressing over the black bean mixture and toss to coat.
4. Serve the salad immediately or refrigerate until ready to serve.

Nutritional Value: Calories: 225 Fat: 13g Saturated Fat: 2g Cholesterol: 0mg Sodium: 10mg Carbohydrates: 27g Fiber: 6g Sugar: 12g Protein: 7g

192. Tomato And Basil Salad

Prep. Time: 5 minutes **Servings:** 5
Ingredients:
- 4 cups cherry tomatoes, halved
- 1/4 cup chopped fresh basil
- 2 tbsp olive oil
- 1 tbsp balsamic vinegar
- 1 tsp honey
- Salt and pepper, to taste

Instructions:
1. In a large bowl, combine the halved cherry tomatoes and chopped basil.
2. In a separate small bowl, whisk together the olive oil, balsamic vinegar, honey, salt, and pepper.
3. Pour the dressing over the tomato mixture and toss to coat evenly.
4. Serve immediately or chill in the refrigerator for at least 30 minutes before serving. Enjoy!

Nutritional Value: Calories: 166 Fat: 2g Saturated Fat: 0g Cholesterol: 0mg Sodium: 288mg Carbohydrates: 17g Fiber: 15g Sugar: 1g Protein: 10g

193. Artichoke And Olive Salad

Prep. Time: 10 minutes **Servings:** 5
Ingredients:
- 1 can of artichoke hearts, drained and quartered
- 1/2 cup of pitted and halved Kalamata olives
- 1/4 cup of chopped parsley
- 1/4 cup of crumbled feta cheese
- 2 tablespoons of lemon juice
- 2 tablespoons of olive oil
- 1 tablespoon of Dijon mustard
- Salt and pepper to taste

Instructions:
1. In a large mixing bowl, combine the artichoke hearts, olives, parsley, and feta cheese.
2. In a small mixing bowl, whisk together the lemon juice, olive oil, Dijon mustard, salt, and pepper to make the dressing.
3. Pour the dressing over the artichoke mixture and toss to coat.
4. Serve the salad immediately or refrigerate until ready to serve.

Nutritional Value: Calories: 191 Fat: 17g Saturated Fat: 4g Cholesterol: 14mg Sodium: 578mg Carbohydrates: 7g Fiber: 3g Sugar: 2g Protein: 3g

194. Cabbage And Peanut Salad

Prep. Time: 10 minutes **Servings:** 6
Ingredients:
- 4 cups finely shredded green cabbage
- 1/2 cup chopped roasted peanuts
- 2 tbsp rice vinegar
- 2 tbsp sesame oil
- 1 tbsp honey
- 1 tsp grated ginger
- Salt and pepper, to taste

Instructions:
1. In a large bowl, combine the shredded green cabbage and chopped roasted peanuts.
2. In a separate small bowl, whisk together the rice vinegar, sesame oil, honey, grated ginger, salt, and pepper.
3. Pour the dressing over the cabbage mixture and toss to coat evenly.
4. Serve immediately or chill in the refrigerator for at least 30 minutes before serving. Enjoy!

195. Carrot And Ginger Salad

Prep. Time: 10 minutes **Servings:** 5
Ingredients:
- 2 cups of grated carrots
- 2 tablespoons of grated fresh ginger
- 1/4 cup of chopped cilantro
- 1/4 cup of chopped toasted sesame seeds
- 2 tablespoons of rice vinegar
- 2 tablespoons of vegetable oil
- 1 tablespoon of honey
- Salt and pepper to taste

Instructions:
1. In a large mixing bowl, combine the grated carrots, grated ginger, cilantro, and sesame seeds.
2. In a small mixing bowl, whisk together the rice vinegar, vegetable oil, honey, salt, and pepper to make the dressing.
3. Pour the dressing over the carrot mixture and toss to coat.
4. Serve the salad immediately or refrigerate until ready to serve.

Nutritional Value: Calories: 157 Fat: 12g Saturated Fat: 2g Cholesterol: 0mg Sodium: 49mg Carbohydrates: 12g Fiber: 2g Sugar: 7g Protein: 2g

196. Squash And Cranberry Salad

Prep. Time: 15 minutes **Servings:** 5
Ingredients:
- 2 cups roasted butternut squash, diced
- 1/2 cup dried cranberries
- 1/4 cup chopped fresh parsley
- 2 tbsp olive oil
- 1 tbsp apple cider vinegar
- 1 tsp honey
- Salt and pepper, to taste

Instructions:
1. In a large bowl, combine the diced roasted butternut squash, dried cranberries, and chopped parsley.
2. In a separate small bowl, whisk together the olive oil, apple cider vinegar, honey, salt, and pepper.
3. Pour the dressing over the squash mixture and toss to coat evenly.
4. Serve immediately or chill in the refrigerator for at least 30 minutes before serving. Enjoy!

197. Cucumber And Cilantro Salad

Prep. Time: 10 minutes **Servings:** 5
Ingredients:
- 2 large cucumbers, thinly sliced
- 1/4 cup of chopped cilantro
- 1/4 cup of chopped toasted pumpkin seeds
- 2 tablespoons of rice vinegar
- 2 tablespoons of vegetable oil
- 1 tablespoon of honey
- Salt and pepper to taste

Instructions:
1. In a large mixing bowl, combine the cucumbers, cilantro, and pumpkin seeds.
2. In a small mixing bowl, whisk together the rice vinegar, vegetable oil, honey, salt, and pepper to make the dressing.
3. Pour the dressing over the cucumber mixture and toss to coat.
4. Serve the salad immediately or refrigerate until ready to serve.

Nutritional Value: Calories: 105 Fat: 9g Saturated Fat: 1g Cholesterol: 0mg Sodium: 22mg Carbohydrates: 5g Fiber: 1g Sugar: 3g Protein: 2g

198. Eggplant And Bell Pepper Salad

Prep. Time: 5 minutes **Servings:** 5
Ingredients:
- 1 large eggplant, diced
- 1 red bell pepper, diced
- 1 yellow bell pepper, diced
- 1/4 cup chopped fresh parsley
- 2 tbsp olive oil
- 1 tbsp red wine vinegar
- 1 tsp honey
- Salt and pepper, to taste

Instructions:
1. In a large bowl, combine the diced eggplant, diced red bell pepper, diced yellow bell pepper, and chopped parsley.
2. In a separate small bowl, whisk together the olive oil, red wine vinegar, honey, salt, and pepper.
3. Pour the dressing over the eggplant mixture and toss to coat evenly.
4. Serve immediately or chill in the refrigerator for at least 30 minutes before serving. Enjoy!

199. Broccoli And Almond Salad

Prep. Time: 10 minutes **Cooking Time:** 10 minutes **Servings:** 3
Ingredients:
- 2 cups of broccoli florets
- 1/4 cup of chopped parsley
- 1/4 cup of chopped toasted almonds
- 2 tablespoons of lemon juice
- 2 tablespoons of olive oil
- 1 tablespoon of Dijon mustard
- Salt and pepper to taste

Instructions:
1. Bring a large pot of salted water to a boil. Add the broccoli florets and cook for 5-7 minutes, or until tender but still firm. Drain and rinse the broccoli under cold water to stop the cooking process.
2. In a large mixing bowl, combine the cooked broccoli, parsley, almonds.
3. In a small mixing bowl, whisk together the lemon juice, olive oil, Dijon mustard, salt, and pepper to make the dressing.
4. Pour the dressing over the broccoli mixture and toss to coat.
5. Serve the salad immediately or refrigerate until ready to serve.

Nutritional Value: Calories: 133 Fat: 12g Saturated Fat: 2g Cholesterol: 0mg Sodium: 78mg Carbohydrates: 6g Fiber: 2g Sugar: 2g Protein: 3g

200. Zucchini And Pine Nut Salad

Prep. Time: 10 minutes **Servings:** 4
Ingredients:
- 2 medium zucchinis, thinly sliced
- 1/2 cup toasted pine nuts
- 1/4 cup chopped fresh basil
- 2 tbsp olive oil
- 1 tbsp lemon juice
- 1 tsp honey
- Salt and pepper, to taste

Instructions:
1. In a large bowl, combine the thinly sliced zucchinis, toasted pine nuts, and chopped basil.
2. In a separate small bowl, whisk together the olive oil, lemon juice, honey, salt, and pepper.
3. Pour the dressing over the zucchini mixture and toss to coat evenly.
4. Serve immediately or chill in the refrigerator for at least 30 minutes before serving. Enjoy!

Nutritional Value: Calories: 138 Fat: 7g Saturated Fat: 1g Cholesterol: 0mg Sodium: 28mg Carbohydrates: 8g Fiber: 14g Sugar: 1g Protein: 5g

201. Beet And Walnut Salad

Prep. Time: 10 minutes **Cooking Time:** 50 minutes **Servings:** 3
Ingredients:
- 4 medium sized beets, peeled and diced
- 1/4 cup of chopped parsley
- 1/4 cup of chopped toasted walnuts
- 2 tablespoons of balsamic vinegar
- 2 tablespoons of olive oil
- 1 tablespoon of honey
- Salt and pepper to taste

Instructions:
1. Preheat the oven to 375°F (190°C). Line a baking sheet with parchment paper.
2. Place the diced beets on the prepared baking sheet and toss with some olive oil, salt, and pepper.
3. Roast the beets for 40-50 minutes, or until tender and golden brown. Remove from the oven and let it cool.
4. In a large mixing bowl, combine the cooked beets, parsley, and walnuts.
5. In a small mixing bowl, whisk together the balsamic vinegar, olive oil, honey, salt, and pepper to make the dressing.
6. Pour the dressing over the beet mixture and toss to coat.
7. Serve the salad immediately or refrigerate until ready to serve.

Nutritional Value: Calories: 164 Fat: 13g Saturated Fat: 2g Cholesterol: 0mg Sodium: 94mg Carbohydrates: 12g Fiber: 3g Sugar: 8g Protein: 3g

202. Green Bean And Pesto Salad

Prep. Time: 20 minutes **Servings:** 4
Ingredients:
- 1 lb green beans, trimmed
- 1/4 cup prepared pesto
- 1/4 cup toasted pine nuts
- 2 tbsp olive oil
- 1 tbsp lemon juice
- Salt and pepper, to taste

Instructions:
1. Bring a pot of salted water to a boil. Add the green beans and cook for about 3-4 minutes or until tender yet still crisp. Drain and rinse under cold water to stop the cooking process.
2. In a large bowl, combine the green beans, pesto, and toasted pine nuts.
3. In a separate small bowl, whisk together the olive oil, lemon juice, salt and pepper.

4. Pour the dressing over the green bean mixture and toss to coat evenly.
5. Serve immediately or chill in the refrigerator for at least 30 minutes before serving. Enjoy!

Nutritional Value: Calories: 155 Fat: 12g Saturated Fat: 2g Cholesterol: 1mg Sodium: 84mg Carbohydrates: 15g Fiber: 12g Sugar: 1g Protein: 6g

203.   Radish And Avocado Salad

Prep. Time: 10 minutes **Servings:** 4
Ingredients:
- 1 bunch of radishes, thinly sliced
- 1 avocado, peeled and diced
- 1/4 cup of chopped cilantro
- 1/4 cup of chopped toasted pumpkin seeds
- 2 tablespoons of lime juice
- 2 tablespoons of olive oil
- 1 tablespoon of honey
- Salt and pepper to taste

Instructions:
1. In a large mixing bowl, combine the radishes, avocado, cilantro, and pumpkin seeds.
2. In a small mixing bowl, whisk together the lime juice, olive oil, honey, salt, and pepper to make the dressing.
3. Pour the dressing over the radish mixture and toss to coat.
4. Serve the salad immediately or refrigerate until ready to serve.

Nutritional Value: Calories: 204 Fat: 18g Saturated Fat: 3g Cholesterol: 0mg Sodium: 71mg Carbohydrates: 12g Fiber: 6g Sugar: 4g Protein: 3g

204.   Cauliflower And Pistachio Salad

Prep. Time: 10 minutes **Servings:** 2

Ingredients:
- 1 medium head cauliflower, chopped
- 1/2 cup chopped pistachios
- 1/4 cup chopped fresh parsley
- 2 tbsp olive oil
- 1 tbsp lemon juice
- 1 tsp honey
- Salt and pepper, to taste

Instructions:
1. In a large bowl, combine the chopped cauliflower, chopped pistachios, and chopped parsley.
2. In a separate small bowl, whisk together the olive oil, lemon juice, honey, salt, and pepper.
3. Pour the dressing over the cauliflower mixture and toss to coat evenly.
4. Serve immediately or chill in the refrigerator for at least 30 minutes before serving. Enjoy!

Nutritional Value: Calories: 156 Fat: 9g Saturated Fat: 1g Cholesterol: 2mg Sodium: 88mg Carbohydrates: 10g Fiber: 15g Sugar: 1g Protein: 9g

205.   Asparagus And Parmesan Salad

Prep. Time: 5 minutes **Cooking Time:** 10 minutes **Servings:** 4
Ingredients:
- 1 pound of asparagus, trimmed and cut into 2-inch pieces
- 1/4 cup of grated Parmesan cheese
- 1/4 cup of chopped parsley
- 2 tablespoons of lemon juice
- 2 tablespoons of olive oil
- 1 tablespoon of Dijon mustard
- Salt and pepper to taste

Instructions:
- Bring a large pot of salted water to a boil. Add the asparagus and cook for 2-3

minutes, or until tender but still firm. Drain and rinse the asparagus under cold water to stop the cooking process.
- In a large mixing bowl, combine the cooked asparagus, Parmesan cheese, parsley.
- In a small mixing bowl, whisk together the lemon juice, olive oil, Dijon mustard, salt, and pepper to make the dressing.
- Pour the dressing over the asparagus mixture and toss to coat.
- Serve the salad immediately or refrigerate until ready to serve.

Nutritional Value: Calories: 131 Fat: 11g Saturated Fat: 3g Cholesterol: 8mg Sodium: 252mg Carbohydrates: 5g Fiber: 2g Sugar: 2g Protein: 5g

206. Pea And Lemon Salad

Prep. Time: 15 minutes **Servings:** 5
Ingredients:
- 2 cups frozen peas, thawed
- 1/4 cup chopped fresh mint
- 2 tbsp olive oil
- 1 tbsp lemon juice
- 1 tsp honey
- Salt and pepper, to taste

Instructions:
1. In a large bowl, combine the thawed peas, chopped mint.
2. In a separate small bowl, whisk together the olive oil, lemon juice, honey, salt, and pepper.
3. Pour the dressing over the peas mixture and toss to coat evenly.
4. Serve immediately or chill in the refrigerator for at least 30 minutes before serving. Enjoy!

Nutritional Value: Calories: 110 Fat: 6g Saturated Fat: 0g Cholesterol: 0mg Sodium: 55mg Carbohydrates: 10g Fiber: 12g Sugar: 5g Protein: 10g

Smoothie

207. Green Goddess Smoothie

Prep. Time: 5 minutes **Servings:** 4
Ingredients:
- 1 cup fresh spinach
- 1 cup fresh kale
- 1/2 ripe avocado
- 1/2 cup fresh parsley
- 1/2 cup fresh cilantro
- 1/2 inch fresh ginger
- 1/2 lime, juiced
- 1 cup unsweetened almond milk or coconut water
- 1/2 banana (optional)

Instructions:
1. Add all ingredients to a blender and blend until smooth.
2. Add more almond milk or water as needed to reach your desired consistency.
3. Taste and adjust seasoning as needed.
4. Serve immediately, garnish with some chopped parsley or cilantro.

Nutritional Value: Calories: 92 Fat: 2g Cholesterol: 0mg Sodium: 90mg Carbohydrates: 6g Fiber: 19g Sugar: 3g Protein: 5g

208. Beryllioses Smoothie

Prep. Time: 5 minutes **Servings:** 2
Ingredients:
- 1 cup frozen mixed berries (strawberries, blueberries, raspberries, blackberries)
- 1 ripe banana
- 1/2 cup plain Greek yogurt
- 1/2 cup almond milk
- 1 tsp honey (optional)

Instructions:
1. Add the frozen berries, banana, Greek yogurt, almond milk, and honey (if using) to a blender.
2. Blend on high speed until smooth and creamy.
3. Pour into a glass and enjoy!

Nutritional Value: Calories: 89 Fat: 1g Cholesterol: 0mg Sodium: 67mg Carbohydrates: 20g Fiber: 24g Sugar: 6g Protein: 4g

209. Mango Madness Smoothie

Prep. Time: 5 minutes **Servings:** 2
Ingredients:
- 1 cup frozen mango chunks
- 1 ripe banana
- 1/2 cup plain Greek yogurt
- 1/2 cup orange juice
- 1 tsp honey (optional)

Instructions:
1. Add the frozen mango, banana, Greek yogurt, orange juice, and honey (if using) to a blender.
2. Blend on high speed until smooth and creamy.
3. Pour into a glass and enjoy!

Nutritional Value: Calories: 101 Fat: 2g Cholesterol: 0mg Sodium: 95mg Carbohydrates: 22g Fiber: 18g Sugar: 7g Protein: 6g

210. Tropical Dream Smoothie

Prep. Time: 5 minutes **Servings:** 3
Ingredients:
- 1 cup frozen pineapple chunks
- 1/2 cup frozen mango chunks
- 1/2 cup frozen papaya chunks
- 1/2 cup coconut milk
- 1/2 cup orange juice
- 1/2 banana (optional)

Instructions:
1. Add all ingredients to a blender and blend until smooth.
2. Add more coconut milk or orange juice as needed to reach your desired consistency.
3. Taste and adjust seasoning as needed.

4. Serve immediately, garnish with some pineapple chunks or a sprinkle of coconut flakes.

Nutritional Value: Calories: 108 Fat: 3g Cholesterol: 1mg Sodium: 94mg Carbohydrates: 15g Fiber: 13g Sugar: 3g Protein: 4g

211. Carrot Ginger Smoothie

Prep. Time: 5 minutes **Servings:** 3
Ingredients:
- 2 cups fresh carrot juice
- 1 inch fresh ginger, peeled and grated
- 1 ripe banana
- 1/2 cup plain yogurt
- 1/4 cup orange juice
- 1 tbsp honey (optional)
- 1/2 tsp vanilla extract (optional)

Instructions:
1. Add all ingredients to a blender and blend until smooth.
2. Add more orange juice as needed to reach your desired consistency.
3. Taste and adjust seasoning as needed.
4. Serve immediately, garnish with some grated ginger or a sprinkle of cinnamon if desired.

Nutritional Value: Calories: 88 Fat: 1g Cholesterol: 0mg Sodium: 65mg Carbohydrates: 26g Fiber: 17g Sugar: 6g Protein: 9g

212. Peach Melba Smoothie

Prep. Time: 5 minutes **Servings:** 3
Ingredients:
- 1 cup frozen peaches
- 1/2 cup frozen raspberries
- 1 ripe banana
- 1/2 cup plain Greek yogurt
- 1/2 cup almond milk
- 1 tsp honey (optional)

Instructions:
1. Add the frozen peaches, raspberries, banana, Greek yogurt, almond milk, and honey (if using) to a blender.
2. Blend on high speed until smooth and creamy.
3. Pour into a glass and enjoy!

Nutritional Value: Calories: 84 Fat: 1g Cholesterol: 0mg Sodium: 88mg Carbohydrates: 10g Fiber: 25g Sugar: 7g Protein: 6g

213. Spinach Apple Smoothie

Prep. Time: 5 minutes **Servings:** 4
Ingredients:
- 2 cups fresh spinach
- 1 medium sized apple, cored and diced
- 1 banana
- 1/2 cup plain Greek yogurt
- 1/4 cup orange juice
- 1 tbsp honey (optional)
- 1/2 tsp vanilla extract (optional)

Instructions:
1. Add all ingredients to a blender and blend until smooth.
2. Add more orange juice as needed to reach your desired consistency.
3. Taste and adjust seasoning as needed.
4. Serve immediately, garnish with some chopped apple or a sprinkle of cinnamon if desired.

Nutritional Value: Calories: 85 Fat: 1g Cholesterol: 1mg Sodium: 109mg Carbohydrates: 11g Fiber: 24g Sugar: 5g Protein: 9g

214. Cucumber Melon Smoothie

Prep. Time: 5 minutes **Servings:** 3
Ingredients:
- 1 cup cubed cantaloupe
- 1/2 cup cucumber, peeled and diced
- 1/2 cup plain Greek yogurt
- 1/2 cup coconut water

- 1 tsp honey (optional)

Instructions:
1. Add the cantaloupe, cucumber, Greek yogurt, coconut water, and honey (if using) to a blender.
2. Blend on high speed until smooth and creamy.
3. Pour into a glass and enjoy!

Nutritional Value: Calories: 94 Fat: 1g Cholesterol: 0mg Sodium: 110mg Carbohydrates: 16g Fiber: 18g Sugar: 1g Protein: 8g

215. Chocolate Banana Smoothie

Prep. Time: 5 minutes **Servings:** 2
Ingredients:
- 1 ripe banana
- 1/2 cup milk or milk alternative
- 1/2 cup plain Greek yogurt
- 2 tbsp unsweetened cocoa powder
- 1 tbsp honey or maple syrup (optional)
- 1/2 tsp vanilla extract (optional)
- 2-3 ice cubes (optional)

Instructions:
1. Add all ingredients to a blender and blend until smooth.
2. Taste and adjust sweetness as needed.
3. Serve immediately, garnish with some cocoa powder or a sprinkle of chocolate chips if desired.

Nutritional Value: Calories: 188 Fat: 4g Cholesterol: 2mg Sodium: 188mg Carbohydrates: 26g Fiber: 13g Sugar: 6g Protein: 9g

216. Avocado Lime Smoothie

Prep. Time: 5 minutes **Servings:** 2
Ingredients:
- 1 ripe avocado
- 1/2 cup plain Greek yogurt
- 1/2 cup coconut milk or almond milk
- 1/2 lime, juiced
- 1 tsp honey (optional)

Instructions:
1. Add the avocado, Greek yogurt, coconut milk or almond milk, lime juice, and honey (if using) to a blender.
2. Blend on high speed until smooth and creamy.
3. Pour into a glass and enjoy!

Nutritional Value: Calories: 190 Fat: 5g Cholesterol: 0mg Sodium: 176mg Carbohydrates: 24g Fiber: 18g Sugar: 3g Protein: 6g

217. Pineapple Coconut Smoothie

Prep. Time: 5 minutes **Servings:** 3
Ingredients:
- 1 cup fresh or frozen pineapple chunks
- 1/2 cup coconut milk
- 1/2 cup plain Greek yogurt
- 1/4 cup unsweetened shredded coconut
- 1 tbsp honey or maple syrup (optional)
- 1/2 tsp vanilla extract (optional)
- 2-3 ice cubes (optional)

Instructions:
1. Add all ingredients to a blender and blend until smooth.
2. Taste and adjust sweetness as needed.
3. Serve immediately, garnish with some shredded coconut or a pineapple chunks if desired.

Nutritional Value: Calories: 136 Fat: 2g Cholesterol: 1mg Sodium: 134mg Carbohydrates: 19g Fiber: 8g Sugar: 2g Protein: 10g

218. Strawberry Basil Smoothie

Prep. Time: 5 minutes **Servings:** 2
Ingredients:

- 1 cup fresh or frozen strawberries
- 1/2 cup plain Greek yogurt
- 1/4 cup fresh basil leaves
- 1/4 cup orange juice
- 1 tbsp honey or maple syrup (optional)
- 2-3 ice cubes (optional)

Instructions:
1. Add all ingredients to a blender and blend until smooth.
2. Taste and adjust sweetness as needed.
3. Serve immediately, garnish with some fresh basil leaves or a strawberry if desired.

Nutritional Value: Calories: 122 Fat: 3g Cholesterol: 1mg Sodium: 24mg Carbohydrates: 15g Fiber: 11g Sugar: 3g Protein: 7g

219. Blueberry Almond Smoothie

Prep. Time: 5 minutes **Servings:** 5
Ingredients:
- 1 cup frozen blueberries
- 1/2 cup almond milk
- 1/4 cup plain Greek yogurt
- 1/4 cup rolled oats
- 1 tbsp almond butter
- 1 tsp honey (optional)

Instructions:
1. Add the blueberries, almond milk, Greek yogurt, rolled oats, almond butter, and honey (if using) to a blender.
2. Blend on high speed until smooth and creamy.
3. Pour into a glass and enjoy!

Nutritional Value: Calories: 155 Fat: 5g Cholesterol: 3mg Sodium: 145mg Carbohydrates: 7g Fiber: 6g Sugar: 1g Protein: 11g

220. Beetroot Apple Smoothie

Prep. Time: 5 minutes **Servings:** 2
Ingredients:
- 1 cup fresh or cooked beetroot, diced
- 1 medium sized apple, cored and diced
- 1/2 cup plain Greek yogurt
- 1/4 cup orange juice
- 1 tbsp honey or maple syrup (optional)
- 1/2 tsp vanilla extract (optional)
- 2-3 ice cubes (optional)

Instructions:
1. Add all ingredients to a blender and blend until smooth.
2. Taste and adjust sweetness as needed.
3. Serve immediately, garnish with some beetroot powder or a sprinkle of cinnamon if desired.

Nutritional Value: Calories: 121 Fat: 4g Cholesterol: 0mg Sodium: 133mg Carbohydrates: 7g Fiber: 10g Sugar: 4g Protein: 3g

221. Kale Kiwi Smoothie

Prep. Time: 5 minutes **Servings:** 2
Ingredients:
- 1 cup packed kale leaves
- 2 kiwis, peeled and chopped
- 1/2 banana
- 1/2 cup almond milk
- 1/4 cup plain Greek yogurt
- 1 tsp honey (optional)

Instructions:
1. Add the kale leaves, kiwis, banana, almond milk, Greek yogurt, and honey (if using) to a blender.
2. Blend on high speed until smooth and creamy.
3. Pour into a glass and enjoy!

Nutritional Value: Calories: 109 Fat: 1g Cholesterol: 0mg Sodium: 66mg Carbohydrates: 22g Fiber: 11g Sugar: 3g Protein: 14g

222. Grapefruit Rosemary Smoothie

Prep. Time: 5 minutes **Servings:** 2
Ingredients:
- 1 grapefruit, peeled and segmented
- 1/2 cup plain Greek yogurt
- 1/4 cup orange juice
- 1 tbsp honey or maple syrup (optional)
- 1 sprig of fresh rosemary
- 2-3 ice cubes (optional)

Instructions:
1. Add all ingredients to a blender and blend until smooth.
2. Taste and adjust sweetness as needed.
3. Serve immediately, garnish with some rosemary sprigs or a grapefruit segment if desired.

Nutritional Value: Calories: 103 Fat: 1g Cholesterol: 0mg Sodium: 100mg Carbohydrates: 8g Fiber: 18g Sugar: 9g Protein: 5g

223. Raspberry Ginger Smoothie

Prep. Time: 5 minutes **Servings:** 3
Ingredients:
- 1 cup fresh or frozen raspberries
- 1/2 cup plain Greek yogurt
- 1/4 cup orange juice
- 1 inch fresh ginger, peeled and grated
- 1 tbsp honey or maple syrup (optional)
- 2-3 ice cubes (optional)

Instructions:
1. Add all ingredients to a blender and blend until smooth.
2. Taste and adjust sweetness as needed.
3. Serve immediately, garnish with some raspberries or grated ginger if desired.

Nutritional Value: Calories: 98 Fat: 1g Cholesterol: 0mg Sodium: 77mg Carbohydrates: 12g Fiber: 8g Sugar: 2g Protein: 10g

224. Orange Mango Smoothie

Prep. Time: 5 minutes **Servings:** 3
Ingredients:
- 1 cup frozen mango chunks
- 1/2 cup orange juice
- 1/2 cup plain Greek yogurt
- 1/4 tsp grated ginger (optional)
- 1 tsp honey (optional)

Instructions:
1. Add the frozen mango, orange juice, Greek yogurt, grated ginger (if using), and honey (if using) to a blender.
2. Blend on high speed until smooth and creamy.
3. Pour into a glass and enjoy!

Nutritional Value: Calories: 102 Fat: 1g Cholesterol: 1mg Sodium: 55mg Carbohydrates: 4g Fiber: 12g Sugar: 4g Protein: 3g

225. Pomegranate Pear Smoothie

Prep. Time: 5 minutes **Servings:** 2
Ingredients:
- 1/2 cup fresh pomegranate arils
- 1 ripe pear, peeled and diced
- 1/2 cup plain Greek yogurt
- 1/4 cup orange juice
- 1 tbsp honey or maple syrup (optional)
- 2-3 ice cubes (optional)

Instructions:
1. Add all ingredients to a blender and blend until smooth.
2. Taste and adjust sweetness as needed.
3. Serve immediately, garnish with some pomegranate arils or a pear slice if desired.

Nutritional Value: Calories: 109 Fat: 0g Cholesterol: 0mg Sodium: 55mg Carbohydrates: 7g Fiber: 14g Sugar: 4g Protein: 3g

226. Acai Berry Smoothie

Prep. Time: 5 minutes **Servings:** 1
Ingredients:
- 1 pack of acai berry puree (found frozen in most health food stores)
- 1/2 cup frozen mixed berries
- 1/2 cup almond milk or coconut milk
- 1/2 banana
- 1 tsp honey (optional)

Instructions:
1. Add the acai berry puree, mixed berries, almond milk or coconut milk, banana, and honey (if using) to a blender.
2. Blend on high speed until smooth and creamy.
3. Pour into a glass and enjoy!

Nutritional Value: Calories: 118 Fat: 2g Cholesterol: 0mg Sodium: 80mg Carbohydrates: 9g Fiber: 10g Sugar: 5g Protein: 7g

227. Cauliflower Turmeric Smoothie

Prep. Time: 5 minutes **Servings:** 2
Ingredients:
- 1 cup fresh or frozen cauliflower florets
- 1/2 inch fresh ginger, peeled and grated
- 1/2 teaspoon of turmeric powder
- 1/2 cup plain Greek yogurt
- 1/4 cup almond milk or coconut milk
- 1 tbsp honey or maple syrup (optional)
- 2-3 ice cubes (optional)

Instructions:
1. Add all ingredients to a blender and blend until smooth.
2. Taste and adjust sweetness as needed.
3. Serve immediately, garnish with some grated ginger or turmeric powder if desired.

Nutritional Value: Calories: 88 Fat: 2g Cholesterol: 9mg Sodium: 50mg Carbohydrates: 6g Fiber: 10g Sugar: 3g Protein: 5g

228. Sweet Potato Pie Smoothie

Prep. Time: 5 minutes **Servings:** 2
Ingredients:
- 1/2 cup cooked and mashed sweet potato
- 1/2 cup plain Greek yogurt
- 1/2 cup unsweetened almond milk
- 1 tsp vanilla extract
- 1 tsp honey (optional)
- 1/4 tsp ground cinnamon
- 1/4 tsp ground nutmeg

Instructions:
1. Add the cooked and mashed sweet potato, Greek yogurt, almond milk, vanilla extract, honey (if using), cinnamon, and nutmeg to a blender.
2. Blend on high speed until smooth and creamy.
3. Pour into a glass and enjoy!

Nutritional Value: Calories: 133 Fat: 2g Cholesterol: 1mg Sodium: 31mg Carbohydrates: 10g Fiber: 9g Sugar: 3g Protein: 7g

229. Radish Cucumber Smoothie

Prep. Time: 5 minutes **Servings:** 3
Ingredients:
- 1 cup fresh radishes, trimmed and diced
- 1/2 cup fresh cucumber, peeled and diced
- 1/2 cup plain Greek yogurt
- 1/4 cup orange juice
- 1 tbsp honey or maple syrup (optional)
- 2-3 ice cubes (optional)

Instructions:
1. Add all ingredients to a blender and blend until smooth.
2. Taste and adjust sweetness as needed.
3. Serve immediately, garnish with some radish slices or cucumber chunks if desired.

Nutritional Value: Calories: 82 Fat: 0g Cholesterol: 0mg Sodium: 44mg Carbohydrates: 6g Fiber: 18g Sugar: 3g Protein: 4g

230. Broccoli Walnut Smoothie

Prep. Time: 5 minutes **Servings:** 3
Ingredients:
- 1 cup packed broccoli florets
- 1/2 cup unsweetened almond milk
- 1/4 cup plain Greek yogurt
- 1 tbsp chopped walnuts
- 1 tsp honey (optional)
- 1/4 tsp ground cinnamon

Instructions:
1. Add the broccoli florets, almond milk, Greek yogurt, chopped walnuts, honey (if using), and cinnamon to a blender.
2. Blend on high speed until smooth and creamy.
3. Pour into a glass and enjoy!

Nutritional Value: Calories: 77 Fat: 0g Cholesterol: 0mg Sodium: 122mg Carbohydrates: 6g Fiber: 14g Sugar: 0g Protein: 9g

231. Asparagus Lemon Smoothie

Prep. Time: 5 minutes **Servings:** 2
Ingredients:
- 1 cup fresh asparagus, trimmed and diced
- 1/2 cup plain Greek yogurt
- 1/4 cup lemon juice
- 1 tbsp honey or maple syrup (optional)
- 2-3 ice cubes (optional)

Instructions:
1. Add all ingredients to a blender and blend until smooth.
2. Taste and adjust sweetness as needed.
3. Serve immediately, garnish with some asparagus chunks or lemon zest if desired.

Nutritional Value: Calories: 91 Fat: 1g Cholesterol: 0mg Sodium: 60mg Carbohydrates: 7g Fiber: 10g Sugar: 1g Protein: 6g

232. Zucchini Basil Smoothie

Prep. Time: 5 minutes **Servings:** 2
Ingredients:
- 1/2 cup grated zucchini
- 1/2 cup plain Greek yogurt
- 1/2 cup unsweetened almond milk
- 1 tbsp fresh basil leaves
- 1 tsp honey (optional)
- 1/4 tsp ground cinnamon

Instructions:
1. Add the grated zucchini, Greek yogurt, almond milk, basil leaves, honey (if using), and cinnamon to a blender.
2. Blend on high speed until smooth and creamy.
3. Pour into a glass and enjoy!

Nutritional Value: Calories: 99 Fat: 1g Cholesterol: 0mg Sodium: 133mg Carbohydrates: 7g Fiber: 21g Sugar: 3g Protein: 6g

233. Sweet Pea Mint Smoothie

Prep. Time: 5 minutes **Servings:** 2
Ingredients:
- 1 cup fresh or frozen sweet peas
- 1/2 cup plain Greek yogurt
- 1/4 cup fresh mint leaves
- 1/4 cup orange juice
- 1 tbsp honey or maple syrup (optional)
- 2-3 ice cubes (optional)

Instructions:
1. Add all ingredients to a blender and blend until smooth.
2. Taste and adjust sweetness as needed.
3. Serve immediately, garnish with some fresh mint leaves or a sweet pea pod if desired.

Nutritional Value: Calories: 82 Fat: 1g Cholesterol: 0mg Sodium: 86mg Carbohydrates: 7g Fiber: 12g Sugar: 1g Protein: 5g

234. Cabbage Ginger Smoothie

Prep. Time: 5 minutes **Servings:** 3
Ingredients:
- 1 cup packed green cabbage leaves
- 1/2 cup coconut water or pineapple juice
- 1/2 inch piece of ginger, peeled and grated
- 1/4 cup plain Greek yogurt
- 1 tsp honey (optional)

Instructions:
1. Add the cabbage leaves, coconut water or pineapple juice, grated ginger, Greek yogurt, and honey (if using) to a blender.
2. Blend on high speed until smooth and creamy.
3. Pour into a glass and enjoy!

Nutritional Value: Calories: 85 Fat: 2g Cholesterol: 0mg Sodium: 88mg Carbohydrates: 6g Fiber: 10g Sugar: 1g Protein: 6g

235. Apple Cinnamon Smoothie

Prep. Time: 5 minutes **Servings:** 1
Ingredients:
- 1 medium sized apple, cored and diced
- 1/2 cup plain Greek yogurt
- 1/4 cup milk or milk alternative
- 1 tsp ground cinnamon
- 1 tbsp honey or maple syrup (optional)
- 1/2 tsp vanilla extract (optional)
- 2-3 ice cubes (optional)

Instructions:
1. Add all ingredients to a blender and blend until smooth.
2. Taste and adjust sweetness as needed.
3. Serve immediately, garnish with some cinnamon powder or a sprinkle of chopped apples if desired.

Nutritional Value: Calories: 66 Fat: 0g Cholesterol: 0mg Sodium: 48mg Carbohydrates: 5g Fiber: 14g Sugar: 1g Protein: 8g

236. Lemon Ginger Smoothie

Prep. Time: 5 minutes **Servings:** 2
Ingredients:
- 1/2 cup plain Greek yogurt
- 1/2 cup almond milk or coconut milk
- 1/2 lemon, juiced
- 1/2-inch piece of ginger, peeled and grated
- 1 tsp honey (optional)

Instructions:
1. Add the Greek yogurt, almond milk or coconut milk, lemon juice, grated ginger, and honey (if using) to a blender.
2. Blend on high speed until smooth and creamy.
3. Pour into a glass and enjoy!

Nutritional Value: Calories: 103 Fat: 2g Cholesterol: 0mg Sodium: 81mg Carbohydrates: 7g Fiber: 8g Sugar: 1g Protein: 6g

237. Cacao Avocado Smoothie

Prep. Time: 5 minutes **Servings:** 2
Ingredients:
- 1 ripe avocado
- 1/2 cup almond milk or coconut milk
- 2 tbsp unsweetened cocoa powder or cacao powder
- 1 tsp honey (optional)
- 1 tsp vanilla extract

Instructions:
1. Add the avocado, almond milk or coconut milk, cocoa powder or cacao powder, honey (if using) and vanilla extract to a blender.
2. Blend on high speed until smooth and creamy.
3. Pour into a glass and enjoy!

Nutritional Value: Calories: 96 Fat: 2g Cholesterol: 1mg Sodium: 99mg Carbohydrates: 6g Fiber: 13g Sugar: 1g Protein: 5g

238. Banana Oat Smoothie

Prep. Time: 5 minutes **Servings:** 2
Ingredients:
- 1 ripe banana
- 1/2 cup rolled oats
- 1/2 cup milk or milk alternative
- 1/2 cup plain Greek yogurt
- 1 tbsp honey or maple syrup (optional)
- 1/2 tsp vanilla extract (optional)
- 2-3 ice cubes (optional)

Instructions:
1. Add all ingredients to a blender and blend until smooth.
2. Taste and adjust sweetness as needed.
3. Serve immediately, garnish with some oats or banana slices if desired.

Nutritional Value: Calories: 104 Fat: 1g Cholesterol: 1mg Sodium: 74mg Carbohydrates: 20g Fiber: 11g Sugar: 3g Protein: 8g

239. Pineapple Spinach Smoothie

Prep. Time: 5 minutes **Servings:** 1
Ingredients:
- 1 cup frozen pineapple chunks
- 1 cup packed spinach leaves
- 1/2 cup coconut water or pineapple juice
- 1/2 banana
- 1 tsp honey (optional)

Instructions:
1. Add the frozen pineapple, spinach leaves, coconut water or pineapple juice, banana, and honey (if using) to a blender.
2. Blend on high speed until smooth and creamy.
3. Pour into a glass and enjoy!

Nutritional Value: Calories: 76 Fat: 0g Cholesterol: mg Sodium: 65mg Carbohydrates: 8g Fiber: 9g Sugar: 2g Protein: 5g

240. Sweet Potato Cinnamon Smoothie

Prep. Time: 5 minutes **Servings:** 3
Ingredients:
- 1 cup cooked and mashed sweet potato
- 1/2 cup plain Greek yogurt
- 1/4 cup milk or milk alternative
- 1 tsp ground cinnamon
- 1 tbsp honey or maple syrup (optional)
- 1/2 tsp vanilla extract (optional)
- 2-3 ice cubes (optional)

Instructions:
1. Add all ingredients to a blender and blend until smooth.
2. Taste and adjust sweetness as needed.
3. Serve immediately, garnish with some cinnamon powder or a sprinkle of sweet potato chunks if desired.

Nutritional Value: Calories: 119 Fat: 2g Cholesterol: 1mg Sodium: 69mg Carbohydrates: 22g Fiber: 9g Sugar: 2g Protein: 9g

241. Mango Lassi Smoothie

Prep. Time: 5 minutes **Servings:** 2
Ingredients:
- 1 cup frozen mango chunks
- 1/2 cup plain Greek yogurt
- 1/4 cup milk (cow, almond, soy or any other milk)
- 1 tsp honey (optional)
- 1/4 tsp ground cardamom (optional)

Instructions:
1. Add the frozen mango, Greek yogurt, milk, honey (if using), and cardamom (if using) to a blender.
2. Blend on high speed until smooth and creamy.

3. Pour into a glass and enjoy!

Nutritional Value: Calories: 124 Fat: 3g Cholesterol: 2mg Sodium: 88mg Carbohydrates: 4g Fiber: 6g Sugar: 6g Protein: 6g

242. Carrot Orange Smoothie

Prep. Time: 5 minutes **Servings:** 3

Ingredients:
- 1 cup fresh or cooked carrots, diced
- 1/2 cup fresh orange juice
- 1/2 cup plain Greek yogurt
- 1 tbsp honey or maple syrup (optional)
- 1/2 tsp vanilla extract (optional)
- 2-3 ice cubes (optional)

Instructions:
1. Add all ingredients to a blender and blend until smooth.
2. Taste and adjust sweetness as needed.
3. Serve immediately, garnish with some grated carrot or orange zest if desired.

Nutritional Value: Calories: 102 Fat: 2g Cholesterol: 1mg Sodium: 76mg Carbohydrates: 6g Fiber: 10g Sugar: 4g Protein: 7g

243. Strawberry Kale Smoothie

Prep. Time: 5 minutes **Servings:** 4

Ingredients:
- 1 cup frozen strawberries
- 1 cup packed kale leaves
- 1/2 banana
- 1/2 cup unsweetened almond milk or coconut milk
- 1/4 cup plain Greek yogurt
- 1 tsp honey (optional)

Instructions:
1. Add the frozen strawberries, kale leaves, banana, almond milk or coconut milk, Greek yogurt, and honey (if using) to a blender.
2. Blend on high speed until smooth and creamy.

3. Pour into a glass and enjoy!

Nutritional Value: Calories: 98 Fat: 0g Cholesterol: 0mg Sodium: 88mg Carbohydrates: 22g Fiber: 14g Sugar: 2g Protein: 3g

244. Papaya Pineapple Smoothie

Prep. Time: 5 minutes **Servings:** 3

Ingredients:
- 1 cup fresh or frozen papaya, diced
- 1/2 cup fresh or frozen pineapple chunks
- 1/2 cup plain Greek yogurt
- 1/4 cup coconut milk
- 1 tbsp honey or maple syrup (optional)
- 2-3 ice cubes (optional)

Instructions:
1. Add all ingredients to a blender and blend until smooth.
2. Taste and adjust sweetness as needed.
3. Serve immediately, garnish with some papaya chunks or pineapple chunks if desired.

Nutritional Value: Calories: 108 Fat: 1g Cholesterol: 0mg Sodium: 44mg Carbohydrates: 3g Fiber: 12g Sugar: 1g Protein: 4g

245. Blackberry Lemon Smoothie

Prep. Time: 5 minutes **Servings:** 2

Ingredients:
- 1 cup fresh or frozen blackberries
- 1/2 cup plain Greek yogurt
- 1/2 cup unsweetened almond milk or coconut milk
- 1/4 cup fresh lemon juice
- 1 tsp honey (optional)

Instructions:
1. Add the blackberries, Greek yogurt, almond milk or coconut milk, lemon juice, and honey (if using) to a blender.
2. Blend on high speed until smooth and creamy.

3. Pour into a glass and enjoy!

Nutritional Value: Calories: 92 Fat: 1g Cholesterol: 3mg Sodium: 91mg Carbohydrates: 5g Fiber: 9g Sugar: 5g Protein: 4g

246. Peach Mango Smoothie

Prep. Time: 5 minutes **Servings:** 3
Ingredients:
- 1 cup fresh or frozen peaches, diced
- 1/2 cup fresh or frozen mango chunks
- 1/2 cup plain Greek yogurt
- 1/4 cup orange juice
- 1 tbsp honey or maple syrup (optional)
- 2-3 ice cubes (optional)

Instructions:
1. Add all ingredients to a blender and blend until smooth.
2. Taste and adjust sweetness as needed.
3. Serve immediately, garnish with some peach slices or mango chunks if desired.

Nutritional Value: Calories: 96 Fat: 1g Cholesterol: 0mg Sodium: 87mg Carbohydrates: 6g Fiber: 9g Sugar: 4g Protein: 7g

247. Cucumber Melon Mint Smoothie

Prep. Time: 5 minutes **Servings:** 2
Ingredients:
- 1/2 cup diced cucumber
- 1/2 cup diced cantaloupe or honeydew melon
- 1/2 cup plain Greek yogurt
- 1/4 cup coconut water or almond milk
- 1 tbsp fresh mint leaves
- 1 tsp honey (optional)

Instructions:
1. Add the diced cucumber, diced cantaloupe or honeydew melon, Greek yogurt, coconut water or almond milk, fresh mint leaves, and honey (if using) to a blender.

2. Blend on high speed until smooth and creamy.
3. Pour into a glass and enjoy!

Nutritional Value: Calories: 97 Fat: 1g Cholesterol: 0mg Sodium: 55mg Carbohydrates: 4g Fiber: 13g Sugar: 1g Protein: 6g

248. Chocolate Hazelnut Smoothie

Prep. Time: 5 minutes **Servings:** 3
Ingredients:
- 1 ripe banana
- 1/2 cup milk or milk alternative
- 1/4 cup hazelnut butter
- 2 tablespoons cocoa powder
- 1 tbsp honey or maple syrup (optional)
- 1/2 tsp vanilla extract (optional)
- 2-3 ice cubes (optional)

Instructions:
1. Add all ingredients to a blender and blend until smooth.
2. Taste and adjust sweetness as needed.

Serve immediately, garnish with some chopped hazelnuts or cocoa powder if desired.

Nutritional Value: Calories: 133 Fat: 6g Cholesterol: 22mg Sodium: 102mg Carbohydrates: 11g Fiber: 6g Sugar: 2g Protein: 9g

249. Avocado Cacao Smoothie

Prep. Time: 5 minutes **Servings:** 2
Ingredients:
- 1 ripe avocado
- 1/2 cup unsweetened almond milk or coconut milk
- 2 tbsp unsweetened cocoa powder or cacao powder
- 1 tsp honey (optional)
- 1 tsp vanilla extract

Instructions:

1. Add the avocado, almond milk or coconut milk, cocoa powder or cacao powder, honey (if using) and vanilla extract to a blender.
2. Blend on high speed until smooth and creamy.
3. Pour into a glass and enjoy!

Nutritional Value: Calories: 142 Fat: 6g Cholesterol: 2mg Sodium: 99mg Carbohydrates: 9g Fiber: 6g Sugar: 5g Protein: 9g

250. Pineapple Coconut Lime Smoothie

Prep. Time: 5 minutes **Servings:** 2
Ingredients:
- 1 cup fresh or frozen pineapple chunks
- 1/2 cup coconut milk
- 1/4 cup lime juice
- 1 tbsp honey or maple syrup (optional)
- 2-3 ice cubes (optional)

Instructions:
1. Add all ingredients to a blender and blend until smooth.
2. Taste and adjust sweetness as needed.
3. Serve immediately, garnish with some pineapple chunks or lime zest if desired.

Nutritional Value: Calories: 98 Fat: 1g Cholesterol: 1mg Sodium: 65mg Carbohydrates: 7g Fiber: 12g Sugar: 4g Protein: 5g

251. Papaya Paradise Smoothie

Prep. Time: 5 minutes **Servings:** 3
Ingredients:
- 1 cup diced papaya
- 1/2 cup coconut milk or almond milk
- 1/4 cup plain Greek yogurt
- 1 tbsp honey (optional)
- 1/4 tsp ground turmeric (optional)
- 1/4 tsp ground cinnamon (optional)

Instructions:

1. Add the diced papaya, coconut milk or almond milk, Greek yogurt, honey (if using), turmeric (if using), and cinnamon (if using) to a blender.
2. Blend on high speed until smooth and creamy.
3. Pour into a glass and enjoy!

Nutritional Value: Calories: 89 Fat: 1g Cholesterol: 0mg Sodium: 87mg Carbohydrates: 10g Fiber: 5g Sugar: 2g Protein: 9g

252. Beetroot Ginger Smoothie

Prep. Time: 5 minutes **Servings:** 3
Ingredients:
- 1 cup fresh or cooked beets, diced
- 1/2 inch fresh ginger, peeled and grated
- 1/2 cup plain Greek yogurt
- 1/4 cup almond milk or coconut milk
- 1 tbsp honey or maple syrup (optional)
- 2-3 ice cubes (optional)

Instructions:
1. Add all ingredients to a blender and blend until smooth.
2. Taste and adjust sweetness as needed.
3. Serve immediately, garnish with some grated ginger or beetroot chunks if desired.

Nutritional Value: Calories: 87 Fat: 1g Cholesterol: 3mg Sodium: 97mg Carbohydrates: 9g Fiber: 11g Sugar: 2g Protein: 6g

253. Kale Banana Smoothie

Prep. Time: 5 minutes **Servings:** 3
Ingredients:
- 1 cup packed kale leaves
- 1 ripe banana
- 1/2 cup unsweetened almond milk or coconut milk
- 1/4 cup plain Greek yogurt
- 1 tsp honey (optional)

Instructions:

1. Add the kale leaves, banana, almond milk or coconut milk, Greek yogurt, and honey (if using) to a blender.
2. Blend on high speed until smooth and creamy.
3. Pour into a glass and enjoy!

Nutritional Value: Calories: 102 Fat: 1g Cholesterol: 1mg Sodium: 48mg Carbohydrates: 18g Fiber: 8g Sugar: 2g Protein: 4g

254. Blackberry Vanilla Smoothie

Prep. Time: 5 minutes **Servings:** 2
Ingredients:
- 1 cup fresh or frozen blackberries
- 1/2 cup plain Greek yogurt
- 1/4 cup milk or milk alternative
- 1 tsp vanilla extract
- 1 tbsp honey or maple syrup (optional)
- 2-3 ice cubes (optional)

Instructions:
1. Add all ingredients to a blender and blend until smooth.
2. Taste and adjust sweetness as needed.
3. Serve immediately, garnish with some blackberries or vanilla powder if desired.

Nutritional Value: Calories: 88 Fat: 2g Cholesterol: 1mg Sodium: 84mg Carbohydrates: 7g Fiber: 7g Sugar: 1g Protein: 8g

255. Orange Mango Ginger Smoothie

Prep. Time: 5 minutes **Servings:** 3
Ingredients:
- 1 cup fresh or frozen mango chunks
- 1/2 cup fresh orange juice
- 1/2 inch fresh ginger, peeled and grated
- 1/4 cup plain Greek yogurt
- 1 tbsp honey or maple syrup (optional)
- 2-3 ice cubes (optional)

Instructions:
1. Add all ingredients to a blender and blend until smooth.
2. Taste and adjust sweetness as needed.
3. Serve immediately, garnish with some mango chunks or ginger slices if desired.

Nutritional Value: Calories: 88 Fat: 3g Cholesterol: 0mg Sodium: 97mg Carbohydrates: 9g Fiber: 9g Sugar: 2g Protein: 8g

256. Raspberry Lime Smoothie

Prep. Time: 5 minutes **Servings:** 4
Ingredients:
- 1 cup frozen raspberries
- 1 ripe lime, peeled and seeded
- 1/2 cup plain yogurt
- 1/2 cup orange juice
- 1/4 cup honey
- 1 cup ice

Instructions:
1. In a blender, combine the raspberries, lime, yogurt, orange juice, honey, and ice.
2. Blend until smooth.
3. Taste and adjust sweetness if necessary.
4. Pour into glasses and serve immediately.
5. Enjoy your Raspberry Lime Smoothie!

Nutritional Value: Calories: 91 Fat: 1g Cholesterol: 2mg Sodium: 72mg Carbohydrates: 5g Fiber: 3g Sugar: 2g Protein: 9g

257. Acai Berry Blueberry Smoothie

Prep. Time: 5 minutes **Servings:** 5
Ingredients:
- 1/2 cup frozen acai berry puree
- 1/2 cup fresh or frozen blueberries
- 1/2 cup plain Greek yogurt
- 1/4 cup almond milk or coconut milk
- 1 tbsp honey or maple syrup (optional)
- 2-3 ice cubes (optional)

Instructions:

1. Add all ingredients to a blender and blend until smooth.
2. Taste and adjust sweetness as needed.
3. Serve immediately, garnish with some blueberries or acai powder if desired.

Nutritional Value: Calories: 94 Fat: 2g Cholesterol: 3mg Sodium: 49mg Carbohydrates: 8g Fiber: 13g Sugar: 2g Protein: 4g

258. Sweet Potato Pie Spiced Smoothie

Prep. Time: 5 minutes **Servings:** 3
Ingredients:
- 1 cup cooked and mashed sweet potato
- 1 ripe banana
- 1/2 cup plain yogurt
- 1/2 cup milk
- 1/4 cup maple syrup
- 1 tsp pumpkin pie spice
- 1 tsp vanilla extract
- 1 cup ice

Instructions:
1. In a blender, combine the sweet potato, banana, yogurt, milk, maple syrup, pumpkin pie spice, vanilla extract and ice.
2. Blend until smooth.
3. Taste and adjust sweetness if necessary.
4. Pour into glasses and serve immediately.
5. Enjoy your Sweet Potato Pie Spiced Smoothie!

Nutritional Value: Calories: 121 Fat: 2g Cholesterol: 0mg Sodium: 98mg Carbohydrates: 23g Fiber: 12g Sugar: 4g Protein: 8g

259. Cauliflower Turmeric Coconut Smoothie

Prep. Time: 5 minutes **Servings:** 3
Ingredients:
- 1 cup fresh or cooked cauliflower florets
- 1/2 inch fresh turmeric, peeled and grated
- 1/4 cup coconut milk
- 1/4 cup plain Greek yogurt
- 1 tbsp honey or maple syrup (optional)
- 2-3 ice cubes (optional)

Instructions:
1. Add all ingredients to a blender and blend until smooth.
2. Taste and adjust sweetness as needed.
3. Serve immediately, garnish with some grated turmeric or cauliflower chunks if desired.

Nutritional Value: Calories: 108 Fat: 1g Cholesterol: 2mg Sodium: 88mg Carbohydrates: 4g Fiber: 9g Sugar: 1g Protein: 7g

260. Broccoli Walnut Smoothie With Vanilla

Prep. Time: 5 minutes **Servings:** 4
Ingredients:
- 1 cup fresh broccoli florets
- 1/2 cup chopped walnuts
- 1 ripe banana
- 1/2 cup plain yogurt
- 1/2 cup milk
- 1 tsp vanilla extract
- 1 tsp honey (optional)
- 1 cup ice

Instructions:
1. In a blender, combine the broccoli florets, walnuts, banana, yogurt, milk, vanilla extract, honey (if using) and ice.
2. Blend until smooth.
3. Taste and adjust sweetness if necessary.
4. Pour into glasses and serve immediately.
5. Enjoy your Broccoli Walnut Smoothie with vanilla!

Nutritional Value: Calories: 132 Fat: 4g Cholesterol: 6mg Sodium: 102mg Carbohydrates: 24g Fiber: 8g Sugar: 4g Protein: 10g

Snacks

261. Baked Sweet Potato Fries

Prep. Time: 15 minutes **Cooking Time:** 30 minutes **Servings:** 4

Ingredients:
- 2 large sweet potatoes, peeled and cut into fries
- 2 tablespoons olive oil
- Salt and pepper, to taste
- Optional: spices such as cumin, paprika, or chili powder

Instructions:
1. Preheat the oven to 425 degrees F (220 degrees C).
2. In a large bowl, toss the sweet potato fries with olive oil, salt, pepper, and any optional spices.
3. Spread the fries out on a baking sheet in a single layer.
4. Bake for 25-30 minutes, flipping the fries halfway through, or until they are crispy and golden brown.
5. Serve hot and enjoy!

Nutritional Value: Calories: 190 Fat: 11g Cholesterol: 15mg Carbohydrates: 25g Fiber: 3g Sugar: 6g Protein: 2g

262. Grilled Zucchini And Bell Pepper Skewers

Prep. Time: 10 minutes **Cooking Time:** 10 minutes **Servings:** 4

Ingredients:
- 2 medium zucchinis, cut into 1-inch chunks
- 2 bell peppers (any color), cut into 1-inch chunks
- 1/4 cup olive oil
- 2 cloves of garlic, minced
- 1 tsp. dried oregano
- 1/2 tsp. salt
- 1/4 tsp. black pepper

Instructions:
1. In a small bowl, mix together the olive oil, garlic, oregano, salt, and black pepper.
2. Thread the zucchini and bell pepper chunks onto skewers.
3. Brush the skewers with the olive oil mixture.
4. Preheat grill to medium-high heat.
5. Grill skewers for 8-10 minutes, turning occasionally, until vegetables are tender and lightly charred.
6. Serve immediately and enjoy!

Nutritional Value: Calories: 167 Fat: 15g Cholesterol: 20mg Carbohydrates: 9g Fiber: 2g Sugar: 4g Protein: 3g

263. Stuffed Portobello Mushrooms

Prep. Time: 15 minutes **Cooking Time:** 25 minutes **Servings:** 5

Ingredients:
- 4 large portobello mushroom caps, stems removed
- 2 tablespoons olive oil
- Salt and pepper, to taste
- 1 small onion, diced
- 2 cloves of garlic, minced
- 1 cup cooked quinoa or rice
- 1 cup diced vegetables of your choice (such as bell peppers, spinach, or zucchini)
- 1/4 cup grated Parmesan cheese
- 1/4 cup chopped fresh herbs (such as parsley or basil)

Instructions:
1. Preheat the oven to 375 degrees F (190 degrees C).

2. In a small bowl, combine the olive oil, salt, and pepper. Brush the mixture onto the mushroom caps, reserving any remaining mixture.
3. In a pan over medium heat, sauté the onion and garlic until softened.
4. Add diced vegetables and stir until vegetables are tender.
5. Remove from heat and mix in cooked quinoa or rice, cheese, and herbs.
6. Stuff the mushroom caps with the quinoa or rice mixture.
7. Place the mushrooms on a baking sheet, and brush the remaining olive oil mixture over the tops.
8. Bake for 20-25 minutes or until the mushrooms are tender and the stuffing is heated through.
9. Serve and enjoy!

Nutritional Value: Calories: 256 Fat: 14g Cholesterol: 31mg Carbohydrates: 21g Fiber: 3g Sugar: 4g Protein: 9g

264. Black Bean And Corn Quesadillas

Prep. Time: 10 minutes **Cooking Time:** 5 minutes **Servings:** 6
Ingredients:
- 1 can of black beans, drained and rinsed
- 1 cup of frozen corn, thawed
- 1/2 red onion, diced
- 1 jalapeño pepper, seeded and diced
- 1/4 cup chopped fresh cilantro
- 1/2 teaspoon ground cumin
- Salt and pepper, to taste
- 1 cup shredded Mexican blend cheese
- 8 flour tortillas
- Olive oil or cooking spray for the pan

Instructions:
1. In a large bowl, combine the black beans, corn, red onion, jalapeño, cilantro, cumin, salt, and pepper.
2. Heat a large skillet over medium heat and coat with olive oil or cooking spray.
3. Take one tortilla and place it on the skillet. Sprinkle 1/8 of the cheese and 1/8 of the bean mixture on one half of the tortilla.
4. Fold the other half of the tortilla over the filling and press down lightly with a spatula.
5. Cook the quesadilla for 2-3 minutes on each side, or until the cheese is melted and the tortilla is golden brown.
6. Remove the quesadilla from the skillet and let it cool for a minute before slicing into wedges.
7. Repeat with the remaining tortillas and filling.
8. Serve hot with salsa, sour cream, or guacamole on the side, if desired.

Nutritional Value: Calories: 381 Fat: 17g Cholesterol: 72mg Carbohydrates: 43g Fiber: 8g Sugar: 4g Protein: 15g

265. Chickpea And Avocado Salad

Prep. Time: 10 minutes **Cooking Time:** 15 minutes **Servings:** 3
Ingredients:
- 1 can of chickpeas, drained and rinsed
- 2 ripe avocados, diced
- 1/2 red onion, finely diced
- 1/4 cup chopped fresh cilantro
- 2 tablespoons fresh lime juice
- 2 tablespoons olive oil
- Salt and pepper, to taste

Instructions:
1. In a large bowl, combine the chickpeas, avocados, red onion, and cilantro.
2. In a small bowl, whisk together the lime juice, olive oil, salt, and pepper to make the dressing.

3. Pour the dressing over the chickpea and avocado mixture and toss to combine.
4. Let the salad sit for at least 15 minutes to allow the flavors to meld together.
5. Taste and adjust seasoning if needed.
6. Serve chilled or at room temperature.

Nutritional Value: Calories: 463 Fat: 38g Cholesterol: 64mg Carbohydrates: 31g Fiber: 12g Sugar: 5g Protein: 10g

266. Spinach And Feta Stuffed Phyllo Cups

Prep. Time: 15 minutes **Cooking Time:** 15 minutes **Servings:** 4

Ingredients:
- 1 package of phyllo cups (15 cups)
- 1 tbsp olive oil
- 1 onion, finely chopped
- 3 cloves of garlic, minced
- 10 oz. frozen spinach, thawed and squeezed dry
- 4 oz. feta cheese, crumbled
- 1/4 cup grated Parmesan cheese
- Salt and pepper to taste

Instructions:
1. Preheat the oven to 350°F (175°C).
2. In a pan, heat olive oil over medium heat. Add onion and garlic, sauté until softened and lightly golden.
3. Add the spinach to the pan and sauté for another 2-3 minutes. Remove from heat and let it cool.
4. In a mixing bowl, combine the spinach mixture, feta cheese, Parmesan cheese, salt and pepper. Mix well.
5. Place the phyllo cups on a baking sheet. Fill each cup with the spinach mixture, about 2 tsp of filling.
6. Bake for 10-12 minutes or until the phyllo cups are golden brown and the filling is heated through.
7. Let it cool for a few minutes before serving. Serve warm and enjoy!

Nutritional Value: Calories: 132 Fat: 9g Cholesterol: 43mg Carbohydrates: 8g Fiber: 1g Sugar: 1g Protein: 6g

267. Cucumber And Dill Yogurt Dip

Prep. Time: 10 minutes **Cooking Time:** None **Servings:** 4

Ingredients:
- 1 cup plain Greek yogurt
- 1/2 cucumber, peeled and grated
- 1/4 cup chopped fresh dill
- 2 cloves of garlic, minced
- 2 tablespoons fresh lemon juice
- Salt and pepper, to taste

Instructions:
1. In a medium bowl, combine the yogurt, grated cucumber, dill, garlic, lemon juice, salt, and pepper.
2. Stir until well combined.
3. Taste and adjust seasoning if needed.
4. Cover and refrigerate for at least 30 minutes to allow the flavors to meld together.
5. Serve chilled with vegetables, crackers, or pita chips for dipping.

Nutritional Value: Calories: 55 Fat: 2g Cholesterol: 6mg Carbohydrates: 4g Fiber: 1g Sugar: 2g Protein: 5g

268. Eggplant Parmesan Bites

Prep. Time: 15 minutes **Cooking Time:** 35 minutes **Servings:** 4

Ingredients:
- 1 medium eggplant, sliced into 1/4-inch rounds
- Salt
- 1/2 cup all-purpose flour
- 2 eggs, beaten

- 1 cup Italian-seasoned breadcrumbs
- 1/4 cup grated Parmesan cheese
- 1/4 cup chopped fresh basil
- 1/4 cup chopped fresh parsley
- 1/4 tsp black pepper
- 1/2 cup vegetable oil
- 1 cup marinara sauce
- 1 cup shredded mozzarella cheese

Instructions:
1. Sprinkle eggplant slices with salt and let sit for 30 minutes. Pat dry with a paper towel to remove excess moisture.
2. In a shallow dish, combine the flour, beaten eggs, breadcrumbs, Parmesan cheese, basil, parsley and black pepper.
3. Heat the vegetable oil in a large skillet over medium-high heat.
4. Dip the eggplant slices into the flour mixture, shaking off any excess, then into the beaten eggs and finally into the breadcrumb mixture, pressing to adhere.
5. Add the eggplant slices to the skillet and cook until golden brown and crispy on both sides, about 3-4 minutes per side. Drain on a paper towel-lined plate.
6. Preheat the oven to 375°F (190°C).
7. Spread 1/4 cup of marinara sauce on the bottom of a baking dish. Place the eggplant slices in a single layer on top of the sauce.
8. Top each eggplant slice with 1 tsp of marinara sauce and 1 tsp of shredded mozzarella cheese.
9. Bake for 20-25 minutes, or until the cheese is melted and bubbly.
10. Let cool for a few minutes before serving. Enjoy!+

Nutritional Value: Calories: 740 Fat: 54g Cholesterol: 144mg Carbohydrates: 42g Fiber: 7g Sugar: 8g Protein: 29g

269. Grilled Eggplant Roll-Ups

Prep. Time: 15 minutes **Cooking Time:** 15 minutes **Servings:** 5

Ingredients:
- 2 large eggplants, cut into 1/4-inch slices
- 2 tablespoons olive oil
- Salt and pepper, to taste
- 1 cup ricotta cheese
- 1/2 cup grated Parmesan cheese
- 1/4 cup chopped fresh basil
- 2 cloves of garlic, minced
- 1 cup marinara sauce

Instructions:
1. Preheat the grill to medium-high heat.
2. Brush the eggplant slices with olive oil, and season with salt and pepper.
3. Grill the eggplant slices for 3-4 minutes on each side, or until tender and grill marks appear.
4. Remove the eggplant slices from the grill and let them cool for a few minutes.
5. In a medium bowl, combine the ricotta cheese, Parmesan cheese, basil, and garlic.
6. Spread about 2 tablespoons of the cheese mixture on each eggplant slice.
7. Roll up the eggplant slices and secure them with toothpicks.
8. Brush the roll-ups with some marinara sauce.
9. Grill the roll-ups for an additional 2-3 minutes on each side, or until the cheese is melted and the roll-ups are heated through.
10. Remove the toothpicks and serve the eggplant roll-ups with additional marinara sauce on the side.

Nutritional Value: Calories: 238 Fat: 18g Cholesterol: 67mg Carbohydrates: 16g Fiber: 6g Sugar: 9g Protein: 11g

270. Lentil And Beetroot Patty

Prep. Time: 10 minutes **Cooking Time:** 25 minutes **Servings:** 4

Ingredients:
- 1 cup dried green or brown lentils
- 3 cups water
- 1 tsp salt
- 2 medium-size beets, grated
- 1 onion, finely chopped
- 2 cloves of garlic, minced
- 1/4 cup breadcrumbs
- 2 tbsp all-purpose flour
- 2 tbsp chopped fresh parsley
- 1 tsp ground cumin
- 1/2 tsp ground black pepper
- Salt to taste
- Vegetable oil for frying

Instructions:
1. Rinse the lentils and place them in a large pot with 3 cups of water and 1 tsp of salt. Bring to a boil, then reduce the heat to low and simmer for 20-25 minutes or until lentils are tender. Drain any excess water and let the lentils cool.
2. In a pan, heat a small amount of oil over medium heat. Add onion and garlic and sauté until softened.
3. In a large mixing bowl, combine the cooked lentils, grated beets, sautéed onion and garlic, breadcrumbs, flour, parsley, cumin, black pepper, and salt. Mix well.
4. Form the mixture into small patties, about 1/2 inch thick.
5. Heat a skillet with a small amount of vegetable oil over medium heat. Add the patties and cook for about 3-4 minutes per side or until golden brown.
6. Serve the patties warm on a bun or with your favorite sauce.

Nutritional Value: Calories: 255 Fat: 7g Cholesterol: 6mg Carbohydrates: 41g Fiber: 12g Sugar: 6g Protein: 14g

271. Zucchini And Carrot Fritters

Prep. Time: 10 minutes **Cooking Time:** 6 minutes **Servings:** 4

Ingredients:
- 2 cups grated zucchini
- 1 cup grated carrots
- 1/2 cup all-purpose flour
- 1/4 cup grated Parmesan cheese
- 2 eggs, lightly beaten
- 2 cloves of garlic, minced
- 2 tbsp chopped fresh parsley
- Salt and pepper to taste
- Vegetable oil for frying

Instructions:
1. In a colander, place the grated zucchini and carrots and sprinkle with salt. Let sit for 10 minutes to release excess moisture. Pat dry with paper towels.
2. In a mixing bowl, combine the zucchini, carrots, flour, Parmesan cheese, eggs, garlic, parsley, salt and pepper. Mix well.
3. Heat a skillet over medium-high heat with a small amount of vegetable oil.
4. Using a spoon or an ice cream scoop, drop the mixture into the skillet by spoonfuls, flattening them slightly. Fry the fritters for 2-3 minutes per side or until golden brown.
5. Drain the fritters on a paper towel-lined plate.
6. Serve the fritters warm with your favorite dipping sauce. Enjoy!

Nutritional Value: Calories: 187 Fat: 9g Cholesterol: 92mg Carbohydrates: 18g Fiber: 2g Sugar: 3g Protein: 10g

272. Spicy Sweet Potato And Black Bean Taquitos

Prep. Time: 10 minutes, **Cooking Time:** 20 minutes **Servings:** 6
Ingredients:
- 3 medium sweet potatoes, peeled and chopped
- 1 tablespoon olive oil
- 1 teaspoon chili powder
- 1/2 teaspoon cumin
- 1/2 teaspoon paprika
- 1/4 teaspoon garlic powder
- 1/4 teaspoon onion powder
- 1/4 teaspoon salt
- 1 can black beans, drained and rinsed
- 1/2 cup corn
- 8 large flour tortillas
- Avocado oil or other high-heat oil, for frying
- Optional toppings: diced red onion, diced tomato, fresh cilantro, diced jalapeno, shredded lettuce, salsa, guacamole, and/or vegan sour cream

Instructions:
1. Preheat oven to 400°F (204°C). Line a baking sheet with parchment paper.
2. In a large bowl, mix together the chopped sweet potatoes, olive oil, chili powder, cumin, paprika, garlic powder, onion powder, and salt.
3. Spread the sweet potato mixture out on the prepared baking sheet.
4. Bake for 15-20 minutes, or until the sweet potatoes are tender.
5. In a large bowl, mix together the roasted sweet potatoes, black beans, and corn.
6. Warm the flour tortillas for about 15 seconds in the microwave or on a griddle.
7. Spoon about 2 tablespoons of the sweet potato mixture down the center of each tortilla.
8. Roll up the tortilla tightly, tucking in the ends.
9. In a large, heavy-bottomed skillet, heat about 1/2 inch of avocado oil or other high-heat oil over medium heat.
10. Fry the taquitos, seam side down, until they are golden brown and crispy, about 2-3 minutes per side.
11. Drain on a paper towel-lined plate.
12. Serve the taquitos hot, garnished with your desired toppings.

Nutritional Value: Calories: 390, Fat: 11g, Protein: 10g, Carbohydrates: 68g, Fiber: 8g, Cholesterol: 0mg, Sodium: 630mg

273. Tomato And Basil Bruschetta

Prep. Time: 15 minutes, **Cooking Time:** 10 minutes **Servings:** 4
Ingredients:
- 8 slices of baguette, 1/2 inch thick
- 1 large ripe tomato, diced
- 1/4 cup fresh basil, chopped
- 2 cloves garlic, minced
- 1/4 teaspoon salt
- 1/4 teaspoon black pepper
- 2 tablespoons extra virgin olive oil
- Balsamic glaze, for drizzling (optional)

Instructions:
1. Preheat oven to 400°F (200°C).
2. Arrange the baguette slices on a baking sheet and bake for 5-7 minutes, or until lightly toasted.
3. In a small bowl, mix together the diced tomato, basil, garlic, salt, pepper, and olive oil.
4. Spoon a generous amount of the tomato mixture onto each slice of toasted baguette.
5. Return the bruschetta to the oven and bake for an additional 2-3 minutes, or until the tomato mixture is hot and bubbly.
6. Remove from the oven and drizzle with balsamic glaze, if desired. Serve hot.

Nutritional Value: Calories: 167, Fat: 9g, Saturated Fat: 1g, Cholesterol: 0mg, Sodium: 386mg, Carbohydrates: 17g, Fiber: 2g, Sugar: 2g, Protein: 4g

274. Vegan Mac And Cheese

Prep. Time: 15 minutes, **Cooking Time:** 15 minutes **Servings:** 4
Ingredients:
- 2 cups of dried macaroni
- 2 tablespoons of olive oil
- 2 tablespoons of flour
- 2 cups of unsweetened plant-based milk
- 2 teaspoons of Dijon mustard
- 1/2 teaspoon of garlic powder
- 1/4 teaspoon of onion powder
- 1/4 teaspoon of turmeric
- Salt and pepper, to taste
- 1/2 cup of nutritional yeast
- 1/2 cup of vegan cheddar cheese
- 1/2 cup of vegan mozzarella cheese

Instructions:
1. Cook macaroni according to the package instructions.
2. In a separate saucepan, heat the olive oil over medium heat.
3. Add the flour and stir constantly for 1 minute.
4. Gradually add the plant-based milk, whisking continuously until the mixture thickens.
5. Stir in the Dijon mustard, garlic powder, onion powder, turmeric, salt, and pepper.
6. Remove from heat and stir in the nutritional yeast, vegan cheddar cheese, and vegan mozzarella cheese.
7. Mix the cooked macaroni with the cheese sauce.
8. Serve immediately.

Nutritional Value:: Calories: 422, Total Fat: 19g, Saturated Fat: 4g, Trans Fat: 0g, Cholesterol: 0mg, Sodium: 230mg, Total Carbohydrates: 47g, Dietary Fiber: 5g, Total Sugars: 5g, Protein: 21g.

275. Creamy Tomato And Lentil Soup

Prep. Time: 10 minutes, **Cooking Time:** 30 minutes **Servings:** 4 **Ingredients:**
- 1 tablespoon olive oil
- 1 onion, chopped
- 2 cloves garlic, minced
- 2 large carrots, peeled and diced
- 2 large stalks celery, diced
- 1 teaspoon dried thyme
- 2 tablespoons tomato paste
- 1 (14.5 oz) can diced tomatoes
- 1 cup green lentils, rinsed and drained
- 4 cups vegetable broth
- Salt and pepper, to taste
- 1/4 cup heavy cream or coconut cream (optional)
- Fresh basil, for garnish (optional)

Instructions:
1. In a large pot, heat the olive oil over medium heat.
2. Add the onion, garlic, carrots, and celery and cook, stirring occasionally, until the vegetables are soft, about 5-7 minutes.
3. Stir in the thyme and tomato paste and cook for an additional minute.
4. Add the diced tomatoes, lentils, and vegetable broth. Bring the mixture to a boil, reduce heat, and let simmer for 20-25 minutes, or until the lentils are soft.
5. Using an immersion blender or transfer the soup to a blender or food processor and blend until smooth.
6. Stir in the heavy cream or coconut cream, if using, and season with salt and pepper to taste.
7. Serve the soup hot, garnished with fresh basil, if desired.

Nutritional Value: (per serving): Calories: 263, Fat: 10g, Saturated Fat: 2g, Cholesterol: 10mg, Sodium: 1,044mg, Carbohydrates: 36g, Fiber: 14g, Sugar: 8g, Protein: 13g

276. Mushroom And Lentil Pâté

Prep. Time: 10 minutes, **Cooking Time:** 25 minutes **Servings:** 4
Ingredients:
- 2 cups chopped mushrooms (cremini or button)
- 1 cup green or brown lentils, rinsed and drained
- 1 small onion, chopped
- 2 garlic cloves, minced

- 1 tbsp olive oil
- 1 tbsp soy sauce
- 1 tsp dried thyme
- 1 tsp dried rosemary
- 1 tsp dried basil
- 1/2 tsp salt
- 1/4 tsp black pepper
- 2 tbsp nutritional yeast (optional)
- 2 tbsp lemon juice
- 1 tbsp tomato paste

Instructions:
1. Preheat oven to 375°F.
2. In a large saucepan, heat the oil over medium heat. Add the onion and garlic and cook until the onion is translucent, about 5 minutes.
3. Add the mushrooms and cook until they release their moisture and start to brown, about 5 minutes.
4. Stir in the lentils, thyme, rosemary, basil, salt, and pepper. Cook for another 2-3 minutes.
5. Transfer the mixture to a food processor and add the nutritional yeast, lemon juice, and tomato paste. Pulse until well combined but still chunky.
6. Spoon the mixture into a small baking dish and smooth out the top.
7. Bake for 25 minutes, or until the top is lightly browned.

Nutritional value: Calories: 165, Fat: 6g, Sodium: 550mg, Carbohydrates: 20g, Fiber: 7g, Protein: 10g

277. Cauliflower And Cashew Cheese

Prep. Time: 10 mins, **Cooking Time:** 25 mins
Servings: 4-6
Ingredients:
- 1 head of cauliflower, cut into florets
- 1 cup raw cashews, soaked overnight or boiled for 15 minutes
- 1/2 cup water
- 3 tablespoons lemon juice
- 2 tablespoons nutritional yeast
- 1 tablespoon tahini
- 2 cloves garlic
- 1 teaspoon salt
- 1/2 teaspoon onion powder
- 1/4 teaspoon smoked paprika
- Pinch of cayenne pepper
- 2-3 tablespoons unsweetened almond milk (as needed)

Instructions:
1. Preheat oven to 375°F (190°C). Line a baking sheet with parchment paper.
2. In a high-speed blender or food processor, combine the soaked and drained cashews, water, lemon juice, nutritional yeast, tahini, garlic, salt, onion powder, smoked paprika, and cayenne pepper. Blend until smooth, scraping down the sides as needed. If the mixture is too thick, add the almond milk 1 tablespoon at a time until it reaches a pourable consistency.
3. Place the cauliflower florets on the prepared baking sheet and bake for 20-25 minutes or until tender and lightly browned.
4. Remove the cauliflower from the oven and let it cool slightly.
5. In a medium saucepan over medium heat, warm the cashew cheese until heated through, stirring constantly.
6. Serve the warm cashew cheese over the roasted cauliflower and enjoy.

Nutritional Value:: Calories: 243, Fat: 18g, Saturated Fat: 3g, Carbohydrates: 15g, Fiber: 4g, Sugar: 4g, Protein: 9g.

278. Sweet Potato And Black Bean Chili

Prep. Time: 10 minutes, **Cooking Time:** 30 minutes **Servings:** 4
Ingredients:
- 1 large sweet potato, peeled and diced
- 1 tablespoon olive oil
- 1 onion, chopped
- 3 garlic cloves, minced
- 2 tablespoons chili powder
- 1 teaspoon paprika
- 1 teaspoon ground cumin
- 1/2 teaspoon salt

- 1 can (14.5 ounces) diced tomatoes, undrained
- 1 can (15 ounces) black beans, drained and rinsed
- 1 cup vegetable broth
- 2 tablespoons chopped fresh cilantro (optional)

Instructions:
1. Heat the oil in a large saucepan over medium heat.
2. Add the sweet potato, onion, and garlic. Cook for 5 minutes, until the onion is soft.
3. Stir in the chili powder, paprika, cumin, and salt. Cook for 1 minute.
4. Add the diced tomatoes with their juice, black beans, and vegetable broth. Bring to a boil.
5. Reduce heat and simmer for 20 minutes, or until the sweet potato is tender.
6. Stir in the cilantro (if using). Serve hot.

Nutritional Value:: Calories: 220, Fat: 5g, Saturated Fat: 1g, Sodium: 700mg, Carbohydrates: 38g, Fiber: 8g, Sugar: 7g, Protein: 9g

279. Vegan Sushi Rolls

Prep. Time: 20 minutes **Cooking Time:** 30 minutes **Servings:** 5

Ingredients:
- 2 cups sushi rice
- 2 cups water
- 2 tablespoons rice vinegar
- 1 tablespoon sugar
- 1 teaspoon salt
- 6 sheets of nori seaweed
- Optional filling Ingredients avocado, cucumber, carrot, bell pepper, tofu, mushrooms, sprouts
- Soy sauce and wasabi, for serving

Instructions:
1. Rinse the sushi rice in a fine mesh strainer until the water runs clear.
2. In a medium saucepan, combine the rice and water. Bring to a boil, then reduce the heat to low, cover, and simmer for 18-20 minutes, or until the water is absorbed and the rice is tender.
3. In a small saucepan, combine the rice vinegar, sugar, and salt. Heat over low heat, stirring until the sugar and salt have dissolved.
4. When the rice is done, remove it from the heat and let it cool for 10 minutes.
5. While the rice is still warm, add the vinegar mixture to the rice and stir gently to combine. Allow the rice to cool completely.
6. To assemble the sushi rolls, place a sheet of nori, shiny side down, on a bamboo sushi rolling mat or a clean, flat surface.
7. Spread a thin layer of rice over the nori, leaving a 1-inch border at the top.
8. Arrange your chosen fillings in a line across the center of the rice.
9. Using the mat or your hands, roll the sushi tightly, pressing to seal the edges.
10. Repeat the process with the remaining nori and filling ingredients.
11. Cut the sushi rolls into bite-size pieces using a sharp knife.
12. Serve with soy sauce and wasabi for dipping.

Nutritional Value: Calories: 355 Fat: 12g Cholesterol: 14mg Carbohydrates: 38g Fiber: 4g Sugar: 4g Protein: 15g

280. Vegan Chili Cheese Fries

Prep. Time: 15 minutes, **Cooking Time:** 30 minutes **Servings:** 4

Ingredients:
- 2 large sweet potatoes, peeled and sliced into thin fries
- 2 tablespoons oil
- Salt and pepper, to taste
- 1 can black beans, drained and rinsed
- 1 large onion, diced
- 2 cloves garlic, minced

- 1 red bell pepper, diced
- 1 teaspoon chili powder
- 1 teaspoon cumin
- 1/2 teaspoon smoked paprika
- 1/2 teaspoon dried oregano
- 1/2 teaspoon dried basil
- 2 tablespoons tomato paste
- 1 cup water
- 1 cup vegan shredded cheese
- Fresh cilantro, for garnish

Instructions:
1. Preheat oven to 400°F. Line a large baking sheet with parchment paper.
2. In a bowl, toss sweet potato fries with oil, salt, and pepper.
3. Spread the fries evenly on the prepared baking sheet and bake for 20-25 minutes, flipping halfway through.
4. Meanwhile, in a large pan, heat some oil over medium heat.
5. Add the onion and garlic and cook for 2-3 minutes, until softened.
6. Add the bell pepper and cook for another 2-3 minutes.
7. Add the black beans, chili powder, cumin, smoked paprika, oregano, basil, tomato paste, and water to the pan. Stir to combine.
8. Bring the mixture to a boil, then reduce heat and let it simmer for 10-15 minutes, until the vegetables are tender.
9. Remove from heat and let it cool slightly.
10. In a small saucepan, heat the vegan cheese until melted.
11. To assemble, place the sweet potato fries on a serving plate.
12. Spoon the black bean chili mixture over the fries.
13. Drizzle the melted cheese over the chili.
14. Garnish with cilantro, if desired.

Nutritional Value:: Calories: 462, Total Fat: 19g, Saturated Fat: 3g, Sodium: 708mg, Carbohydrates: 59g, Fiber: 14g, Sugar: 9g, Protein: 14g.

281. Grilled Eggplant And Halloumi Skewers

Prep. Time: 10 minutes, **Cooking Time:** 15 minutes **Servings:** 4

Ingredients:
- 2 medium eggplants, sliced into rounds
- 8 oz. halloumi cheese, cut into 1-inch cubes
- 8 skewers
- 1/4 cup olive oil
- 1 tsp. dried oregano
- 1 tsp. dried basil
- Salt and pepper, to taste
- Lemon wedges, for serving

Instructions:
1. Soak the skewers in water for 30 minutes to prevent burning.
2. In a small bowl, whisk together the olive oil, oregano, basil, salt, and pepper.
3. Alternately thread the eggplant rounds and halloumi cubes onto the skewers.
4. Brush the skewers with the olive oil mixture.
5. Heat a grill or grill pan to high heat.
6. Grill the skewers for 8-10 minutes, turning occasionally, until the eggplant is tender and the halloumi is slightly charred.
7. Serve the skewers hot with lemon wedges.

Nutritional Value: Calories: 280, Total Fat: 24 g, Saturated Fat: 15 g, Cholesterol: 48 mg, Sodium: 640 mg, Total Carbohydrates: 9 g, Dietary Fiber: 4 g, Sugar: 5 g, Protein: 12 g

282. Carrot And Ginger Soup

Prep. Time: 10 minutes **Cooking Time:** 25 minutes **Servings:** 4

Ingredients:
- 1 tablespoon olive oil
- 1 onion, chopped
- 2 garlic cloves, minced
- 2 inches ginger, peeled and grated
- 4 medium carrots, peeled and sliced
- 4 cups vegetable broth
- Salt and pepper, to taste

- 1 tablespoon lemon juice
- Chopped fresh parsley, for garnish

Instructions:
1. In a large pot, heat the olive oil over medium heat.
2. Add the onion and cook until soft, about 5 minutes.
3. Add the garlic and ginger and cook for another minute.
4. Add the carrots and vegetable broth to the pot and bring to a boil.
5. Reduce the heat and let the soup simmer until the carrots are tender, about 20 minutes.
6. Use an immersion blender or transfer the soup to a blender to puree until smooth.
7. Season with salt, pepper, and lemon juice.
8. Serve hot, garnished with fresh parsley.

Nutritional Value:: Calories: 96, Fat: 4g, Saturated Fat: 1g, Sodium: 845mg, Carbohydrates: 14g, Fiber: 4g, Sugar: 7g, Protein: 2g

283. Vegan Lentil Shepherd's Pie

Prep. Time: 20 minutes **Cooking Time:** 50 minutes **Servings:** 5

Ingredients:
- 1 large onion, chopped
- 3 cloves garlic, minced
- 2 carrots, chopped
- 2 celery stalks, chopped
- 8 oz. mushrooms, sliced
- 1 1/2 cups dried green or brown lentils, rinsed
- 2 tbsp tomato paste
- 2 tsp dried thyme
- 1 tsp dried rosemary
- 1 tsp dried basil
- 4 cups vegetable broth
- Salt and pepper to taste
- 4 large potatoes, peeled and chopped
- 3 tbsp non-dairy butter or margarine
- 1/2 cup unsweetened non-dairy milk
- 1 tbsp olive oil

Instructions:

1. In a large pot, heat the olive oil over medium heat. Add the onion, garlic, carrots, celery, and mushrooms and cook until the vegetables are tender, about 8 minutes.
2. Stir in the lentils, tomato paste, thyme, rosemary, basil, vegetable broth, salt, and pepper. Bring the mixture to a boil, then reduce heat and let it simmer until the lentils are tender, about 30 minutes.
3. Preheat the oven to 375°F. Grease a 9-inch baking dish.
4. Meanwhile, boil the potatoes in a pot of water until tender, about 10 minutes. Drain and mash with the non-dairy butter or margarine and non-dairy milk. Season with salt and pepper.
5. Transfer the lentil mixture to the prepared baking dish. Spoon the mashed potatoes over the lentil mixture, spreading it evenly.
6. Bake the shepherd's pie in the preheated oven for 30 minutes, or until the potatoes are lightly browned on top.

Nutritional Value:: Calories: 348 Total Fat: 8 g Saturated Fat: 2 g Cholesterol: 0 mg Sodium: 487 mg Total Carbohydrates: 56 g Dietary Fiber: 17 g Sugar: 6 g Protein: 18 g

284. Stuffed Sweet Potatoes

Prep. Time: 30 mins, **Cooking Time:** 30 mins **Servings:** 4

Ingredients:
- 4 medium sweet potatoes
- 1 tablespoon olive oil
- 1 yellow onion, chopped
- 2 garlic cloves, minced
- 1 teaspoon grated ginger
- 1 teaspoon ground cumin
- 1 teaspoon chili powder
- Salt and pepper to taste
- 2 cups cooked black beans
- 1 cup corn kernels
- 1/4 cup chopped cilantro
- 2 tablespoons lime juice
- 4 ounces crumbled feta cheese

- 4 tablespoons vegan sour cream (optional)

Instructions:
1. Preheat oven to 400°F.
2. Prick sweet potatoes all over with a fork and place on a baking sheet. Bake for 45-50 minutes or until soft.
3. While sweet potatoes are cooking, heat olive oil in a large skillet over medium heat. Add the onion, garlic, ginger, cumin, chili powder, salt and pepper. Cook until the onion is soft, about 5 minutes.
4. Stir in black beans, corn, cilantro, and lime juice. Cook for a few more minutes until heated through.
5. Once sweet potatoes are done, slice each one lengthwise and scoop out the insides into a large bowl. Mash with a fork.
6. Fill each sweet potato skin with some of the bean and corn mixture and top with crumbled feta cheese.
7. Place the stuffed sweet potatoes back on the baking sheet and return to the oven for 10-15 minutes until heated through.
8. Serve with a dollop of vegan sour cream, if desired.

Nutritional Value: Calories: 410, Total Fat: 14g, Saturated Fat: 4g, Cholesterol: 19mg, Sodium: 557mg, Total Carbohydrates: 66g, Dietary Fiber: 11g, Sugar: 11g, Protein: 13g

285. Indian-Style Lentil And Vegetable Stew

Prep. Time: 10 minutes **Cooking Time:** 30 minutes **Servings:** 4

Ingredients:
- 1 tablespoon vegetable oil
- 1 onion, diced
- 2 cloves garlic, minced
- 1 tablespoon grated ginger
- 1 tablespoon curry powder
- 1 teaspoon ground cumin
- 1 teaspoon ground coriander
- 1/4 teaspoon ground turmeric
- 1/4 teaspoon cayenne pepper
- 1 cup dried green or brown lentils, rinsed and drained
- 4 cups vegetable broth
- 1 can diced tomatoes
- 1 cup diced carrots
- 1 cup diced potatoes
- 1 cup frozen peas
- 1/4 cup chopped fresh cilantro
- Salt and pepper to taste
- Optional toppings: plain yogurt, chopped fresh cilantro, naan bread

Instructions:
1. In a large pot, heat the oil over medium heat. Add the onion, garlic, and ginger and sauté until softened, about 5 minutes.
2. Add the curry powder, cumin, coriander, turmeric, and cayenne pepper and stir to combine. Cook for an additional 2-3 minutes, or until fragrant.
3. Add the lentils, vegetable broth, diced tomatoes, carrots, potatoes, and peas to the pot. Bring to a boil, then reduce the heat and simmer for 20-25 minutes, or until the lentils are tender and the vegetables are cooked through.
4. Stir in the cilantro, salt, and pepper.
5. Serve hot with plain yogurt, chopped fresh cilantro, and naan bread, if desired.

Nutritional Value: Calories: 198 Fat: 6g Cholesterol: 2mg Carbohydrates: 39g Fiber: 27g Sugar: 3g Protein: 18g

286. Vegan Lentil And Vegetable Shepherd's Pie

Prep. Time: 20 minutes **Cooking Time:** 60 minutes **Servings:** 6

Ingredients:
- 1 large onion, chopped
- 2 cloves garlic, minced
- 3 carrots, diced
- 3 celery stalks, diced
- 1 cup green or brown lentils, rinsed

- 3 cups vegetable broth
- 2 cups diced potatoes
- 1 cup frozen peas
- 1 cup frozen corn
- 1 tablespoon tomato paste
- 1 teaspoon dried thyme
- 1 teaspoon dried rosemary
- Salt and pepper, to taste
- 3 tablespoons olive oil
- 4 tablespoons vegan butter
- 1/4 cup all-purpose flour
- 2 cups almond or soy milk

Instructions:
1. Preheat oven to 400°F.
2. In a large saucepan, heat 2 tablespoons of olive oil over medium heat.
3. Add the onion, garlic, carrots, and celery and cook until the vegetables are soft and translucent, about 10 minutes.
4. Add the lentils and vegetable broth to the saucepan, bring to a boil, then reduce heat to low and simmer for 20-25 minutes, or until the lentils are tender.
5. In a separate pot, boil the potatoes until tender, then mash them with the remaining tablespoon of olive oil and 2 tablespoons of vegan butter.
6. In a separate saucepan, melt the remaining 2 tablespoons of vegan butter over medium heat.
7. Whisk in the flour and cook for 2-3 minutes, until the mixture turns a light golden brown.
8. Slowly pour in the almond or soy milk, whisking constantly, until the mixture thickens and becomes smooth.
9. Stir in the frozen peas and corn, tomato paste, thyme, rosemary, salt, and pepper into the lentil mixture.
10. Transfer the lentil mixture to a 9x13 inch baking dish.
11. Spoon the mashed potatoes over the lentil mixture, spreading it evenly to cover the top.
12. Bake for 20-25 minutes, or until the top is golden and the filling is heated through.
13. Serve hot and enjoy!

Nutritional Value:: Calories: 325 Fat: 14g Saturated Fat: 3g Cholesterol: 0mg Sodium: 400mg Total Carbohydrates: 43g Fiber: 8g Sugar: 8g Protein: 10g

287. Sweet Potato And Black Bean Chili

Prep. Time: 15 minutes **Cooking Time:** 30 minutes **Servings:** 4

Ingredients:
- 2 tbsp olive oil
- 1 onion, diced
- 2 cloves of garlic, minced
- 2 medium sweet potatoes, peeled and diced
- 1 red bell pepper, diced
- 2 cups cooked black beans
- 1 cup vegetable broth
- 1 can (14.5 oz) diced tomatoes
- 1 tsp ground cumin
- 1 tsp chili powder
- 1/4 tsp cayenne pepper (optional)
- Salt and pepper, to taste
- Toppings: sour cream, cheddar cheese, green onions, cilantro

Instructions:
1. In a large pot or Dutch oven, heat the olive oil over medium heat. Add the onion and garlic and cook until softened, about 5 minutes.
2. Add the sweet potatoes and red bell pepper and cook for another 5 minutes.
3. Stir in the black beans, vegetable broth, diced tomatoes, cumin, chili powder, cayenne pepper (if using), salt, and pepper. Bring to a simmer.
4. Reduce the heat to low and let the chili simmer for 20-25 minutes, or until the sweet potatoes are tender.
5. Serve the chili in bowls and top with sour cream, cheddar cheese, green onions, and cilantro.

Nutritional Value: Calories: 388 Fat: 7g Cholesterol: 8mg Carbohydrates: 34g Fiber: 18g Sugar: 6g Protein: 25g

288. Vegetable And Lentil Curry

Prep. Time: 10 mins, **Cooking Time:** 25 mins
Servings: 4
Ingredients:
- 1 tbsp vegetable oil
- 1 medium onion, diced
- 3 cloves garlic, minced
- 1 tbsp fresh ginger, grated
- 2 medium carrots, diced
- 2 medium bell peppers, diced
- 1 can (14.5 oz) diced tomatoes
- 1 cup green or brown lentils, rinsed and drained
- 1 tsp salt
- 1 tsp cumin powder
- 1 tsp coriander powder
- 1 tsp turmeric
- 1 tsp garam masala
- 1/2 tsp chili powder
- 1 cup water
- Fresh cilantro for garnish (optional)

Instructions:
1. In a large saucepan or Dutch oven, heat the oil over medium heat.
2. Add the onion, garlic, and ginger and cook until softened, about 5 minutes.
3. Stir in the carrots and bell peppers and cook for 5 more minutes.
4. Add the tomatoes, lentils, salt, cumin, coriander, turmeric, garam masala, chili powder, and water. Stir to combine.
5. Bring the mixture to a boil, then reduce the heat to low, cover and simmer until the lentils are tender, about 20 minutes.
6. Serve over rice or with naan bread, garnished with cilantro, if desired.

Nutritional Value:: Calories: 250, Fat: 7g, Carbohydrates: 39g, Protein: 12g, Fiber: 13g.

289. Vegan Lentil And Vegetable Stew

Prep. Time: 15 minutes **Cooking Time:** 25 minutes **Servings:** 4
Ingredients:
- 1 tbsp olive oil
- 1 onion, diced
- 2 cloves of garlic, minced
- 1 cup green or brown lentils, rinsed and drained
- 2 cups vegetable broth
- 1 can diced tomatoes
- 1 cup diced carrots
- 1 cup diced potatoes
- 1 cup diced celery
- 1 cup diced bell pepper
- 1 tsp dried thyme
- 1 tsp dried rosemary
- 1 tsp dried oregano
- Salt and pepper, to taste
- 2 cups kale or spinach, chopped
- 1 cup cooked quinoa or brown rice (optional)

Instructions:
1. In a large pot or Dutch oven, heat the olive oil over medium heat. Add the onion and garlic and cook until softened, about 5 minutes.
2. Add the lentils, vegetable broth, diced tomatoes, carrots, potatoes, celery, bell pepper, thyme, rosemary, oregano, salt, and pepper. Bring to a simmer.
3. Reduce the heat to low and let the stew simmer for 20-25 minutes, or until the lentils and vegetables are tender.
4. Stir in the kale or spinach and let it wilt for a minute or two.
5. Serve the stew in bowls, over a bed of cooked quinoa or brown rice if desired.
6. Enjoy!

Nutritional Value: Calories: 197 Fat: 8g Cholesterol: 7mg Carbohydrates: 10g Fiber: 14g Sugar: 1g Protein: 18g

290. Roasted Cauliflower And Chickpea Salad

Prep. Time: 20 minutes **Cooking Time:** 30 minutes **Servings:** 4
Ingredients:
- 1 head of cauliflower, cut into florets
- 1 can chickpeas, rinsed and drained
- 2 tbsp olive oil
- 1 tsp ground cumin
- 1 tsp smoked paprika
- Salt and pepper, to taste
- 1/4 cup chopped parsley
- 2 tbsp lemon juice
- 2 tbsp tahini
- 2 cloves of garlic, minced
- 1/4 cup water

Instructions:
1. Preheat the oven to 400°F (200°C).
2. On a baking sheet, toss the cauliflower florets and chickpeas with the olive oil, cumin, smoked paprika, salt and pepper. Roast for 25-30 minutes, or until the cauliflower is tender and slightly browned.
3. In a small bowl, mix together the parsley, lemon juice, tahini, garlic and water to make the dressing.
4. In a large bowl, combine the roasted cauliflower and chickpeas. Toss with the dressing.
5. Serve the salad warm or at room temperature, garnished with additional parsley if desired.

Nutritional Value: Calories: 106 Fat: 4g Cholesterol: 1mg Carbohydrates: 10g Fiber: 24g Sugar: 4g Protein: 12g

291. Grilled Eggplant And Zucchini Rolls

Prep. Time: 15 minutes **Cooking Time:** 5 minutes **Servings:** 4
Ingredients:
- 2 medium eggplants, sliced lengthwise into 1/4 inch slices
- 2 medium zucchinis, sliced lengthwise into 1/4 inch slices
- 2 tbsp olive oil
- Salt and pepper, to taste
- 1 cup cooked rice
- 1 can (14.5 oz) diced tomatoes, drained
- 1 cup cooked lentils
- 1/4 cup chopped fresh basil
- 1/4 cup chopped fresh parsley
- 1/4 cup chopped fresh oregano
- 2 cloves of garlic, minced
- 1 tsp dried thyme
- 1 tsp paprika
- 1 tsp chili powder
- 1 tsp cumin
- 1 tsp coriander
- 2 tbsp tomato paste
- 1 tbsp balsamic vinegar
- 1 tbsp lemon juice

Instructions:
1. Preheat the grill to medium heat.
2. Brush the eggplant and zucchini slices with olive oil and season with salt and pepper.
3. Grill the eggplant and zucchini slices for 2-3 minutes on each side until they are slightly charred and tender.
4. In a large bowl, mix together the cooked rice, diced tomatoes, cooked lentils, basil, parsley, oregano, garlic, thyme, paprika, chili powder, cumin, coriander, tomato paste, balsamic vinegar, and lemon juice.
5. Spoon about 2 tbsp of the mixture onto each eggplant slice and roll up tightly, securing with toothpicks.
6. Place the rolled eggplant and zucchini in a large casserole dish and bake in a preheated 350°F oven for 25-30 minutes, or until heated through.

7. Serve hot with a side of crusty bread, if desired. Enjoy!

Nutritional Value: Calories: 181 Fat: 7g Saturated Fat: 1g Cholesterol: 0mg Sodium: 198mg Carbohydrates: 26g Fiber: 7g Sugar: 7g Protein: 8g

292. Grilled Eggplant And Zucchini Skewers

Prep. Time: 10 minutes **Cooking Time:** 10 minutes **Servings:** 5

Ingredients:
- 2 medium eggplants, cut into 1-inch cubes
- 2 medium zucchini, cut into 1-inch cubes
- Salt and pepper, to taste
- 1/4 cup olive oil
- 1/4 cup chopped fresh basil
- 2 cloves of garlic, minced
- Bamboo skewers (soaked in water for at least 30 minutes)

Instructions:
1. Preheat grill to medium-high heat.
2. Thread the eggplant and zucchini cubes onto the skewers, alternating between the two vegetables.
3. In a small bowl, mix together the olive oil, basil, garlic, salt and pepper.
4. Brush the skewers with the mixture.
5. Grill the skewers for 8-10 minutes, turning occasionally, or until the vegetables are tender and slightly charred.
6. Serve the skewers warm, garnished with additional chopped basil if desired.

Nutritional Value: Calories: 172 Fat: 5g Cholesterol: 31mg Carbohydrates: 23g Fiber: 18g Sugar: 1g Protein: 17g

293. Roasted Portobello Mushroom And Red Pepper Skewers

Prep. Time: 10 minutes **Cooking Time:** 20 minutes **Servings:** 4

Ingredients:
- 4 large portobello mushroom caps, stems removed
- 2 red bell peppers, cut into 1-inch squares
- Salt and pepper, to taste
- 2 tbsp olive oil
- 2 cloves of garlic, minced
- 1 tsp dried thyme
- Bamboo skewers (soaked in water for at least 30 minutes)

Instructions:
1. Preheat oven to 425°F (220°C).
2. Thread the mushroom caps and red pepper squares onto the skewers, alternating between the two vegetables.
3. In a small bowl, mix together the olive oil, garlic, thyme, salt and pepper.
4. Brush the skewers with the mixture.
5. Place the skewers on a baking sheet and roast for 15-20 minutes, turning occasionally, or until the vegetables are tender and slightly browned.
6. Serve the skewers warm, garnished with additional thyme if desired.
7. Enjoy!

Nutritional Value: Calories: 118 Fat: 6g Cholesterol: 3mg Carbohydrates: 14g Fiber: 8g Sugar: 3g Protein: 15g

294. Vegetable And Lentil Lasagna

Prep. Time: 15 minutes **Cooking Time:** 25 minutes **Servings:** 4

Ingredients:
- 1 tbsp olive oil
- 1 onion, diced

- 2 cloves of garlic, minced
- 1 cup green or brown lentils, rinsed and drained
- 1 can diced tomatoes
- 2 cups vegetable broth
- 1 tsp dried oregano
- 1 tsp dried basil
- Salt and pepper, to taste
- 1 cup frozen spinach, thawed and squeezed dry
- 1 cup chopped mushrooms
- 1 cup diced bell pepper
- 1 cup diced zucchini
- 8-10 lasagna noodles
- 1 cup ricotta cheese
- 1 cup shredded mozzarella cheese
- 1/4 cup grated Parmesan cheese

Instructions:
1. Preheat the oven to 375°F (190°C).
2. In a large pot or Dutch oven, heat the olive oil over medium heat. Add the onion and garlic and cook until softened, about 5 minutes.
3. Stir in the lentils, diced tomatoes, vegetable broth, oregano, basil, salt and pepper. Bring to a simmer.
4. Reduce the heat to low and let the sauce simmer for 20-25 minutes, or until the lentils are tender.
5. In a large bowl, mix together the spinach, mushrooms, bell pepper and zucchini.
6. Spread a thin layer of the lentil sauce on the bottom of a 9x13 inch baking dish.
7. Place a layer of lasagna noodles on top of the sauce. Spread a layer of ricotta cheese over the noodles, then add a layer of the vegetable mixture, and a layer of the lentil sauce. Repeat the layers until all the ingredients are used up, ending with a layer of lentil sauce.
8. Sprinkle the mozzarella cheese and Parmesan cheese on top.
9. Cover the lasagna with foil and bake for 25 minutes. Remove the foil and bake for another 25 minutes, or until the cheese is melted and bubbly.
10. Let the lasagna cool for 10-15 minutes before slicing and serving.
11. Enjoy!

Nutritional Value: Calories: 299 Fat: 12g Cholesterol: 54mg Carbohydrates: 28g Fiber: 14g Sugar: 7g Protein: 22g

295. Vegan Lentil And Vegetable Pot Pie

Prep. Time: 15 minutes **Cooking Time:** 40 minutes **Servings:** 6

Ingredients:
- 2 tbsp olive oil
- 1 large onion, chopped
- 2 large carrots, peeled and diced
- 2 large stalks celery, diced
- 3 cloves garlic, minced
- 2 cups green or brown lentils, rinsed and drained
- 4 cups vegetable broth
- 1 tsp dried thyme
- 1 tsp dried rosemary
- 2 large potatoes, peeled and diced
- 2 cups frozen mixed vegetables (peas, carrots, corn, green beans)
- Salt and pepper, to taste
- 1 cup all-purpose flour
- 1 cup unsweetened plant-based milk (such as almond or soy)
- 2 pre-made pie crusts
- 1 tbsp nutritional yeast (optional)

Instructions:
1. Preheat your oven to 400°F.
2. In a large pot, heat the olive oil over medium heat. Add the onion, carrots, celery, and garlic and cook until softened, about 5 minutes.
3. Add the lentils, broth, thyme, rosemary, and potatoes to the pot and bring to a boil. Reduce heat to low and simmer until the lentils are tender, about 30 minutes.

4. Stir in the frozen vegetables, season with salt and pepper to taste, and cook for 5 minutes more.
5. In a separate bowl, whisk together the flour and plant-based milk until smooth. Stir the mixture into the pot and continue cooking until the mixture thickens, about 5 minutes.
6. Transfer the lentil and vegetable mixture to a 9x13 inch baking dish.
7. Roll out one of the pie crusts and place it on top of the mixture, trimming any excess.
8. Roll out the second pie crust and cut it into strips. Arrange the strips in a lattice pattern on top of the first crust.
9. Bake the pot pie for 25-30 minutes, or until the crust is golden brown and the filling is hot and bubbly.
10. Let the pot pie cool for 10 minutes before serving.

Nutritional Value:: Calories: 380 Fat: 15g Saturated Fat: 2g Carbohydrates: 52g Fiber: 10g Sugar: 4g Protein: 12g

296. Vegetable And Lentil Stir Fry

Prep. Time: 10 minutes **Cooking Time:** 15 minutes **Servings:** 5

Ingredients:
- 1 cup green lentils, cooked
- 2 cups mixed vegetables (e.g. carrots, bell peppers, onions, snow peas)
- 1 tablespoon olive oil
- 2 cloves of garlic, minced
- 2 tablespoons soy sauce
- 2 teaspoons cornstarch
- Salt and pepper to taste
- Chopped cilantro, for garnish

Instructions:
1. Wash and chop the mixed vegetables into bite-sized pieces.
2. Heat the olive oil in a large wok or pan over medium heat.
3. Add the garlic and cook for 30 seconds, or until fragrant.
4. Add the chopped vegetables and cook for 5-7 minutes, or until they start to soften.
5. Add the cooked lentils and continue to stir fry for another 2-3 minutes.
6. In a small bowl, whisk together the soy sauce and cornstarch.
7. Pour the mixture into the wok and stir to combine with the vegetables and lentils.
8. Season with salt and pepper to taste.
9. Cook for an additional 2-3 minutes, or until the sauce has thickened.
10. Garnish with chopped cilantro and serve hot.

Nutritional Value:: Calories: 246 Fat: 6g Carbs: 39g Protein: 12g Fiber: 11g Vegan Lentil And

297. Vegetable Pie

Prep. Time: 10 minutes **Cooking Time:** 60 minutes **Servings:** 5

Ingredients:
- 2 cups green or brown lentils
- 3-4 cups of water or vegetable broth
- 2 large carrots, peeled and diced
- 2 large potatoes, peeled and diced
- 1 large onion, chopped
- 2 cloves of garlic, minced
- 1 large red pepper, diced
- 2 cups frozen peas
- 2 tablespoons olive oil
- 2 tablespoons tomato paste
- 1 teaspoon dried thyme
- 1 teaspoon dried rosemary
- 1 teaspoon dried oregano
- Salt and pepper to taste
- 2 sheets of puff pastry
- 1 tablespoon plant-based milk (optional)

Instructions:
1. Preheat the oven to 375°F (190°C).
2. In a large saucepan, bring the lentils and water or broth to a boil. Reduce heat to low and let simmer until lentils are soft and most of the liquid is absorbed, about 20-30 minutes.
3. In a large skillet, heat the olive oil over medium heat. Add the onion and cook

until soft and translucent, about 5 minutes.
4. Add the garlic, diced carrots, diced potatoes, red pepper, and frozen peas to the skillet. Cook for an additional 5 minutes, until vegetables are slightly soft.
5. Stir in the tomato paste and herbs. Season with salt and pepper to taste.
6. Stir in the cooked lentils and continue to cook over medium heat for an additional 5 minutes.
7. Roll out one sheet of puff pastry and place it in the bottom of a 9-inch (23cm) pie dish.
8. Pour the lentil and vegetable mixture over the pastry in the pie dish.
9. Roll out the second sheet of puff pastry and place it on top of the pie, crimping the edges to seal.
10. Brush the top of the pastry with plant-based milk, if desired.
11. Bake the pie for 25-30 minutes, or until the pastry is golden brown and puffed.
12. Serve warm and enjoy!

Nutritional Value: Calories: 346 Fat: 18g Carbohydrates: 37g Protein: 12g Sodium: 267mg Fiber: 8g

298. Vegan Lentil And Vegetable Spaghetti

Prep. Time: 10 minutes **Cooking Time:** 20 minutes **Servings:** 2

Ingredients:
- 8 ounces spaghetti
- 1 tablespoon olive oil
- 1 medium onion, diced
- 3 garlic cloves, minced
- 2 medium carrots, diced
- 2 medium zucchinis, diced
- 1 red bell pepper, diced
- 1 cup cooked lentils
- 1 can diced tomatoes (14 ounces)
- 1 teaspoon dried basil
- 1 teaspoon dried oregano
- Salt and pepper, to taste
- 1/4 cup chopped fresh parsley
- Fresh grated Parmesan cheese (optional)

Instructions:
1. Cook the spaghetti according to the package instructions. Reserve 1/2 cup of pasta water, then drain the spaghetti.
2. In a large saucepan, heat the olive oil over medium heat. Add the onion and garlic and cook for 3-4 minutes until softened.
3. Add the carrots, zucchinis, and red bell pepper and cook for another 5 minutes until tender.
4. Stir in the cooked lentils, diced tomatoes, basil, oregano, salt, and pepper. Bring the mixture to a simmer and let it cook for 10 minutes.
5. If the sauce is too thick, add some of the reserved pasta water to thin it out.
6. Toss the spaghetti with the lentil and vegetable sauce. Serve in bowls, garnished with fresh parsley and grated Parmesan cheese, if desired.

Nutritional Value: Calories: 380 Fat: 9g Carbohydrates: 62g Protein: 17g Fiber: 12g

299. Vegan Lentil And Vegetable Spaghetti Sauce

Prep. Time: 10 minutes **Cooking Time:** 40 minutes **Servings:** 4

Ingredients:
- 1 cup green lentils
- 4 cups vegetable broth
- 1 onion, diced
- 2 carrots, diced
- 2 celery stalks, diced
- 2 cloves of garlic, minced
- 2 cups of mushrooms (or bell peppers, zucchini, or eggplant)
- 1 can diced tomatoes
- 2 tablespoons olive oil
- 2 teaspoon dried oregano
- 2 teaspoon dried basil
- Salt and pepper, to taste
- Fresh parsley or basil, for garnish (optional)

Instructions:
1. Rinse the lentils and pick out any debris.
2. In a large pot or Dutch oven, heat the olive oil over medium heat. Add the onion, carrots, celery, and garlic and sauté until softened, about 5 minutes.
3. Add the oregano and basil and stir for another minute.
4. Add the vegetable broth, diced tomatoes, and lentils. Bring the mixture to a boil, then reduce the heat to low and let simmer for about 20-25 minutes, or until the lentils are tender.
5. Add the chopped vegetables and continue to simmer for another 10-15 minutes, or until the vegetables are cooked through.
6. Season with salt and pepper, to taste.
7. Serve hot, over cooked spaghetti noodles, garnished with fresh parsley or basil, if desired.
8. Enjoy!

Nutritional Value: Calories: 62 Fat: 6g Cholesterol: 3mg Carbohydrates: 18g Fiber: 19g Sugar: 4g Protein: 9g

300. Vegan Lentil And Vegetable Pizza

Prep. Time: 15 minutes **Cooking Time:** 15 minutes **Servings:** 5

Ingredients:
- 1 pre-made or homemade pizza dough
- 1/2 cup tomato sauce or pizza sauce
- 1/2 cup cooked green or brown lentils
- 1 cup diced vegetables (such as bell peppers, mushrooms, and zucchini)
- 1/4 cup diced red onion
- 1/4 teaspoon dried oregano
- 1/4 teaspoon red pepper flakes (optional)
- Salt and pepper, to taste
- Vegan cheese or nutritional yeast (optional)

Instructions:
1. Preheat the oven to 425°F (220°C).
2. Roll out the pizza dough to desired thickness on a lightly floured surface.
3. Transfer the dough to a baking sheet or pizza stone.
4. Spread the tomato sauce or pizza sauce over the dough, leaving a little bit of space around the edges for the crust.
5. Sprinkle the cooked lentils, diced vegetables, red onion, oregano, red pepper flakes (if using), salt, and pepper on top of the sauce.
6. If using, sprinkle on some vegan cheese or nutritional yeast for extra flavor.
7. Bake the pizza for 12-15 minutes or until the crust is golden brown and the cheese is melted (if using).
8. Let cool for a few minutes before slicing and serving.

Nutritional Value: Calories: 300 Fat: 12g Cholesterol: 14mg Carbohydrates: 40g Fiber: 13g Sugar: 6g Protein: 10g

301. Vegan Lentil And Vegetable Shepherd's Pie

Prep. Time: 10 minutes **Cooking Time:** 45 minutes **Servings:** 5

Ingredients:
- 1 tablespoon olive oil
- 1 large onion, diced
- 3 garlic cloves, minced
- 1 large carrot, peeled and diced
- 2 large celery stalks, diced
- 1 large red bell pepper, diced
- 8 ounces cremini mushrooms, sliced
- 1 cup green or brown lentils, rinsed and drained
- 2 cups vegetable broth
- 1 tablespoon tomato paste
- 1 teaspoon dried thyme
- 1 teaspoon dried rosemary
- Salt and pepper to taste
- 4 large russet potatoes, peeled and cubed

- 1/2 cup unsweetened almond milk
- 2 tablespoons vegan butter
- 2 tablespoons chopped fresh parsley

Instructions:
1. Preheat oven to 375°F (190°C).
2. Heat the olive oil in a large pot over medium heat. Add the onion, garlic, carrot, celery, red bell pepper, and mushrooms. Cook until vegetables are tender, about 10 minutes.
3. Stir in the lentils, vegetable broth, tomato paste, thyme, rosemary, salt, and pepper. Bring to a boil, then reduce heat to low and simmer for 25-30 minutes, or until lentils are tender.
4. Meanwhile, boil the potatoes in a large pot of salted water until tender, about 15 minutes. Drain and return to the pot. Mash the potatoes with the almond milk, vegan butter, parsley, salt, and pepper.
5. Transfer the lentil and vegetable mixture to a 9x13-inch baking dish. Spread the mashed potatoes over the top of the lentil mixture.
6. Bake for 30 minutes, or until the potatoes are golden brown.

Nutritional Value: Calories: 270 Total Fat: 8g Saturated Fat: 2g Cholesterol: 0mg Sodium: 310mg Total Carbohydrates: 44g Dietary Fiber: 9g Sugars: 4g Protein: 11g

302. Vegan Lentil And Vegetable Curry Pasta

Prep. Time: 15 minutes **Cooking Time:** 25 minutes **Servings:** 4

Ingredients:
- 8 oz of pasta of your choice
- 1 tablespoon coconut oil or vegetable oil
- 1 onion, diced
- 2 cloves garlic, minced
- 1 tablespoon curry powder
- 1 teaspoon ground cumin
- 1/2 teaspoon ground turmeric
- 1/2 teaspoon ground coriander
- 1/4 teaspoon cayenne pepper (optional)
- 1 cup diced vegetables (such as bell peppers, carrots, and eggplant)
- 1 cup cooked green or brown lentils
- 1 can of coconut milk
- 1/2 cup vegetable broth
- Salt and pepper to taste
- Fresh cilantro or basil, for serving

Instructions:
1. Cook pasta according to package instructions and set aside.
2. In a large skillet or pan, heat the coconut oil or vegetable oil over medium-high heat.
3. Add the onion and garlic and cook until softened, about 5 minutes.
4. Stir in the curry powder, cumin, turmeric, coriander, and cayenne pepper (if using) and cook for another 1-2 minutes until fragrant.
5. Add the diced vegetables and cook for an additional 5 minutes.
6. Stir in the cooked lentils, coconut milk, and vegetable broth. Bring to a simmer and let cook for about 10 minutes, or until the vegetables are tender and the sauce has thickened.
7. Season with salt and pepper to taste.
8. Once the sauce is heated through, add the cooked pasta to the skillet or pan, and toss to coat the pasta in the curry sauce.
9. Serve the curry pasta with fresh cilantro or basil on top.

Nutritional Value: Calories: 367 Fat: 18g Cholesterol: Carbohydrates: 55g Fiber: 10g Protein: 17g

303. Vegan Lentil And Vegetable Curry Pizza

Prep. Time: 15 minutes **Cooking Time:** 15 minutes **Servings:** 6

Ingredients:
- 1 pre-made or homemade pizza dough

- 1/2 cup tomato sauce or pizza sauce
- 1/2 cup cooked green or brown lentils
- 1 cup diced vegetables (such as bell peppers, mushrooms, and zucchini)
- 1/4 cup diced red onion
- 1 tablespoon curry powder
- 1 teaspoon ground cumin
- 1/4 teaspoon ground turmeric
- 1/4 teaspoon ground coriander
- Salt and pepper, to taste
- Vegan cheese or nutritional yeast (optional)
- Fresh cilantro or basil, for serving

Instructions:
1. Preheat the oven to 425°F (220°C).
2. Roll out the pizza dough to desired thickness on a lightly floured surface.
3. Transfer the dough to a baking sheet or pizza stone.
4. Spread the tomato sauce or pizza sauce over the dough, leaving a little bit of space around the edges for the crust.
5. Sprinkle the cooked lentils, diced vegetables, red onion, curry powder, cumin, turmeric, coriander, salt, and pepper on top of the sauce.
6. If using, sprinkle on some vegan cheese or nutritional yeast for extra flavor.
7. Bake the pizza for 12-15 minutes or until the crust is golden brown and the cheese is melted (if using).
8. Let cool for a few minutes before slicing and serving.
9. Garnish with fresh cilantro or basil before serving.

Nutritional Value: Calories: 288 Fat: 14g Cholesterol: 19mg Carbohydrates: 41g Fiber: 8g Sugar: 6g Protein: 9g

Dinner

304. Lentil And Vegetable Curry

Prep. Time: 15 minutes **Cooking Time:** 30 minutes **Servings:** 4
Ingredients:
- 1 cup of green lentils, rinsed
- 2 cups of water
- 1 onion, diced
- 3 cloves of garlic, minced
- 1 tablespoon of ginger, grated
- 2 tablespoons of vegetable oil
- 1 tablespoon of curry powder
- 1 teaspoon of ground cumin
- 1 teaspoon of ground coriander
- 1/4 teaspoon of cayenne pepper (optional)
- 1 can of diced tomatoes
- 1 cup of diced carrots
- 1 cup of diced potatoes
- 1 cup of frozen peas
- Salt and pepper to taste
- Fresh cilantro for garnish

Instructions:
1. In a large pot, bring the lentils and water to a boil. Reduce heat and simmer for 20-25 minutes or until the lentils are tender. Drain any excess water and set aside.
2. In a large pan, heat the oil over medium heat. Add the onions, garlic, and ginger and cook for 2-3 minutes or until softened.
3. Stir in the curry powder, cumin, coriander, and cayenne pepper (if using) and cook for 1-2 minutes or until fragrant.
4. Add the diced tomatoes, carrots, potatoes, and frozen peas to the pan and bring to a simmer.
5. Cover the pan and cook for 10-15 minutes or until the vegetables are tender.
6. Stir in the cooked lentils and season with salt and pepper to taste.
7. Garnish with fresh cilantro and serve over rice or with naan bread.

Nutritional Value: Calories: 264, Fat: 6g, Carbohydrates: 44g, Protein: 12g, Fiber: 12g, Iron: 4mg

305. Vegetable Lasagna

Prep. Time: 30 minutes **Cooking Time:** 45 minutes **Servings:** 8
Ingredients:
- 1 pound of lasagna noodles
- 2 cups of fresh spinach, chopped
- 1 cup of diced bell peppers (red, yellow, green)
- 1 cup of diced zucchini
- 1 cup of diced mushrooms
- 1 cup of diced onion
- 2 cloves of garlic, minced
- 2 cups of marinara sauce
- 2 cups of ricotta cheese
- 1 cup of grated mozzarella cheese
- 1/4 cup of grated Parmesan cheese
- 2 eggs
- Salt and pepper to taste

Instructions:
1. Preheat the oven to 375°F (190°C).
2. Cook lasagna noodles according to package instructions, drain and set aside.
3. In a large pan, heat some oil over medium heat. Add the spinach, bell peppers, zucchini, mushrooms, onion, and garlic and sauté for 5-7 minutes or until softened.
4. In a mixing bowl, mix together the ricotta cheese, 1/2 cup of mozzarella cheese, 1/4 cup of Parmesan cheese, eggs, salt and pepper.
5. Spread 1/4 cup of marinara sauce on the bottom of a 9x13 inch baking dish.

6. Place a single layer of lasagna noodles on top of the sauce, spread 1/3 of the cheese mixture over the noodles and then 1/3 of the vegetable mixture.
7. Repeat the layering two more times, making sure to end with a layer of sauce and cheese on top.
8. Cover the dish with aluminum foil and bake for 25 minutes.
9. Remove the foil and sprinkle the remaining mozzarella and Parmesan cheese over the top.
10. Return the dish to the oven and bake for an additional 15-20 minutes or until the cheese is melted and the lasagna is bubbly.
11. Let it cool for 10-15 minutes before serving.

Nutritional Value: Calories: 380, Fat: 14g, Carbohydrates: 42g, Protein: 19g, Fiber: 3g, Iron: 3mg.

306. Eggplant Parmesan

Prep. Time: 30 minutes **Cooking Time:** 30 minutes **Servings:** 6

Ingredients:
- 2 medium eggplants, sliced into 1/4 inch rounds
- 1 cup all-purpose flour
- 2 eggs, beaten
- 1 cup Italian-seasoned breadcrumbs
- 1/2 cup vegetable oil
- 1 cup marinara sauce
- 1 cup shredded mozzarella cheese
- 1/4 cup grated Parmesan cheese
- Salt and pepper to taste
- Fresh basil leaves (for garnish)

Instructions:
1. Preheat the oven to 350°F (175°C).
2. Season eggplant slices with salt and pepper.
3. Place flour, eggs, and breadcrumbs in three separate shallow dishes.
4. Dip eggplant slices in flour, then egg, then breadcrumbs, pressing to adhere.
5. Heat vegetable oil in a large skillet over medium-high heat.
6. Fry eggplant slices until golden brown, about 3-4 minutes per side.
7. Remove eggplant from skillet and place on a paper towel-lined plate to remove excess oil.
8. Spread 1/4 cup of marinara sauce on the bottom of a baking dish.
9. Place the fried eggplant slices on top of the sauce.
10. Top with mozzarella cheese, and Parmesan cheese.
11. Bake for 20-25 minutes, or until cheese is melted and bubbly.
12. Garnish with fresh basil leaves before serving.

Nutritional Value: Calories: 401, Fat: 27g, Cholesterol: 84mg, Sodium: 646mg, Carbohydrates: 22g, Protein: 14g.

307. Chickpea And Spinach Stew

Prep. Time: 30 minutes **Cooking Time:** 15 minutes **Servings:** 4

Ingredients:
- 1 tablespoon of olive oil
- 1 onion, diced
- 3 cloves of garlic, minced
- 1 tablespoon of ginger, grated
- 1 teaspoon of ground cumin
- 1 teaspoon of ground coriander
- 1/4 teaspoon of turmeric
- 1/4 teaspoon of cayenne pepper (optional)
- 1 can of chickpeas, rinsed and drained
- 1 cup of vegetable broth
- 1 can of diced tomatoes
- 4 cups of fresh spinach

- Salt and pepper to taste
- Fresh cilantro for garnish

Instructions:
1. In a large pot or Dutch oven, heat the olive oil over medium heat. Add the onion, garlic, and ginger and cook for 2-3 minutes or until softened.
2. Stir in the cumin, coriander, turmeric, and cayenne pepper (if using) and cook for 1-2 minutes or until fragrant.
3. Add the chickpeas, vegetable broth, and diced tomatoes to the pot and bring to a simmer.
4. Reduce the heat to low and let it cook for 5-10 minutes.
5. Stir in the fresh spinach and cook for another 2-3 minutes or until the spinach is wilted.
6. Season with salt and pepper to taste.
7. Garnish with fresh cilantro and serve over rice or with flatbread.

Nutritional Value: Calories: 190, Fat: 5g, Carbohydrates: 30g, Protein: 9g, Fiber: 8g, Iron: 4mg.

308. Zucchini And Corn Fritters

Prep. Time: 15 minutes **Cooking Time:** 15 minutes **Servings:** 4

Ingredients:
- 2 medium zucchini, grated
- 1/2 cup corn kernels (fresh or frozen)
- 2 green onions, thinly sliced
- 1/4 cup all-purpose flour
- 2 eggs, beaten
- 1/4 cup grated Parmesan cheese
- 2 cloves of garlic, minced
- 2 tbsp chopped fresh parsley
- Salt and pepper to taste
- Vegetable oil for frying

Instructions:
1. In a mixing bowl, combine the grated zucchini, corn kernels, green onions, flour, eggs, Parmesan cheese, garlic, parsley, salt and pepper.
2. Heat vegetable oil in a large skillet over medium-high heat.
3. Use a tablespoon to drop the mixture into the skillet in small mounds, flattening them slightly with a spatula.
4. Cook the fritters until golden brown, about 2-3 minutes per side.
5. Remove fritters from skillet and place on a paper towel-lined plate to remove excess oil.
6. Serve the fritters warm with your favorite dipping sauce.

Nutritional Value: Calories: 200, Fat: 12g, Cholesterol: 111mg, Sodium: 179mg, Carbohydrates: 14g, Protein: 8g.

309. Quinoa And Black Bean Burrito Bowls

Prep. Time: 10 minutes **Cooking Time:** 20 minutes **Servings:** 4

Ingredients:
- 1 cup of quinoa, rinsed
- 2 cups of water
- 1 tablespoon of olive oil
- 1 onion, diced
- 2 cloves of garlic, minced
- 1 red bell pepper, diced
- 1 can of black beans, rinsed and drained
- 1 teaspoon of ground cumin
- 1 teaspoon of chili powder
- Salt and pepper to taste
- 1 avocado, diced
- 1 tomato, diced
- 1/4 cup of chopped cilantro
- 1 lime, cut into wedges
- For serving: shredded lettuce, shredded cheese, sour cream or plain yogurt, hot sauce (optional)

Instructions:

1. In a medium saucepan, bring the quinoa and water to a boil. Reduce heat, cover and simmer for 15-20 minutes or until the quinoa is tender and the water is absorbed.
2. In a large skillet, heat the olive oil over medium heat. Add the onion, garlic, and red bell pepper and sauté for 2-3 minutes or until softened.
3. Stir in the black beans, cumin, chili powder, and season with salt and pepper to taste.
4. Cook for another 5-7 minutes or until heated through.
5. To assemble the bowls, divide the cooked quinoa among four bowls.
6. Top with the black bean mixture, avocado, tomato, and cilantro.
7. Serve with lime wedges, shredded lettuce, shredded cheese, sour cream or plain yogurt and hot sauce (if desired).

Nutritional Value: Calories: 340, Fat: 12g, Carbohydrates: 47g, Protein: 12g, Fiber: 11g, Iron: 4mg.

310. Pesto Pasta Salad

Prep. Time: 10 minutes **Cooking Time:** 5 minutes **Servings:** 4
Ingredients:
- 8 oz pasta of your choice (penne, fusilli, or farfalle)
- 1/2 cup basil pesto
- 1/2 cup cherry tomatoes, halved
- 1/2 cup diced mozzarella cheese
- 1/4 cup sliced black olives
- 2 tbsp extra-virgin olive oil
- Salt and pepper to taste
- Fresh basil leaves (for garnish)

Instructions:
1. Cook pasta according to package instructions, then drain and rinse with cold water.
2. In a mixing bowl, combine the cooked pasta, pesto, cherry tomatoes, mozzarella cheese, black olives, olive oil, salt, and pepper.
3. Toss until pasta is evenly coated.
4. Garnish with fresh basil leaves before serving.
5. Serve pasta salad chilled or at room temperature.

Nutritional Value: Calories: 464, Fat: 29g, Cholesterol: 30mg, Sodium: 704mg, Carbohydrates: 39g, Protein: 14g.

311. Cauliflower And Chickpea Curry

Prep. Time: 10 minutes **Cooking Time:** 20 minutes **Servings:** 4
Ingredients:
- 1 tablespoon of vegetable oil
- 1 onion, diced
- 3 cloves of garlic, minced
- 1 tablespoon of ginger, grated
- 2 tablespoons of curry powder
- 1 teaspoon of ground cumin
- 1 teaspoon of ground coriander
- 1/4 teaspoon of turmeric
- 1/4 teaspoon of cayenne pepper (optional)
- 1 head of cauliflower, cut into florets
- 1 can of chickpeas, rinsed and drained
- 1 cup of vegetable broth
- 1 can of diced tomatoes
- Salt and pepper to taste
- Fresh cilantro for garnish

Instructions:
1. In a large pot or Dutch oven, heat the oil over medium heat. Add the onion, garlic, and ginger and cook for 2-3 minutes or until softened.
2. Stir in the curry powder, cumin, coriander, turmeric, and cayenne pepper

(if using) and cook for 1-2 minutes or until fragrant.
3. Add the cauliflower, chickpeas, vegetable broth, and diced tomatoes to the pot and bring to a simmer.
4. Reduce the heat to low and let it cook for 10-15 minutes or until the cauliflower is tender.
5. Season with salt and pepper to taste.
6. Garnish with fresh cilantro and serve over rice or with naan bread.

Nutritional Value: Calories: 180, Fat: 5g, Carbohydrates: 27g, Protein: 8g, Fiber: 8g, Iron: 4mg.

312. Lentil And Beetroot Patty

Prep. Time: 30 minutes **Cooking Time:** 15 minutes **Servings:** 6
Ingredients:
- 1 cup dried green or brown lentils
- 2 cups water
- 1 large beetroot, peeled and grated
- 1/2 cup diced onion
- 2 cloves of garlic, minced
- 1/4 cup breadcrumbs
- 1 egg
- 2 tbsp chopped fresh parsley
- Salt and pepper to taste
- Vegetable oil for frying

Instructions:
1. Rinse the lentils and add them to a pot with 2 cups of water. Bring to a boil and then reduce the heat to a simmer. Cook for about 20-25 minutes, or until lentils are tender. Drain any excess water.
2. In a mixing bowl, combine the cooked lentils, grated beetroot, onion, garlic, breadcrumbs, egg, parsley, salt, and pepper.
3. Mix everything together until well combined.
4. Form the mixture into small patties.
5. Heat vegetable oil in a large skillet over medium-high heat.
6. Fry the patties until golden brown, about 2-3 minutes per side.
7. Remove the patties from skillet and place on a paper towel-lined plate to remove excess oil.
8. Serve the patties with your favorite dipping sauce or as a burger patty.

Nutritional Value: Calories: 164, Fat: 4g, Cholesterol: 37mg, Sodium: 56mg, Carbohydrates: 24g, Protein: 8g.

313. Grilled Zucchini And Bell Pepper Skewers

Prep. Time: 15 minutes **Cooking Time:** 15 minutes **Servings:** 4
Ingredients:
- 2 zucchini, sliced into 1/2-inch thick rounds
- 2 bell peppers, cut into 1-inch pieces
- 1/4 cup of olive oil
- 2 cloves of garlic, minced
- 2 tablespoons of fresh lemon juice
- 1 teaspoon of dried oregano
- Salt and pepper to taste
- Fresh parsley or basil for garnish
- Skewers (soaked in water for 30 minutes)

Instructions:
1. Preheat grill to medium-high heat or preheat a grill pan over medium-high heat.
2. In a small bowl, mix together the olive oil, garlic, lemon juice, oregano, salt and pepper.
3. Thread the zucchini rounds and bell pepper pieces onto skewers.
4. Brush the skewers with the marinade and let them sit for at least 15 minutes.
5. Grill the skewers for 8-10 minutes per side, or until the vegetables are tender and slightly charred.

6. Garnish with fresh parsley or basil, and serve as a side dish or as a main dish with a side of rice or quinoa.

Nutritional Value Calories: 130, Fat: 12g, Carbohydrates: 6g, Protein: 2g, Fiber: 2g, Iron: 1mg.

314. Vegetable Samosas

Prep. Time: 30 minutes **Cooking Time:** 30 minutes **Servings:** 8

Ingredients:
- 2 cups all-purpose flour
- 1/2 tsp salt
- 1/4 cup vegetable oil
- 1/4 cup water
- 2 cups diced mixed vegetables (potatoes, carrots, peas, onions)
- 1 tsp cumin powder
- 1 tsp coriander powder
- 1 tsp garam masala powder
- Salt and pepper to taste
- Vegetable oil for frying

Instructions:
1. In a mixing bowl, combine the flour, salt and vegetable oil. Mix well and gradually add water to make a dough.
2. Knead the dough for about 5 minutes, then cover and let it rest for 30 minutes.
3. In a skillet over medium heat, add some oil and sauté the diced vegetables until they are cooked through.
4. Add cumin powder, coriander powder, garam masala powder, salt and pepper and cook for an additional 2-3 minutes.
5. Remove the skillet from heat and let the mixture cool.
6. Divide the dough into 8 equal portions.
7. Roll out each portion into a circle, about 6 inches in diameter.
8. Cut each circle in half to make two semi-circles.
9. Place 2 tablespoons of the vegetable mixture on one end of each semi-circle.
10. Fold the semi-circle to form a triangle, then press the edges to seal.
11. Heat oil in a deep pan or wok.
12. Fry the samosas until golden brown, about 2-3 minutes per side.
13. Remove the samosas from the oil and place on a paper towel-lined plate to remove excess oil.
14. Serve the samosas hot with your favorite dipping sauce.

Nutritional Value: Calories: 196, Fat: 10g, Cholesterol: 0mg, Sodium: 123mg, Carbohydrates: 23g, Protein: 3g

315. Roasted Brussels Sprouts With Balsamic Glaze

Prep. Time: 10 minutes **Cooking Time:** 25 minutes **Servings:** 4

Ingredients:
- 1 1/2 pounds of Brussels sprouts, trimmed and halved
- 2 tablespoons of olive oil
- Salt and pepper to taste
- For the Balsamic Glaze:
- 1/2 cup of balsamic vinegar
- 2 tablespoons of honey
- 1 clove of garlic, minced
- 1/4 teaspoon of red pepper flakes (optional)
- Salt and pepper to taste

Instructions:
1. Preheat the oven to 400°F (200°C).
2. In a large bowl, toss the Brussels sprouts with olive oil, salt and pepper.
3. Spread the Brussels sprouts in a single layer on a baking sheet.
4. Roast in the preheated oven for 25-30 minutes, or until tender and golden brown, flipping halfway through.

5. While the Brussels sprouts are roasting, make the balsamic glaze. In a small saucepan, combine the balsamic vinegar, honey, garlic, red pepper flakes (if using), salt and pepper.
6. Bring the mixture to a boil over medium-high heat, then reduce the heat to medium-low and let it simmer for 8-10 minutes, or until the glaze has thickened and reduced by half.
7. Remove from heat and let it cool for a few minutes.
8. Once the Brussels sprouts are cooked, remove them from the oven and toss them with the balsamic glaze.
9. Serve immediately.

Nutritional Value: Calories: 150, Fat: 7g, Carbohydrates: 19g, Protein: 4g, Fiber: 4g, Iron: 2mg.

316. Roasted Cauliflower Bites

Prep. Time: 10 minutes **Cooking Time:** 20 minutes **Servings:** 4
Ingredients:
- 1 head of cauliflower, cut into florets
- 2 tbsp olive oil
- 1 tsp smoked paprika
- 1 tsp garlic powder
- Salt and pepper to taste

Instructions:
1. Preheat the oven to 425°F (220°C).
2. In a mixing bowl, combine the cauliflower florets, olive oil, smoked paprika, garlic powder, salt, and pepper.
3. Toss until the cauliflower is evenly coated.
4. Spread the cauliflower on a baking sheet lined with parchment paper.
5. Roast for 20-25 minutes, or until the cauliflower is tender and lightly browned.
6. Serve the cauliflower bites warm as a side dish or as a snack.

Nutritional Value: Calories: 84, Fat: 7g, Cholesterol: 0mg, Sodium: 116mg, Carbohydrates: 6g, Protein: 2g

317. Carrot And Ginger Soup

Prep. Time: 15 minutes **Cooking Time:** 25 minutes **Servings:** 4
Ingredients:
- 2 tablespoons of olive oil
- 1 onion, diced
- 2 cloves of garlic, minced
- 2 tablespoons of ginger, grated
- 1 teaspoon of ground cumin
- 1 teaspoon of ground coriander
- 1/4 teaspoon of cayenne pepper (optional)
- 6 cups of peeled and chopped carrots
- 4 cups of vegetable broth
- Salt and pepper to taste
- Fresh cilantro or parsley for garnish
- plain yogurt or sour cream as a topping (optional)

Instructions:
1. In a large pot or Dutch oven, heat the olive oil over medium heat. Add the onion, garlic, and ginger and cook for 2-3 minutes or until softened.
2. Stir in the cumin, coriander, and cayenne pepper (if using) and cook for 1-2 minutes or until fragrant.
3. Add the carrots, vegetable broth, and bring to a simmer.
4. Reduce the heat to low and let it cook for 20-25 minutes or until the carrots are tender.
5. Remove from heat and let it cool for a few minutes.
6. Using an immersion blender or a regular blender, puree the soup until smooth.
7. Reheat the soup if necessary and season with salt and pepper to taste.
8. Garnish with fresh cilantro or parsley, and if desired, add a dollop of plain

yogurt or sour cream on top before serving.

Nutritional Value: Calories: 120, Fat: 7g, Carbohydrates: 14g, Protein: 2g, Fiber: 4g, Iron: 1mg.

318. Vegetable And Lentil Pot Pie

Prep. Time: 30 minutes **Cooking Time:** 30 minutes **Servings:** 6
Ingredients:
- 1 cup dried green or brown lentils
- 2 cups water
- 2 tbsp olive oil
- 1 onion, diced
- 2 cloves of garlic, minced
- 2 cups diced mixed vegetables (carrots, potatoes, peas, corn)
- 1 tsp thyme
- 1 tsp rosemary
- Salt and pepper to taste
- 1 cup vegetable broth
- 1/4 cup all-purpose flour
- 1 sheet of puff pastry, thawed

Instructions:
1. Rinse the lentils and add them to a pot with 2 cups of water. Bring to a boil and then reduce the heat to a simmer. Cook for about 20-25 minutes, or until lentils are tender. Drain any excess water.
2. In a skillet over medium heat, add the olive oil and sauté the onion and garlic until softened.
3. Add the mixed vegetables, thyme, rosemary, salt and pepper and sauté for an additional 5 minutes.
4. Stir in the cooked lentils and vegetable broth, bring to a simmer and let it cook for 5 minutes.
5. Stir in the flour and cook for an additional 2-3 minutes.
6. Pour the mixture into a 9-inch pie dish.
7. Place the thawed puff pastry sheet on top of the mixture, tucking in the edges.
8. Cut a few slits in the puff pastry to allow steam to escape.
9. Bake in preheated oven at 375°F (190°C) for 25-30 minutes or until the pastry is golden brown.
10. Let it cool for 5 minutes before serving.

Nutritional Value: Calories: 405, Fat: 18g, Cholesterol: 0mg, Sodium: 551mg, Carbohydrates: 45g, Protein: 15g.

319. Black Bean And Sweet Potato Chili

Prep. Time: 15 minutes **Cooking Time:** 35 minutes **Servings:** 6
Ingredients:
- 2 tablespoons of olive oil
- 1 onion, diced
- 3 cloves of garlic, minced
- 1 tablespoon of chili powder
- 2 teaspoons of ground cumin
- 1 teaspoon of smoked paprika
- 1/4 teaspoon of cayenne pepper (optional)
- 1 large sweet potato, peeled and diced
- 2 cans of black beans, rinsed and drained
- 1 can of diced tomatoes
- 4 cups of vegetable broth
- Salt and pepper to taste
- Fresh cilantro or parsley for garnish
- shredded cheese, sour cream or plain yogurt, diced avocado as topping (optional)

Instructions:
1. In a large pot or Dutch oven, heat the olive oil over medium heat. Add the onion and garlic, and cook for 2-3 minutes or until softened.
2. Stir in the chili powder, cumin, smoked paprika, and cayenne pepper (if using) and cook for 1-2 minutes or until fragrant.

3. Add the sweet potato, black beans, diced tomatoes, vegetable broth, bring to a simmer.
4. Reduce the heat to low and let it cook for 30-35 minutes or until the sweet potato is tender.
5. Season with salt and pepper to taste.
6. Garnish with fresh cilantro or parsley, and if desired, add shredded cheese, sour cream or plain yogurt, diced avocado on top before serving.

Nutritional Value: Calories: 240, Fat: 5g, Carbohydrates: 39g, Protein: 12g, Fiber: 14g, Iron: 4mg.

320. Grilled Eggplant And Bell Pepper Sandwich

Prep. Time: 10 minutes **Cooking Time:** 20 minutes **Servings:** 4
Ingredients:
- 2 medium eggplants, sliced into 1/2-inch thick rounds
- 2 bell peppers, sliced
- 3 tablespoons of olive oil
- 2 cloves of garlic, minced
- 2 tablespoons of balsamic vinegar
- 1 teaspoon of dried oregano
- Salt and pepper to taste
- 8 slices of rustic bread
- 1/2 cup of pesto
- 4 slices of fresh mozzarella cheese
- 4 leaves of fresh basil

Instructions:
1. Preheat the grill to medium-high heat or preheat a grill pan over medium-high heat.
2. In a small bowl, mix together 2 tablespoons of olive oil, garlic, balsamic vinegar, oregano, salt and pepper.
3. Brush the eggplant and bell pepper slices with the marinade and let them sit for at least 10 minutes.
4. Grill the eggplant and bell pepper slices for 8-10 minutes per side, or until tender and slightly charred.
5. Toast the bread slices on the grill or in a toaster.
6. Spread pesto on four slices of toast.
7. Place a slice of mozzarella cheese, grilled eggplant, grilled bell pepper, and basil leaf on top of the pesto.

321. Falafel Balls With Tahini Sauce

Prep. Time: 30 minutes **Cooking Time:** 15 minutes **Servings:** 3
Ingredients
for Falafel:
- 1 can (15 oz) chickpeas, rinsed and drained
- 1/2 cup chopped fresh parsley
- 1/4 cup chopped fresh cilantro
- 2 cloves of garlic, minced
- 1/4 cup all-purpose flour
- 1 tsp cumin powder
- 1 tsp coriander powder
- Salt and pepper to taste
- Vegetable oil for frying

for Tahini Sauce:
- 1/2 cup tahini
- 2 tbsp lemon juice
- 1 clove of garlic, minced
- 1/4 tsp salt
- 3-4 tbsp water

Instructions: f
1. In a food processor, pulse the chickpeas, parsley, cilantro, garlic, flour, cumin powder, coriander powder, salt and pepper until it forms a coarse mixture.
2. Form the mixture into small balls.
3. Heat vegetable oil in a deep pan or wok.
4. Fry the falafel balls until golden brown, about 2-3 minutes per side.

5. Remove the falafel balls from the oil and place on a paper towel-lined plate to remove excess oil.
6. In a mixing bowl, whisk together the tahini, lemon juice, garlic, salt and water.
7. Add more water if needed to reach the desired consistency.
8. Serve the falafel balls with the tahini sauce as a dip.

Nutritional Value: Calories: 444, Fat: 30g, Cholesterol: 0mg, Sodium: 651mg, Carbohydrates: 32g, Protein: 16g

322. Stuffed Bell Peppers With Quinoa And Black Beans

Prep. Time: 30 minutes **Cooking Time:** 30 minutes **Servings:** 4

Ingredients:
- 4 bell peppers, halved and seeded
- 1 cup quinoa
- 2 cups vegetable broth
- 1 can (15 oz) black beans, rinsed and drained
- 1/2 cup diced onion
- 1/2 cup diced red bell pepper
- 2 cloves of garlic, minced
- 1 tbsp olive oil
- 1 tsp cumin powder
- 1 tsp smoked paprika
- Salt and pepper to taste
- 1 cup shredded cheddar cheese
- Fresh cilantro leaves (for garnish)

Instructions:
1. Preheat the oven to 375°F (190°C).
2. In a saucepan, combine the quinoa and vegetable broth. Bring to a boil, then reduce the heat to a simmer. Cover and cook for about 15-20 minutes, or until the quinoa is tender and the liquid has been absorbed.
3. In a skillet over medium heat, add the olive oil, onion, red bell pepper, garlic, cumin powder, smoked paprika, salt and pepper. Sauté until vegetables are tender, about 5 minutes.
4. Stir in the black beans and cooked quinoa.
5. Stuff the pepper halves with the quinoa and bean mixture.
6. Place the stuffed pepper halves in a baking dish.
7. Top each pepper with shredded cheese.
8. Bake for 20-25 minutes, or until the cheese is melted and bubbly.
9. Garnish with cilantro leaves before serving.

Nutritional Value: Calories: 329, Fat: 10g, Cholesterol: 6mg, Sodium: 432mg, Carbohydrates: 38g, Protein: 27g

323. Spinach And Ricotta Stuffed Shells

Prep. Time: 20 minutes **Cooking Time:** 40 minutes **Servings:** 8

Ingredients:
- 1 (12-ounce) package of jumbo pasta shells
- 1 (10-ounce) package of frozen spinach, thawed and squeezed dry
- 1 (15-ounce) container of ricotta cheese
- 1 cup of grated mozzarella cheese
- 1/4 cup of grated Parmesan cheese
- 2 eggs
- 2 cloves of garlic, minced
- Salt and pepper to taste
- 4 cups of marinara sauce
- Additional grated mozzarella cheese for topping

Instructions:
1. Preheat oven to 375°F (190°C).
2. Cook pasta shells according to package instructions, drain and set aside.

3. In a large mixing bowl, mix together the spinach, ricotta cheese, mozzarella cheese, Parmesan cheese, eggs, garlic, salt and pepper.
4. Spread 1 cup of marinara sauce on the bottom of a 9x13 inch baking dish.
5. Stuff each pasta shell with the cheese mixture and place them in the baking dish.
6. Pour the remaining marinara sauce over the shells.
7. Sprinkle additional mozzarella cheese over the top.
8. Cover the dish with aluminum foil and bake for 25 minutes.
9. Remove the foil and bake for an additional 15-20 minutes or until the cheese is melted and the shells are bubbly.
10. Let it cool for 10-15 minutes before serving.

Nutritional Value: Calories: 380, Fat: 14g, Carbohydrates: 42g, Protein: 19g, Fiber: 3g, Iron: 3mg.

324. Vegetable And Paneer Korma

Prep. Time: 20 minutes **Cooking Time:** 25 minutes **Servings:** 4
Ingredients:
- 2 tbsp vegetable oil
- 1 onion, diced
- 2 cloves of garlic, minced
- 1 tbsp ginger, grated
- 1 tsp cumin powder
- 1 tsp coriander powder
- 1 tsp garam masala powder
- 1 tsp turmeric powder
- 1 tsp red chili powder (optional)
- Salt and pepper to taste
- 1 cup diced mixed vegetables (carrots, potatoes, bell peppers, peas)
- 1 cup diced paneer cheese
- 1 cup plain yogurt
- 1/4 cup heavy cream
- 2 tbsp chopped fresh cilantro (for garnish)

Instructions:
1. Heat the oil in a large skillet over medium heat.
2. Add the onion, garlic, and ginger and sauté until softened, about 5 minutes.
3. Add the cumin, coriander, garam masala, turmeric, red chili powder, salt and pepper and cook for an additional 2-3 minutes.
4. Add the mixed vegetables and sauté until they are slightly softened, about 5-7 minutes.
5. Stir in the diced paneer cheese, yogurt, and cream.
6. Bring the mixture to a simmer and let it cook for 10-15 minutes or until the sauce thickens and the vegetables are tender.
7. Adjust the seasoning if needed.
8. Garnish with fresh cilantro before serving.
9. Serve the Vegetable and Paneer Korma with rice or naan bread for a complete meal.

Nutritional Value: Calories: 303, Fat: 20g, Cholesterol: 61mg, Sodium: 234mg, Carbohydrates: 18g, Protein: 13g

325. Stuffed Okra With Peanut And Tamarind Sauce

Prep. Time: 15 minutes **Cooking Time:** 30 minutes **Servings:** 4
Ingredients:
- 24 okra pods
- 1 cup of ground peanuts
- 1/4 cup of grated coconut
- 1/4 cup of chopped cilantro
- 1/4 cup of chopped mint
- 1 teaspoon of chili powder

- 1 teaspoon of ground cumin
- Salt and pepper to taste
- For the peanut and tamarind sauce:
- 1/2 cup of creamy peanut butter
- 2 tablespoons of tamarind paste
- 2 tablespoons of brown sugar
- 2 cloves of garlic, minced
- 1 tablespoon of grated ginger
- 1 teaspoon of ground cumin
- Salt and pepper to taste
- Water as needed

Instructions:
1. Preheat the oven to 375°F (190°C).
2. Cut off the tops of the okra pods and scoop out the seeds with a spoon.
3. In a medium mixing bowl, mix together the ground peanuts, grated coconut, cilantro, mint, chili powder, cumin, salt, and pepper.
4. Stuff the mixture into the okra pods.
5. Place the stuffed okra pods on a baking sheet and bake for 25-30 minutes or until tender.
6. While the okra is baking, make the peanut and tamarind sauce. In a small saucepan, whisk together the peanut butter, tamarind paste, brown sugar, garlic, ginger, cumin, salt and pepper. Add water as needed to thin the sauce.
7. Heat the sauce over medium heat, stirring frequently, until warmed through.
8. Serve the stuffed okra with the peanut and tamarind sauce on the side.

Nutritional Value: Calories: 440, Fat: 34g, Carbohydrates: 28g, Protein: 12g, Fiber: 7g, Iron: 3mg

326. Chana Masala

Prep. Time: 15 minutes **Cooking Time:** 45 minutes **Servings:** 6

Ingredients:
- 1 tablespoon of vegetable oil
- 1 onion, diced
- 3 cloves of garlic, minced
- 1 tablespoon of ginger, grated
- 2 tablespoons of chana masala spice mix
- 1 teaspoon of ground cumin
- 1 teaspoon of ground coriander
- 1/4 teaspoon of turmeric
- 1/4 teaspoon of cayenne pepper (optional)
- 1 can of chickpeas, rinsed and drained
- 1 can of diced tomatoes
- 1 cup of water
- Salt and pepper to taste
- Fresh cilantro for garnish
- Cooked rice or naan bread for serving

Instructions:
1. In a large pot or Dutch oven, heat the oil over medium heat. Add the onion, garlic, and ginger and cook for 2-3 minutes or until softened.
2. Stir in the chana masala spice mix, cumin, coriander, turmeric, and cayenne pepper (if using) and cook for 1-2 minutes or until fragrant.
3. Add the chickpeas, diced tomatoes, and water and bring to a simmer.
4. Reduce the heat to low and let it cook for 30-35 minutes or until the sauce has thickened and the chickpeas are tender.
5. Season with salt and pepper to taste.
6. Garnish with fresh cilantro and serve over rice or with naan bread.

Nutritional Value: Calories: 150, Fat: 5g, Carbohydrates: 21g, Protein: 6g, Fiber: 5g, Iron: 2mg.

327. Tofu And Broccoli Stir-Fry

Prep. Time: 15 minutes **Cooking Time:** 15 minutes **Servings:** 3

Ingredients:
- 1 block of firm tofu, drained and cut into small cubes

- 2 tbsp vegetable oil
- 2 cloves of garlic, minced
- 1 tbsp ginger, grated
- 1 head of broccoli, cut into florets
- 2 tbsp soy sauce
- 1 tbsp hoisin sauce
- 1 tbsp rice vinegar
- 1 tsp sesame oil
- 1 tsp sugar
- Salt and pepper to taste
- Sesame seeds (for garnish)

Instructions:
1. Heat the vegetable oil in a large skillet or wok over high heat.
2. Add the tofu and stir-fry for 5-7 minutes, or until it is golden brown.
3. Remove the tofu from the skillet and set it aside.
4. Add garlic and ginger to the skillet and stir-fry for 1-2 minutes.
5. Add the broccoli and stir-fry for an additional 3-5 minutes, or until it is tender but still crisp.
6. In a small bowl, mix together the soy sauce, hoisin sauce, rice vinegar, sesame oil, sugar, salt, and pepper.
7. Add the sauce to the skillet and stir-fry for 1-2 minutes.
8. Add the tofu back to the skillet and toss everything together until the tofu is evenly coated with the sauce.
9. Garnish with sesame seeds before serving.
10. Serve the Tofu and Broccoli stir-fry with rice or noodles for a complete meal.

Nutritional Value: Calories: 228, Fat: 17g, Cholesterol: 0mg,

328. Grilled Eggplant Rolls With Ricotta And Basil

Prep. Time: 20 minutes **Cooking Time:** 25 minutes **Servings:** 8

Ingredients:
- 2 medium eggplants, sliced lengthwise into 1/4-inch thick slices
- 2 tablespoons of olive oil
- Salt and pepper to taste
- 1 cup of ricotta cheese
- 1/4 cup of grated Parmesan cheese
- 2 cloves of garlic, minced
- 1/4 cup of chopped fresh basil
- 8 slices of prosciutto
- Additional chopped basil for garnish

Instructions:
1. Preheat grill to medium-high heat or preheat a grill pan over medium-high heat.
2. Brush the eggplant slices with olive oil, and season with salt and pepper.
3. Grill the eggplant slices for 3-4 minutes per side, or until tender and slightly charred.
4. Remove the eggplant from the grill and let them cool slightly.
5. In a mixing bowl, combine the ricotta cheese, Parmesan cheese, garlic, chopped basil, salt, and pepper.
6. Place a spoonful of the cheese mixture on each eggplant slice, then roll it up with a slice of prosciutto.
7. Return the rolls to the grill and cook for an additional 2-3 minutes or until the prosciutto is slightly crisp.
8. Serve the eggplant rolls warm, garnished with additional chopped basil.

Nutritional Value: Calories: 130, Fat: 9g, Carbohydrates: 6g, Protein: 7g, Fiber: 2g, Iron: 1mg.

329. Sweet Potato And Black Bean Tacos

Prep. Time: 20 minutes **Cooking Time:** 25 minutes **Servings:** 5

Ingredients:

- 1 large sweet potato, peeled and diced
- 2 tbsp olive oil
- Salt and pepper to taste
- 1 onion, diced
- 2 cloves of garlic, minced
- 1 tsp cumin powder
- 1 tsp smoked paprika
- 1 can (15 oz) black beans, rinsed and drained
- 1/4 cup water
- 8-10 corn tortillas
- Toppings of your choice (shredded cheese, salsa, avocado, sour cream, cilantro)

Instructions:
1. Preheat the oven to 425°F (220°C).
2. Toss the sweet potato with olive oil, salt, and pepper.
3. Spread the sweet potato on a baking sheet lined with parchment paper.
4. Roast for 20-25 minutes, or until the sweet potato is tender and lightly browned.
5. In a skillet over medium heat, add some oil and sauté the onion and garlic until softened.
6. Add the cumin powder, smoked paprika, salt, and pepper and cook for an additional 2-3 minutes.
7. Stir in the black beans and water, bring it to a simmer and cook for an additional 5 minutes.
8. Heat the tortillas in a skillet or microwave.
9. To assemble the tacos, place a few tablespoons of the sweet potato mixture and black bean mixture on each tortilla.

Nutritional Value: Calories: 299, Fat: 12g, Cholesterol: 13mg, Sodium: 388mg, Carbohydrates: 35g, Protein: 19g

330. Cauliflower And Pea Curry

Prep. Time: 15 minutes **Cooking Time:** 25 minutes **Servings:** 5

Ingredients:
- 2 tablespoons of vegetable oil
- 1 onion, diced
- 2 cloves of garlic, minced
- 2 tablespoons of ginger, grated
- 1 tablespoon of curry powder
- 1 teaspoon of ground cumin
- 1 teaspoon of ground coriander
- 1/4 teaspoon of turmeric
- 1/4 teaspoon of cayenne pepper (optional)
- 1 head of cauliflower, chopped into florets
- 1 cup of frozen peas
- 1 can of diced tomatoes
- 1 cup of coconut milk
- Salt and pepper to taste
- Fresh cilantro for garnish
- Cooked rice or naan bread for serving

Instructions:
1. In a large pot or Dutch oven, heat the oil over medium heat. Add the onion, garlic, and ginger and cook for 2-3 minutes or until softened.
2. Stir in the curry powder, cumin, coriander, turmeric, and cayenne pepper (if using) and cook for 1-2 minutes or until fragrant.
3. Add the cauliflower, frozen peas, diced tomatoes, and coconut milk and bring to a simmer.
4. Reduce the heat to low and let it cook for 20-25 minutes or until the cauliflower is tender.
5. Season with salt and pepper to taste.
6. Garnish with fresh cilantro and serve over rice or with naan bread.

Nutritional Value: Calories: 290, Fat: 20g, Carbohydrates: 22g, Protein: 7g, Fiber: 6g, Iron: 3mg.

331. Lentil And Vegetable Shepherd's Pie

Prep. Time: 30 minutes **Cooking Time:** 30 minutes **Servings:** 6
Ingredients:
- 1 cup dried green or brown lentils
- 2 cups water
- 2 tbsp olive oil
- 1 onion, diced
- 2 cloves of garlic, minced
- 2 cups diced mixed vegetables (carrots, potatoes, peas, corn)
- 1 tsp thyme
- 1 tsp rosemary
- Salt and pepper to taste
- 1 cup vegetable broth
- 1/4 cup all-purpose flour
- 3 cups mashed potatoes

Instructions:
1. Rinse the lentils and add them to a pot with 2 cups of water. Bring to a boil and then reduce the heat to a simmer. Cook for about 20-25 minutes, or until lentils are tender. Drain any excess water.
2. In a skillet over medium heat, add the olive oil and sauté the onion and garlic until softened.
3. Add the mixed vegetables, thyme, rosemary, salt and pepper and sauté for an additional 5 minutes.
4. Stir in the cooked lentils and vegetable broth, bring to a simmer and let it cook for 5 minutes.
5. Stir in the flour and cook for an additional 2-3 minutes.
6. Pour the mixture into a 9-inch pie dish.
7. Spread the mashed potatoes on top of the mixture, spreading it evenly and making sure to cover the entire surface.
8. Bake in preheated oven at 375°F (190°C) for 25-30 minutes or until the mashed potatoes are golden brown.
9. Let it cool for 5 minutes before serving.

Nutritional Value: Calories: 444, Fat: 14g, Cholesterol: 0mg, Sodium: 716mg, Carbohydrates: 63g, Protein: 18g.

332. Vegetable Moussaka

Prep. Time: 20 minutes **Cooking Time:** 40 minutes **Servings:** 9
Ingredients:
- 2 tablespoons of olive oil
- 1 onion, diced
- 2 cloves of garlic, minced
- 2 cups of diced eggplant
- 2 cups of diced zucchini
- 1 cup of diced bell peppers
- 1 can of diced tomatoes
- 1 teaspoon of dried oregano
- 1 teaspoon of dried basil
- 1/4 teaspoon of ground nutmeg
- Salt and pepper to taste
- For the béchamel sauce:
- 4 tablespoons of butter
- 4 tablespoons of all-purpose flour
- 3 cups of milk
- 1/2 cup of grated Parmesan cheese
- 1/2 cup of grated mozzarella cheese
- 2 eggs

Instructions:
1. Preheat oven to 375°F (190°C).
2. In a large skillet, heat olive oil over medium heat. Add the onion, garlic, eggplant, zucchini, and bell peppers and cook for 8-10 minutes or until tender.

3. Stir in the diced tomatoes, oregano, basil, nutmeg, salt, and pepper. Cook for an additional 5-7 minutes.
4. To make the béchamel sauce, in a medium saucepan, melt the butter over medium heat. Whisk in the flour and cook

Nutritional Value: Calories: 287, Fat: 15g, Cholesterol: 7mg, Sodium: 322mg, Carbohydrates: 31g, Protein: 12g

333. Lentil And Pumpkin Curry

Prep. Time: 20 minutes **Cooking Time:** 25 minutes **Servings:** 5
Ingredients:
- 1 cup dried green or brown lentils
- 2 cups water
- 2 tbsp vegetable oil
- 1 onion, diced
- 2 cloves of garlic, minced
- 1 tbsp ginger, grated
- 1 tsp cumin powder
- 1 tsp coriander powder
- 1 tsp turmeric powder
- 1 tsp garam masala powder
- Salt and pepper to taste
- 1 cup diced pumpkin
- 1 can (14 oz) diced tomatoes
- 1 cup coconut milk
- Fresh cilantro leaves (for garnish)

Instructions:
1. Rinse the lentils and add them to a pot with 2 cups of water. Bring to a boil and then reduce the heat to a simmer. Cook for about 20-25 minutes, or until lentils are tender. Drain any excess water.
2. In a large pot or Dutch oven, heat the oil over medium heat.
3. Add the onion, garlic, and ginger and sauté until softened, about 5 minutes.
4. Add the cumin, coriander, turmeric, garam masala powder, salt, and pepper and cook for an additional 2-3 minutes.
5. Stir in the diced pumpkin, diced tomatoes, and coconut milk. Bring the mixture to a boil and then reduce the heat to a simmer.
6. Cover and let it cook for 15-20 minutes, or until the pumpkin is tender.
7. Stir in the cooked lentils and cook for an additional 5 minutes.
8. Adjust the seasoning if needed.
9. Garnish with fresh cilantro before serving.
10. Serve the Lentil and Pumpkin Curry with rice or naan bread for a complete meal.

Nutritional Value: Calories: 393, Fat: 24g, Cholesterol: 0mg, Sodium: 312mg, Carbohydrates: 34g, Protein: 16g.

334. Stuffed Eggplant With Quinoa And Feta

Prep. Time: 30 minutes **Cooking Time:** 0 minutes **Servings:** 4
Ingredients:
- 2 large eggplants
- 2 tablespoons of olive oil
- 1 onion, diced
- 2 cloves of garlic, minced
- 1 cup of cooked quinoa
- 1/2 cup of crumbled feta cheese
- 1/4 cup of chopped fresh parsley
- 1/4 cup of chopped fresh mint
- Salt and pepper to taste
- For the tomato sauce:
- 1 tablespoon of olive oil
- 1 onion, diced
- 2 cloves of garlic, minced
- 1 can of diced tomatoes
- 1 teaspoon of dried oregano
- 1 teaspoon of dried basil
- Salt and pepper to taste
- Additional crumbled feta cheese for garnish

Instructions:
1. Preheat oven to 375°F (190°C).
2. Cut the eggplants in half lengthwise and scoop out the flesh, leaving about 1/4 inch of flesh on the skin. Chop the scooped out eggplant and set it aside.
3. In a large skillet, heat 2 tablespoons of olive oil over medium heat. Add the onion, garlic, and reserved eggplant flesh and cook for 8-10 minutes or until tender.
4. Stir in the cooked quinoa, feta cheese, parsley, mint, salt, and pepper.
5. Stuff the mixture into the eggplant halves and place them in a baking dish.
6. To make the tomato sauce, in a medium saucepan, heat 1 tablespoon of olive oil over medium heat. Add the onion, garlic, diced tomatoes, oregano, basil, salt.
7. Serve

Nutritional Value: Calories: 301, Fat: 14g, Cholesterol: 21mg, Sodium: 777mg, Carbohydrates: 30g, Protein: 18g

335. Vegetarian Chili Cheese Fries

Prep. Time: 10 minutes **Cooking Time:** 35 minutes **Servings:** 4

Ingredients:
- 2 cups of frozen french fries
- 1 tablespoon of olive oil
- 1 onion, diced
- 2 cloves of garlic, minced
- 1 red bell pepper, diced
- 1 can of black beans, rinsed and drained
- 1 can of diced tomatoes
- 1 tablespoon of chili powder
- 1 teaspoon of ground cumin
- 1/4 teaspoon of cayenne pepper (optional)
- Salt and pepper to taste
- 1 cup of shredded cheddar cheese
- Fresh cilantro or parsley for garnish
- sour cream or plain yogurt as topping (optional)

Instructions:
1. Preheat oven to 425°F (220°C).
2. Spread the frozen french fries on a baking sheet and bake for 25-30 minutes or until crispy and golden.
3. In a large skillet, heat the olive oil over medium heat. Add the onion, garlic, and red bell pepper and cook for 2-3 minutes or until softened.
4. Stir in the black beans, diced tomatoes, chili powder, cumin, and cayenne pepper (if using) and cook for an additional 5-7 minutes or until heated through.
5. Season with salt and pepper to taste.
6. Once the french fries are done, remove them from the oven, and turn the oven on to broil.
7. Spread the black bean mixture over the french fries and top with shredded cheddar cheese.
8. Broil for 2-3 minutes or until the cheese is melted and bubbly.
9. Garnish and serve

Nutritional Value: Calories: 422, Fat: 36g, Cholesterol: 12mg, Sodium: 201mg, Carbohydrates: 34g, Protein: 19g

336. Pan-Seared Portobello Mushrooms With Balsamic Glaze

Prep. Time: 10 minutes **Cooking Time:** 20 minutes **Servings:** 4

Ingredients:
- 4 large Portobello mushroom caps, gills removed
- 2 tbsp olive oil
- Salt and pepper to taste
- 1/4 cup balsamic vinegar
- 2 tbsp brown sugar
- 2 cloves of garlic, minced

- 1 tbsp fresh thyme leaves

Instructions:
1. Heat a large skillet over medium-high heat.
2. Brush the mushroom caps with olive oil and season with salt and pepper.
3. Add the mushrooms, gill side up, to the skillet.
4. Cook for about 6-8 minutes, or until the mushrooms are tender and starting to release their liquid.
5. Turn the mushrooms over and cook for an additional 2-3 minutes.
6. Remove the mushrooms from the skillet and set them aside.
7. In a small saucepan, combine the balsamic vinegar, brown sugar, garlic, and thyme. Bring the mixture to a boil, then reduce the heat to a simmer.
8. Cook for about 8-10 minutes or until the glaze has thickened.
9. Return the mushrooms to the skillet and spoon the glaze over the mushrooms.
10. Cook for an additional 1-2 minutes or until the glaze is heated through.
11. Serve the mushrooms immediately, garnished with additional thyme if desired.
12. Serve the Pan-Seared Portobello Mushrooms with Balsamic Glaze as a side dish or as a main course with a salad or over pasta or rice.

Nutritional Value: Calories: 235, Fat: 18g, Cholesterol: 12mg, Sodium: 281mg, Carbohydrates: 28g, Protein: 19g

337. Vegetable And Cashew Korma

Prep. Time: 10 minutes **Cooking Time:** 30 minutes **Servings:** 5

Ingredients:
- 2 tablespoons of vegetable oil
- 1 onion, diced
- 2 cloves of garlic, minced
- 1 tablespoon of ginger, grated
- 1 cup of diced vegetables (such as carrots, potatoes, bell peppers, and zucchini)
- 2 tablespoons of korma curry paste
- 1 teaspoon of ground cumin
- 1 teaspoon of ground coriander
- 1/4 teaspoon of turmeric
- 1/4 teaspoon of cayenne pepper (optional)
- 1 cup of coconut milk
- 1/2 cup of cashews, soaked and blended into a paste
- Salt and pepper to taste
- Fresh cilantro for garnish
- Cooked rice or naan bread for serving

Instructions:
1. In a large pot or Dutch oven, heat the oil over medium heat. Add the onion, garlic, and ginger and cook for 2-3 minutes or until softened.
2. Stir in the diced vegetables, korma curry paste, cumin, coriander, turmeric, and cayenne pepper (if using) and cook for 1-2 minutes or until fragrant.
3. Stir in the coconut milk and cashew paste, bring to a simmer.
4. Reduce the heat to low and let it cook for 20-25 minutes or until the vegetables are tender.
5. Season with salt and pepper to taste.
6. Garnish with fresh cilantro and serve over rice or with naan bread.

Nutritional Value: Calories: 252, Fat: 18g, Cholesterol: 10mg, Sodium: 2441mg, Carbohydrates: 29g, Protein: 9g

338. Vegetarian Lentil And Vegetable Pot Pie

Prep. Time: 45 minutes **Cooking Time:** 45 minutes **Servings:** 6

Ingredients:
- 1 cup dried green or brown lentils
- 2 cups water
- 2 tbsp vegetable oil
- 1 onion, diced
- 2 cloves of garlic, minced
- 2 cups diced mixed vegetables (carrots, potatoes, peas, corn)
- 1 tsp thyme
- 1 tsp rosemary
- Salt and pepper to taste
- 1 cup vegetable broth
- 1/4 cup all-purpose flour
- 3 cups puff pastry, thawed
- 1 egg, beaten (for egg wash)

Instructions:
1. Rinse the lentils and add them to a pot with 2 cups of water. Bring to a boil and then reduce the heat to a simmer. Cook for about 20-25 minutes, or until lentils are tender. Drain any excess water.
2. In a skillet over medium heat, add the vegetable oil and sauté the onion and garlic until softened.
3. Add the mixed vegetables, thyme, rosemary, salt, and pepper and sauté for an additional 5 minutes.
4. Stir in the cooked lentils and vegetable broth, bring to a simmer and let it cook for 5 minutes.
5. Stir in the flour and cook for an additional 2-3 minutes.
6. Pour the mixture into a 9-inch pie dish.
7. Preheat the oven to 375°F (190°C)
8. Roll out the puff pastry sheet on a lightly floured surface.
9. Place the pastry sheet on top of the mixture, pressing the edges to seal.
10. Brush the pastry with the beaten egg.
11. Cut a few slits in the top of the

Nutritional Value: Calories: 198, Fat: 8g, Cholesterol: 12mg, Sodium: 281mg, Carbohydrates: 35g, Protein: 21g

339. Black Bean And Sweet Potato Enchiladas

Prep. Time: 20 minutes **Cooking Time:** 40 minutes **Servings:** 8

Ingredients:
- 2 tablespoons of vegetable oil
- 1 onion, diced
- 2 cloves of garlic, minced
- 1 teaspoon of ground cumin
- 1/2 teaspoon of dried oregano
- 1/4 teaspoon of cayenne pepper (optional)
- 1 can of black beans, rinsed and drained
- 1 large sweet potato, peeled and diced
- Salt and pepper to taste
- 8 corn tortillas
- 2 cups of enchilada sauce
- 1 cup of shredded cheddar cheese
- Fresh cilantro or scallions for garnish
- sour cream or plain yogurt as topping (optional)

Instructions:
1. Preheat oven to 375°F (190°C).
2. In a large skillet, heat the oil over medium heat. Add the onion, garlic, cumin, oregano, and cayenne pepper (if using) and cook for 2-3 minutes or until softened.
3. Stir in the black beans and sweet potato and cook for 10-15 minutes or until the sweet potato is tender. Season with salt and pepper to taste.
4. Spread about 1/4 cup of enchilada sauce on the bottom of a 9x13 inch baking dish.
5. Place a spoonful of the black bean and sweet potato mixture on each tortilla, roll it up and place it seam side down in the baking dish.

6. Pour the remaining enchilada sauce over the top of the enchiladas, and sprinkle with shredded cheese.
7. Bake for 20-25 minutes or until the cheese is melted and the enchiladas are heated through.
8. Garnish with fresh cilantro or scallions, and serve with sour cream or plain yogurt on the side if desired.

Nutritional Value: Calories: 350, Fat: 14g, Carbohydrates: 43g, Protein: 12g, Fiber: 8g, Iron: 2mg.

340. Tomato And Eggplant Gratin

Prep. Time: 20 minutes **Cooking Time:** 40 minutes **Servings:** 4
Ingredients:
- 2 medium eggplants, sliced into 1/4-inch rounds
- Salt and pepper to taste
- 2 tbsp olive oil
- 3 cloves of garlic, minced
- 2 cups diced tomatoes
- 1/4 cup grated Parmesan cheese
- 1/4 cup breadcrumbs
- 2 tbsp chopped fresh basil

Instructions:
1. Preheat the oven to 375°F (190°C).
2. Layer the eggplant slices in a colander, sprinkling each layer with salt. Let them sit for 30 minutes to release the bitter liquid. Rinse and pat dry.
3. Heat the olive oil in a large skillet over medium heat.
4. Add the eggplant slices and sauté for about 5-7 minutes on each side, or until they are golden brown and tender.
5. Remove the eggplant slices from the skillet and set them aside.
6. Add the garlic to the skillet and sauté for 1-2 minutes.
7. Add the diced tomatoes, bring the mixture to a simmer and let it cook for 10-15 minutes.
8. Season the tomato mixture with salt and pepper.
9. Spread half of the eggplant slices in an even layer in the bottom of a 9-inch baking dish.
10. Spread half of the tomato mixture over the eggplant.
11. Repeat the layers with the remaining eggplant slices and tomato mixture.
12. In a small bowl, mix together the Parmesan cheese, breadcrumbs, and basil.
13. Sprinkle the mixture on top of the gratin.
14. Bake for 25 minutes

Nutritional Value: Calories: 188, Fat: 12g, Cholesterol: 13mg, Sodium: 541mg, Carbohydrates: 28g, Protein: 19g

341. Vegetable And Lentil Soup

Prep. Time: 15 minutes **Cooking Time:** 45 minutes **Servings:** 6
Ingredients:
- 2 tablespoons of olive oil
- 1 onion, diced
- 2 cloves of garlic, minced
- 2 cups of diced vegetables (such as carrots, potatoes, celery, bell peppers)
- 1 cup of green or brown lentils, rinsed and picked over
- 1 teaspoon of dried thyme
- 1 teaspoon of dried rosemary
- 1/4 teaspoon of cayenne pepper (optional)
- 8 cups of vegetable or chicken broth
- Salt and pepper to taste
- Fresh parsley or cilantro for garnish

Instructions:
1. In a large pot or Dutch oven, heat the oil over medium heat. Add the onion and garlic and cook for 2-3 minutes or until softened.

2. Stir in the diced vegetables, lentils, thyme, rosemary, and cayenne pepper (if using) and cook for 1-2 minutes or until fragrant.
3. Add the broth and bring to a simmer.
4. Reduce the heat to low and let it cook for 30-40 minutes or until the lentils and vegetables are tender.
5. Season with salt and pepper to taste.
6. Garnish with fresh parsley or cilantro and serve.

Nutritional Value: Calories: 260, Fat: 8g, Carbohydrates: 36g, Protein: 12g, Fiber: 12g, Iron: 4mg.

342. Vegetarian Lentil And Vegetable Curry

Prep. Time: 20 minutes **Cooking Time:** 25 minutes **Servings:** 5
Ingredients:
- 1 cup dried green or brown lentils
- 2 cups water
- 2 tbsp vegetable oil
- 1 onion, diced
- 2 cloves of garlic, minced
- 1 tbsp ginger, grated
- 1 tsp cumin powder
- 1 tsp coriander powder
- 1 tsp turmeric powder
- 1 tsp garam masala powder
- Salt and pepper to taste
- 2 cups diced mixed vegetables (carrots, potatoes, bell peppers, peas)
- 1 can (14 oz) diced tomatoes
- 1 cup coconut milk
- Fresh cilantro leaves (for garnish)

Instructions:
1. Rinse the lentils and add them to a pot with 2 cups of water. Bring to a boil and then reduce the heat to a simmer. Cook for about 20-25 minutes, or until lentils are tender. Drain any excess water.
2. In a large pot or Dutch oven, heat the oil over medium heat.
3. Add the onion, garlic, and ginger and sauté until softened, about 5 minutes.
4. Add the cumin, coriander, turmeric, garam masala powder, salt, and pepper and cook for an additional 2-3 minutes.
5. Stir in the mixed vegetables, diced tomatoes, and coconut milk. Bring the mixture to a boil and then reduce the heat to a simmer.
6. Cover and let it cook for 15-20 minutes, or until the vegetables are tender.
7. Stir in the cooked lentils and cook for an additional 5 minutes.
8. Adjust the seasoning if needed.
9. Garnish with fresh cilantro before serving.
10. Serve the Vegetarian Lentil and Vegetable Curry over rice or with naan bread for a complete meal.

Nutritional Value: Calories: 393, Fat: 24g, Cholesterol: 0mg, Sodium: 312mg, Carbohydrates: 34g, Protein: 16g.

343. Vegetable And Lentil Curry Pot Pie

Prep. Time: 20 minutes **Cooking Time:** 40 minutes **Servings:** 8
Ingredients:
- 2 tablespoons of vegetable oil
- 1 onion, diced
- 2 cloves of garlic, minced
- 2 cups of diced vegetables (such as carrots, potatoes, bell peppers)
- 1 cup of green or brown lentils, rinsed and picked over
- 2 tablespoons of curry powder
- 1 teaspoon of ground cumin
- 1 teaspoon of ground coriander

- 1/4 teaspoon of turmeric
- 1/4 teaspoon of cayenne pepper (optional)
- 2 cups of vegetable or chicken broth
- Salt and pepper to taste
- 2 sheets of puff pastry, thawed
- 1 egg, beaten

Instructions:
1. Preheat oven to 400°F (200°C).
2. In a large pot or Dutch oven, heat the oil over medium heat. Add the onion and garlic and cook for 2-3 minutes or until softened.
3. Stir in the diced vegetables, lentils, curry powder, cumin, coriander, turmeric, and cayenne pepper (if using) and cook for 1-2 minutes or until fragrant.
4. Stir in the broth and bring to a simmer.
5. Reduce the heat to low and let it cook for 30-40 minutes or until the lentils and vegetables are tender.
6. Season with salt and pepper to taste.
7. Transfer the curry mixture to a 9x13 inch baking dish, and top with puff pastry, tucking the edges into the sides of the dish.
8. Brush the top of the puff pastry with beaten egg.
9. Bake for 25-30 minutes or until the puff pastry is golden brown and puffed.

Nutritional Value: Calories: 400, Fat: 20g, Carbohydrates: 42g, Protein: 12g, Fiber: 10g, Iron: 4mg.

344. Vegetable Jalfrezi

Prep. Time: 10 minutes **Cooking Time:** 30 minutes **Servings:** 4
Total Time: 40 minutes, **Prep. Time:** 10 minutes, **Cooking Time:** 30 minutes **Servings:** 4
Ingredients:
- 2 tablespoons of vegetable oil
- 1 onion, sliced
- 2 cloves of garlic, minced
- 1 tablespoon of ginger, grated
- 1 green bell pepper, sliced
- 1 red bell pepper, sliced
- 1 cup of diced vegetables (such as carrots, potatoes, zucchini)
- 1 teaspoon of ground cumin
- 1 teaspoon of ground coriander
- 1/4 teaspoon of turmeric
- 1/4 teaspoon of cayenne pepper (optional)
- 1 can of diced tomatoes
- 1 cup of frozen peas
- Salt and pepper to taste
- Fresh cilantro for garnish
- Cooked rice or naan bread for serving

Instructions:
1. In a large skillet or wok, heat the oil over medium-high heat. Add the onion, garlic, and ginger and cook for 2-3 minutes or until softened.
2. Stir in the bell peppers and diced vegetables, cumin, coriander, turmeric, and cayenne pepper (if using) and cook for an additional 2-3 minutes or until fragrant.
3. Stir in the diced tomatoes and peas, bring to a simmer.
4. Reduce the heat to low and let it cook for 15-20 minutes or until the vegetables are tender and the sauce is thickened.
5. Season with salt and pepper to taste.
6. Garnish with fresh cilantro and serve over rice or with naan bread.
7. Jalfrezi is a spicy dish, if you prefer a milder dish you can reduce the amount of cayenne pepper or eliminate it.

Nutritional Value: Calories: 322, Fat: 13g, Cholesterol: 14mg, Sodium: 266mg, Carbohydrates: 38g, Protein: 24g

345. Vegetarian Lentil And Vegetable Curry Pie

Prep. Time: 45 minutes **Cooking Time:** 45 minutes **Servings:** 6
Ingredients:
- 1 cup dried green or brown lentils
- 2 cups water
- 2 tbsp vegetable oil
- 1 onion, diced
- 2 cloves of garlic, minced
- 1 tbsp ginger, grated
- 1 tsp cumin powder
- 1 tsp coriander powder
- 1 tsp turmeric powder
- 1 tsp garam masala powder
- Salt and pepper to taste
- 2 cups diced mixed vegetables (carrots, potatoes, bell peppers, peas)
- 1 can (14 oz) diced tomatoes
- 1 cup coconut milk
- 1 sheet of puff pastry, thawed
- Egg wash (1 beaten egg mixed with 1 tbsp water)
- Fresh cilantro leaves (for garnish)

Instructions:
1. Rinse the lentils and add them to a pot with 2 cups of water. Bring to a boil and then reduce the heat to a simmer. Cook for about 20-25 minutes, or until lentils are tender. Drain any excess water.
2. In a large pot or Dutch oven, heat the oil over medium heat.
3. Add the onion, garlic, and ginger and sauté until softened, about 5 minutes.
4. Add the cumin, coriander, turmeric, garam masala powder, salt, and pepper and cook for an additional 2-3 minutes.
5. Stir in the mixed vegetables, diced tomatoes, and coconut milk. Bring the mixture to a boil and then reduce the heat to a simmer.
6. Cover and let it cook for 15-20 minutes, or until the vegetables are tender.
7. Stir in the cooked lentils and cook for an additional 5 minutes.
8. Adjust the seasoning if needed.
9. Preheat the oven to 375°F (190°C).
10. Roll out the puff pastry sheet on a lightly floured surface.
11. Place the lentil and vegetable mixture into a 9-inch pie dish.
12. Place the puff pastry sheet on top of the mixture, pressing the edges to seal.
13. Brush the pastry with egg wash.
14. Bake for 25-30 minutes or until the pastry is golden brown.
15. Let it cool for 5 minutes before serving

Nutritional Value: Calories: 320, Fat: 26g, Cholesterol: 14mg, Sodium: 311mg, Carbohydrates: 38g, Protein: 24g

346. Vegetable And Paneer Tikka Masala

Prep. Time: 15 minutes **Cooking Time:** 30 minutes **Servings:** 4
Ingredients:
- 2 tablespoons of vegetable oil
- 1 onion, finely chopped
- 2 cloves of garlic, minced
- 1 tablespoon of ginger, grated
- 1 tablespoon of tomato paste
- 1 teaspoon of ground cumin
- 1 teaspoon of ground coriander
- 1/2 teaspoon of garam masala
- 1/4 teaspoon of turmeric
- 1/4 teaspoon of cayenne pepper (optional)
- 1 can of diced tomatoes
- 1 cup of diced vegetables (such as bell peppers, carrots, and cauliflower)
- 1 cup of cubed paneer cheese
- 1 cup of heavy cream
- Salt and pepper to taste

- Fresh cilantro for garnish
- Cooked rice or naan bread for serving

Instructions:
1. In a large skillet or pot, heat the oil over medium heat. Add the onion, garlic, and ginger and cook for 2-3 minutes or until softened.
2. Stir in the tomato paste, cumin, coriander, garam masala, turmeric, and cayenne pepper (if using) and cook for an additional 1-2 minutes or until fragrant.
3. Stir in the diced tomatoes and diced vegetables, bring to a simmer.
4. Add the cubed paneer cheese and heavy cream, stir to combine.
5. Let it cook for 10-15 minutes or until the sauce thickens and the vegetables are tender.
6. Season with salt and pepper to taste.
7. Garnish with fresh cilantro and serve over rice or with naan bread.
8. This dish is typically a bit spicy, you can adjust the cayenne pepper to your liking.

Nutritional Value: Calories: 470, Fat: 38g, Carbohydrates: 15g, Protein: 18g, Fiber: 4g, Iron: 2mg.

347. Vegetable And Lentil Dal

Prep. Time: 20 minutes **Cooking Time:** 25 minutes **Servings:** 5

Ingredients:
- 1 cup dried green or brown lentils
- 2 cups water
- 2 tbsp vegetable oil
- 1 onion, diced
- 2 cloves of garlic, minced
- 1 tbsp ginger, grated
- 1 tsp cumin seeds
- 1 tsp mustard seeds
- 1 tsp turmeric powder
- 1 tsp garam masala powder
- Salt and pepper to taste
- 2 cups diced mixed vegetables (carrots, potatoes, bell peppers, peas)
- 1 can (14 oz) diced tomatoes
- 1 cup coconut milk
- Fresh cilantro leaves (for garnish)

Instructions:
1. Rinse the lentils and add them to a pot with 2 cups of water. Bring to a boil and then reduce the heat to a simmer. Cook for about 20-25 minutes, or until lentils are tender. Drain any excess water.
2. In a large pot or Dutch oven, heat the oil over medium heat.
3. Add the cumin seeds and mustard seeds and cook until they start to pop.
4. Add the onion, garlic, and ginger and sauté until softened, about 5 minutes.
5. Add the turmeric, garam masala powder, salt, and pepper and cook for an additional 2-3 minutes.
6. Stir in the mixed vegetables, diced tomatoes, and coconut milk. Bring the mixture to a boil and then reduce the heat to a simmer.
7. Cover and let it cook for 15-20 minutes, or until the vegetables are tender.
8. Stir in the cooked lentils and cook for an additional 5 minutes.
9. Adjust the seasoning if needed.
10. Garnish with fresh cilantro before serving.
11. Serve the Vegetable and Lentil Dal over rice or with naan bread for a complete meal.

Nutritional Value: Calories: 393, Fat: 24g, Cholesterol: 0mg, Sodium: 312mg, Carbohydrates: 34g, Protein: 16g

348. Vegetable And Paneer Biryani

Prep. Time: 20 minutes **Cooking Time:** 40 minutes **Servings:** 6

Ingredients:
- 1 cup Basmati rice
- 2 cups water
- 2 tbsp vegetable oil
- 1 onion, diced
- 2 cloves of garlic, minced
- 1 tbsp ginger, grated
- 1 tsp cumin powder
- 1 tsp coriander powder
- 1 tsp turmeric powder
- 1 tsp garam masala powder
- Salt and pepper to taste
- 2 cups diced mixed vegetables (carrots, potatoes, bell peppers, peas)
- 1 can (14 oz) diced tomatoes
- 1 cup vegetable broth
- 1 cup crumbled paneer cheese
- 1/4 cup chopped fresh cilantro (for garnish)

Instructions:
1. Rinse the rice and add it to a pot with 2 cups of water. Bring to a boil and then reduce the heat to a simmer. Cover and cook for about 18-20 minutes, or until the rice is tender.
2. In a large pot or Dutch oven, heat the oil over medium heat.
3. Add the onion, garlic, and ginger and sauté until softened, about 5 minutes.
4. Add the cumin, coriander, turmeric, garam masala powder, salt, and pepper and cook for an additional 2-3 minutes.
5. Stir in the mixed vegetables, diced tomatoes, and vegetable broth. Bring the mixture to a boil and then reduce the heat to a simmer.
6. Cover and let it cook for 15-20 minutes, or until the vegetables are tender.
7. Stir in the cooked rice and crumbled paneer cheese, mix well.
8. Adjust the seasoning if needed.
9. Garnish with fresh cilantro before serving.

Nutritional Value: Calories: 288, Fat: 14g, Cholesterol: 4mg, Sodium: 211mg, Carbohydrates: 28g, Protein: 9g

349. Vegetable And Lentil Frittata

Prep. Time: 10 minutes **Cooking Time:** 20 minutes **Servings:** 4

Ingredients:
- 8 eggs
- 1/4 cup of milk
- Salt and pepper to taste
- 2 tablespoons of olive oil
- 1 onion, diced
- 2 cloves of garlic, minced
- 2 cups of diced vegetables (such as bell peppers, zucchini, mushrooms, spinach)
- 1/2 cup of cooked green or brown lentils
- 1/4 cup of grated cheese (optional)
- Fresh herbs for garnish (such as parsley or chives)

Instructions:
1. In a large bowl, whisk together the eggs, milk, salt, and pepper.
2. In a large skillet, heat the olive oil over medium heat. Add the onion and garlic and cook for 2-3 minutes or until softened.
3. Add the diced vegetables and cook for an additional 2-3 minutes or until they start to soften.
4. Stir in the cooked lentils.
5. Pour the egg mixture over the vegetables and lentils.
6. Cook the frittata for 2-3 minutes or until the eggs start to set around the edges.
7. Sprinkle grated cheese on top if using.
8. Place the skillet under the broiler and cook for 2-3 minutes or until the top is golden and the eggs are set.

9. Garnish with fresh herbs before serving.
10. You can customize this recipe with your favorite vegetables and lentils, you can also add some spices or herbs for extra flavor.

Nutritional Value: Calories: 250, Fat: 18g, Carbohydrates: 8g, Protein: 14g, Fiber: 4g, Iron: 4mg.

350. Vegetable And Lentil Chili

Prep. Time: 15 minutes **Cooking Time:** 85 minutes **Servings:** 6
Ingredients:
- 1 tablespoon of olive oil
- 1 medium onion (chopped)
- 2 cloves of garlic (minced)
- 1 red bell pepper (chopped)
- 1 green bell pepper (chopped)
- 1 teaspoon of ground cumin
- 1 teaspoon of dried oregano
- 1 teaspoon of smoked paprika
- 1/2 teaspoon of cayenne pepper (optional)
- 2 cups of vegetable broth
- 1 (14.5 oz) can diced tomatoes
- 1 (15 oz) can black beans (drained and rinsed)
- 1 (15 oz) can kidney beans (drained and rinsed)
- 1 cup of uncooked green or brown lentils (rinsed)
- Salt and pepper (to taste)
- Optional toppings: sour cream, shredded cheddar cheese, chopped green onions or cilantro

Instructions:
1. In a large pot, heat the olive oil over medium heat. Add the onion, garlic, and bell peppers and cook until softened, about 5-7 minutes.
2. Stir in the cumin, oregano, paprika, and cayenne pepper (if using) and cook for an additional 1-2 minutes.
3. Add the vegetable broth, diced tomatoes, black beans, kidney beans, and lentils.
4. Bring the mixture to a boil, then reduce the heat and let it simmer, covered, for about 1 hour or until the lentils are tender.
5. Season with salt and pepper to taste.
6. Serve the chili in bowls and top with sour cream, shredded cheese, green onions, or cilantro, if desired.

Nutritional Value: Calories: 305, Fat: 3g, Protein: 18g, Carbohydrates: 54g, Fiber: 15g, Cholesterol: 0mg, Sodium: 556mg.

351. Vegetable And Lentil Stew

Prep. Time: 15 minutes **Cooking Time:** 45 minutes **Servings:** 4
Ingredients:
- 2 tablespoons of olive oil
- 1 onion, diced
- 2 cloves of garlic, minced
- 2 cups of diced vegetables (such as carrots, potatoes, celery, and bell peppers)
- 1 cup of green or brown lentils, rinsed and picked over
- 1 teaspoon of ground cumin
- 1 teaspoon of ground coriander
- 1/4 teaspoon of turmeric
- 1/4 teaspoon of cayenne pepper (optional)
- 1 can of diced tomatoes
- 2 cups of vegetable or chicken broth
- Salt and pepper to taste
- Fresh cilantro or parsley for garnish
- Cooked rice or bread for serving

Instructions:
1. In a large pot or Dutch oven, heat the oil over medium heat. Add the onion and garlic and cook for 2-3 minutes or until softened.

2. Stir in the diced vegetables, lentils, cumin, coriander, turmeric, and cayenne pepper (if using) and cook for 1-2 minutes or until fragrant.
3. Stir in the diced tomatoes and broth, bring to a simmer.
4. Reduce the heat to low, cover and let it cook for 35-40 minutes or until the lentils and vegetables are tender and the sauce is thickened.
5. Season with salt and pepper to taste.
6. Garnish with fresh cilantro or parsley before serving.
7. Serve with cooked rice or bread.
8. You can add more vegetables or spices to this recipe, depending on your preferences.

Nutritional Value: Calories: 300, Fat: 9g, Carbohydrates: 46g, Protein: 12g, Fiber: 14g, Iron: 4mg.

352. Vegetable And Lentil Curry

Prep. Time: 15 minutes **Cooking Time:** 45 minutes **Servings:** 4
Ingredients:
- 2 tablespoons of vegetable oil
- 1 onion, diced
- 2 cloves of garlic, minced
- 2 cups of diced vegetables (such as carrots, potatoes, bell peppers, and eggplant)
- 1 cup of green or brown lentils, rinsed and picked over
- 1 teaspoon of ground cumin
- 1 teaspoon of ground coriander
- 1/2 teaspoon of ground turmeric
- 1/4 teaspoon of cayenne pepper (optional)
- 1 can of diced tomatoes or 2 cups of tomato puree
- 2 cups of vegetable broth
- Salt and pepper to taste
- Fresh cilantro or parsley for garnish
- Cooked rice or naan bread for serving

Instructions:
1. In a large pot or Dutch oven, heat the oil over medium heat. Add the onion and garlic and cook for 2-3 minutes or until softened.
2. Stir in the diced vegetables, lentils, cumin, coriander, turmeric, and cayenne pepper (if using) and cook for 1-2 minutes or until fragrant.
3. Stir in the diced tomatoes or tomato puree and broth, bring to a simmer.
4. Reduce the heat to low, cover and let it cook for 35-40 minutes or until the lentils and vegetables are tender and the sauce is thickened.
5. Season with salt and pepper to taste.
6. Garnish with fresh cilantro or parsley before serving.
7. Serve with cooked rice or naan bread.
8. You can add more vegetables or spices to this recipe, depending on your preferences.

Nutritional Value: Calories: 300, Fat: 9g, Carbohydrates: 46g, Protein: 12g, Fiber: 14g, Iron: 4mg.

353. Vegetable And Lentil Lasagna

Prep. Time: 30 minutes **Cooking Time:** 45 minutes **Servings:** 8
Ingredients:
- 1 tablespoon of olive oil
- 1 medium onion (chopped)
- 2 cloves of garlic (minced)
- 1 cup of sliced mushrooms
- 1 zucchini (sliced)
- 1 eggplant (sliced)
- 1 teaspoon of dried basil
- 1 teaspoon of dried oregano
- Salt and pepper (to taste)

- 1 (15 oz) can of crushed tomatoes
- 1/2 cup of uncooked green or brown lentils (rinsed)
- 1 cup of vegetable broth
- 12 lasagna noodles
- 1 cup of ricotta cheese
- 1 cup of shredded mozzarella cheese
- 1/4 cup of grated Parmesan cheese

Instructions:
1. Preheat the oven to 375°F (190°C).
2. In a large pan, heat the olive oil over medium heat. Add the onion, garlic, mushrooms, zucchini, eggplant, basil, oregano, and a pinch of salt and pepper. Cook until the vegetables are tender, about 8-10 minutes.
3. Stir in the crushed tomatoes, lentils, and vegetable broth. Bring to a simmer and cook for about 10-15 minutes or until the lentils are tender.
4. Cook the lasagna noodles according to the package instructions until al dente. Drain and rinse with cold water.
5. In a mixing bowl, combine the ricotta cheese, 1/2 cup of mozzarella cheese, and 1/4 cup of Parmesan cheese.
6. Spread a thin layer of the vegetable and lentil mixture on the bottom of a 9x13 inch baking dish.
7. Place 3 lasagna noodles on top of the vegetable mixture. Spread a third of the cheese mixture over the noodles. Repeat the layers two more times, ending with a layer of the cheese mixture.
8. Sprinkle the remaining 1/2 cup of mozzarella cheese on top.
9. Cover the baking dish with foil and bake for 25 minutes. Then remove the foil and bake for an additional 15-20 minutes or until the cheese is golden brown and bubbly.
10. Let it cool for a few minutes before slicing and serving.

Nutritional Value: Calories: 312, Fat: 10g, Protein: 17g, Carbohydrates: 38g, Fiber: 7g, Cholesterol: 32mg, Sodium: 380mg.

354. Vegetable And Lentil Enchiladas

Prep. Time: 20 minutes **Cooking Time:** 25 minutes **Servings:** 4

Ingredients:
- 1 tablespoon of vegetable oil
- 1 onion, diced
- 2 cloves of garlic, minced
- 2 cups of diced vegetables (such as zucchini, bell peppers, and mushrooms)
- 1 cup of green or brown lentils, rinsed and picked over
- 1 teaspoon of ground cumin
- 1 teaspoon of ground coriander
- 1/2 teaspoon of ground turmeric
- 1/4 teaspoon of cayenne pepper (optional)
- 1 can of enchilada sauce
- Salt and pepper to taste
- 8-10 corn tortillas
- 1 cup of shredded cheese (cheddar or Monterey jack)
- Fresh cilantro or parsley for garnish
- Sour cream or guacamole for serving

Instructions:
1. Preheat the oven to 375 F (190 C)
2. In a skillet, heat the oil over medium heat. Add the onion and garlic and cook for 2-3 minutes or until softened.
3. Stir in the diced vegetables, lentils, cumin, coriander, turmeric, and cayenne pepper (if using) and cook for 5-7 minutes or until the vegetables are tender. Season with salt and pepper to taste.
4. Spread a thin layer of enchilada sauce on the bottom of a 9x13 inch baking dish.

171

5. To assemble the enchiladas, spoon about 2 tablespoons of the vegetable and lentil mixture onto each tortilla, roll it up and place it seam-side down in the baking dish.
6. Pour the remaining enchilada sauce over the top of the enchiladas and sprinkle with shredded cheese.
7. Bake for 25 minutes or until the cheese is melted and the enchiladas are heated through.
8. Garnish with fresh cilantro or parsley before serving.
9. Serve with sour cream or guacamole.
10. You can add more vegetables or spices to this recipe, depending on your preferences.

Nutritional Value: Calories: 300, Fat: 9g, Carbohydrates: 46g, Protein: 12g, Fiber: 14g, Iron: 4mg.

355. Vegetable And Lentil Burrito Bowls

Prep. Time: 15 minutes **Cooking Time:** 30 minutes **Servings:** 4

Ingredients:
- 1 tablespoon of olive oil
- 1 medium onion (chopped)
- 2 cloves of garlic (minced)
- 1 red bell pepper (chopped)
- 1 yellow bell pepper (chopped)
- 1 teaspoon of ground cumin
- 1 teaspoon of chili powder
- 1 teaspoon of smoked paprika
- Salt and pepper (to taste)
- 1 cup of uncooked green or brown lentils (rinsed)
- 2 cups of vegetable broth
- 1 cup of corn
- 1 cup of diced tomatoes
- 1/2 cup of chopped cilantro
- 4 cups of cooked brown rice
- Optional toppings: shredded cheddar cheese, sour cream, diced avocado, salsa

Instructions:
1. In a large pot, heat the olive oil over medium heat. Add the onion, garlic, bell peppers, cumin, chili powder, and smoked paprika, and season with salt and pepper. Cook until the vegetables are softened, about 5-7 minutes.
2. Stir in the lentils, vegetable broth, corn and diced tomatoes. Bring the mixture to a boil, then reduce the heat and let it simmer for about 20-25 minutes or until the lentils are tender.
3. Stir in the cilantro.
4. To assemble the burrito bowls, divide the cooked rice among four bowls. Top with the lentil mixture and any desired toppings.
5. Serve and enjoy!

Nutritional Value: Calories: 361, Fat: 6g, Protein: 14g, Carbohydrates: 62g, Fiber: 12g, Cholesterol: 0mg, Sodium: 437mg.

356. Vegetable And Lentil Stir-Fry

Prep. Time: 10 minutes **Cooking Time:** 20 minutes **Servings:** 4

Ingredients:
- 1 tablespoon of vegetable oil
- 1 onion, diced
- 2 cloves of garlic, minced
- 1 cup of diced vegetables (such as carrots, bell peppers, broccoli, and mushrooms)
- 1 cup of green or brown lentils, rinsed and picked over
- 1 teaspoon of soy sauce
- 1 teaspoon of rice vinegar
- 1 teaspoon of sesame oil
- 1 teaspoon of grated ginger

- 1/4 teaspoon of red pepper flakes (optional)
- Salt and pepper to taste
- 2 cups of cooked rice for serving
- Sesame seeds and green onions for garnish

Instructions:
1. In a skillet, heat the oil over high heat. Add the onion and garlic and cook for 2-3 minutes or until softened.
2. Stir in the diced vegetables and cook for 2-3 minutes or until the vegetables are tender.
3. Stir in the lentils, soy sauce, rice vinegar, sesame oil, ginger, and red pepper flakes (if using) and cook for 5-7 minutes or until the lentils are tender. Season with salt and pepper to taste.
4. Serve the stir-fry over cooked rice.
5. Garnish with sesame seeds and green onions.
6. You can add more vegetables or spices to this recipe, depending on your preferences.

Nutritional Value: Calories: 400, Fat: 8g, Carbohydrates: 72g, Protein: 14g, Fiber: 14g, Iron: 4mg.

357. Vegetable And Lentil Korma

Prep. Time: 20 minutes **Cooking Time:** 40 minutes **Servings:** 4

Ingredients:
- 1 tablespoon of vegetable oil
- 1 medium onion (chopped)
- 2 cloves of garlic (minced)
- 1 tablespoon of ginger (minced)
- 1 teaspoon of ground cumin
- 1 teaspoon of ground coriander
- 1 teaspoon of turmeric
- 1/2 teaspoon of cinnamon
- 1/4 teaspoon of ground cloves
- Salt and pepper (to taste)
- 1 cup of uncooked green or brown lentils (rinsed)
- 2 cups of vegetable broth
- 1 (14 oz) can of diced tomatoes
- 1 cup of frozen mixed vegetables (peas, carrots, green beans)
- 1/2 cup of coconut milk
- 1/4 cup of chopped cilantro
- Optional toppings: yogurt, sliced almonds

Instructions:
1. In a large pot, heat the vegetable oil over medium heat. Add the onion, garlic, and ginger and cook until softened, about 5-7 minutes.
2. Stir in the cumin, coriander, turmeric, cinnamon, cloves, and a pinch of salt and pepper. Cook for an additional 1-2 minutes.
3. Stir in the lentils, vegetable broth, diced tomatoes, mixed vegetables, and bring the mixture to a simmer.
4. Reduce the heat to low and let it simmer, covered, for about 20-25 minutes or until the lentils are tender.
5. Stir in the coconut milk and cilantro.
6. Adjust the seasoning to taste and serve over rice or with naan bread. Garnish with yogurt and sliced almonds, if desired.

Nutritional Value: Calories: 305, Fat: 12g, Protein: 12g, Carbohydrates: 36g, Fiber: 9g, Cholesterol: 0mg, Sodium: 556mg.

358. Vegetable And Lentil Curry Pie

Prep. Time: 30 minutes **Cooking Time:** 60 minutes **Servings:** 6

Ingredients:
- 2 tablespoons of vegetable oil
- 1 onion, diced

- 2 cloves of garlic, minced
- 1 tablespoon of grated ginger
- 1 teaspoon of ground cumin
- 1 teaspoon of ground coriander
- 1 teaspoon of ground turmeric
- 1/4 teaspoon of cayenne pepper (optional)
- Salt and pepper to taste
- 2 cups of diced vegetables (such as carrots, bell peppers, broccoli, and mushrooms)
- 1 cup of green or brown lentils, rinsed and picked over
- 1 can of diced tomatoes
- 1 cup of vegetable broth
- 1/4 cup of heavy cream
- 1/4 cup of chopped fresh cilantro or parsley
- 1 sheet of puff pastry, thawed
- 1 egg, beaten

Instructions:

1. Preheat the oven to 375 degrees F (190 degrees C).
2. In a skillet, heat the oil over high heat. Add the onion, garlic and ginger and cook for 2-3 minutes or until softened.
3. Stir in the cumin, coriander, turmeric, cayenne pepper (if using) and cook for 1-2 minutes or until fragrant. Season with salt and pepper to taste.
4. Stir in the diced vegetables and cook for 2-3 minutes or until the vegetables are tender.
5. Stir in the lentils, diced tomatoes, vegetable broth and bring to a boil. Reduce the heat and simmer for 15-20 minutes or until the lentils are tender. Stir in the heavy cream and cilantro or parsley.
6. Place the mixture in a baking dish and top it with the puff pastry sheet. Brush the pastry with the beaten egg.
7. Bake for 25-30 minutes or until the pastry is golden brown and puffed.
8. Let cool for 10 minutes before serving.
9. You can add more vegetables or spices to this recipe, depending on your preferences.

Nutritional Value: Calories: 400, Fat: 20g, Carbohydrates: 40g, Protein: 12g, Fiber: 8g, Iron: 4mg

Desserts

359. Vegan Chocolate Mousse

Prep. Time: 15 minutes **Cooking Time:** None
Servings: 4
Ingredients:
- 1 can of full-fat coconut milk, chilled overnight
- 1/2 cup of powdered sugar
- 1/2 cup of unsweetened cocoa powder
- 1 teaspoon of vanilla extract
- 1/4 teaspoon of salt
- Vegan chocolate chips or grated chocolate for garnish (optional)

Instructions:
1. Open the can of chilled coconut milk and scoop out the solidified cream on top, leaving the watery liquid behind.
2. In a large mixing bowl, beat the coconut cream with an electric mixer until it becomes smooth and fluffy.
3. Gradually add the powdered sugar, cocoa powder, vanilla extract, and salt and continue to beat until well combined.
4. Divide the mousse into 4 serving glasses or ramekins.
5. Cover and chill in the refrigerator for at least 10 minutes or until set.
6. Garnish with vegan chocolate chips or grated chocolate before serving, if desired.
7. Note: If you don't have access to canned coconut milk or prefer not to use it, you can also use soaked cashews or silken tofu as a base for this recipe.

Nutritional Value: Calories: 260, Fat: 24g, Carbohydrates: 15g, Protein: 2g, Fiber: 2g.

360. Fruit Sorbet

Prep. Time: 10 minutes **Freezing Time:** 4 hours
Servings: 4
Ingredients:
- 3 cups of fresh fruit of your choice (such as berries, peaches, mango, pineapple)
- 1/2 cup of sugar
- 1/2 cup of water
- 1 tablespoon of lemon juice
- Optional: 1 tablespoon of liqueur or 1/2 teaspoon of vanilla extract

Instructions:
1. In a small saucepan, bring the sugar and water to a boil. Stir until the sugar is dissolved. Remove from heat and let it cool.
2. In a blender or food processor, puree the fruit until smooth. Add the sugar syrup, lemon juice, and any optional ingredients (such as liqueur or vanilla extract) and blend until well combined.
3. Pour the mixture into a shallow container and freeze for about 2 hours.
4. Remove the mixture from the freezer and use a fork to break up any ice crystals that have formed. Return to the freezer and repeat this process every 30 minutes for 2 more hours or until the sorbet is frozen and has a smooth consistency.
5. To serve, scoop the sorbet into bowls or glasses and let it sit at room temperature for a few minutes to soften before eating.

Nutritional Value: Calories: 156, Fat: 0g, Protein: 0g, Carbohydrates: 39g, Fiber: 1g, Cholesterol: 0mg, Sodium: 1mg.

361. Vegan Apple Crisp

Prep. Time: 10 minutes, **Cooking Time:** 40 minutes **Servings:** 6
Ingredients:
- 6 cups of peeled and thinly sliced apples
- 3/4 cup of rolled oats
- 1/2 cup of all-purpose flour
- 1/2 cup of brown sugar
- 1/4 cup of vegan butter or coconut oil

- 1 teaspoon of ground cinnamon
- 1/4 teaspoon of salt

Instructions:
1. Preheat the oven to 375°F (190°C).
2. In a large mixing bowl, combine the sliced apples, cinnamon, and 1/4 cup of brown sugar.
3. In another mixing bowl, combine the rolled oats, all-purpose flour, 1/4 cup of brown sugar, vegan butter or coconut oil, and salt. Mix until crumbly.
4. Transfer the apple mixture to a 9x9 inch (23x23 cm) baking dish.
5. Spread the oat mixture over the apples.
6. Bake for 40 minutes, or until the top is golden brown and the apples are tender.
7. Serve warm with your favorite vegan ice cream or whipped cream (optional)
8. Note: You can also use other types of fruit such as peaches, pears, or berries in place of the apples.

Nutritional Value: Calories: 250, Fat: 9g, Carbohydrates: 43g, Protein: 2g, Fiber: 3g.

362. Vegan Chocolate Chip Cookies

Prep. Time: 10 minutes **Cooking Time:** 15 minutes **Servings:** 12

Ingredients:
- 1 cup of all-purpose flour
- 1/2 teaspoon of baking powder
- 1/2 teaspoon of baking soda
- 1/2 teaspoon of salt
- 1/2 cup of vegan butter, at room temperature
- 1/2 cup of granulated sugar
- 1/4 cup of brown sugar
- 1 teaspoon of vanilla extract
- 1 flax egg (1 tablespoon of ground flaxseed mixed with 3 tablespoons of water)
- 1 cup of vegan chocolate chips

Instructions:
1. Preheat the oven to 350°F (175°C). Line a baking sheet with parchment paper.
2. In a medium bowl, whisk together the flour, baking powder, baking soda, and salt.
3. In a large bowl, beat together the vegan butter, granulated sugar, brown sugar, and vanilla extract until light and fluffy.
4. Add the flax egg and mix until well combined.
5. Gradually add the dry ingredients to the wet ingredients and mix until a dough forms.
6. Fold in the chocolate chips.
7. Use a cookie scoop or spoon to drop dough balls onto the prepared baking sheet.
8. Bake for 12-15 minutes or until the edges are golden brown.
9. Remove from the oven and let the cookies cool on the baking sheet for 5 minutes before transferring them to a wire rack to cool completely.

Nutritional Value: Calories: 168, Fat: 10g, Protein: 2g, Carbohydrates: 20g, Fiber: 1g, Cholesterol: 0mg, Sodium: 126mg.

363. Vegan Carrot Cake

Prep. Time: 30 minutes **Cooking Time:** 1 hour **Servings:** 8-10

Ingredients:
- 2 cups of all-purpose flour
- 2 teaspoons of baking powder
- 1 teaspoon of baking soda
- 1 teaspoon of ground cinnamon
- 1/2 teaspoon of ground nutmeg
- 1/4 teaspoon of ground ginger
- 1/4 teaspoon of ground allspice
- 1/2 teaspoon of salt
- 1 1/2 cups of grated carrots
- 1/2 cup of unsweetened applesauce

- 1/2 cup of almond milk
- 1/2 cup of maple syrup
- 1/2 cup of brown sugar
- 1/4 cup of vegetable oil
- 2 teaspoons of vanilla extract
- Frosting:
- 1 cup of vegan cream cheese
- 1/4 cup of vegan butter
- 1 teaspoon of vanilla extract
- 2 cups of powdered sugar
- 1/4 teaspoon of ground cinnamon

Instructions:
1. Preheat the oven to 350°F (175°C). Grease and flour a 9-inch round cake pan.
2. In a medium bowl, whisk together the flour, baking powder, baking soda, cinnamon, nutmeg, ginger, allspice, and salt.
3. In a separate large bowl, mix together the grated carrots, applesauce, almond milk, maple syrup, brown sugar, vegetable oil, and vanilla extract.
4. Gradually add the dry ingredients to the wet ingredients and mix until well combined.
5. Pour the batter into the prepared cake pan and bake for 50-60 minutes or until a toothpick inserted into the center comes out clean.
6. Let the cake cool in the pan for 10 minutes before transferring it to a wire rack to cool completely.
7. While the cake is cooling, prepare the frosting. In a large bowl, beat together the vegan cream cheese, vegan butter, vanilla extract, powdered sugar, and cinnamon until smooth and creamy.
8. Once the cake has cooled completely, frost the top of the cake with the cream cheese frosting.
9. Serve and enjoy.

Nutritional Value (per serving, without frosting): Calories: 264, Fat: 10g, Protein: 3g, Carbohydrates: 42g, Fiber: 2g, Cholesterol: 0mg, Sodium: 308mg.

364. Vegan Banana Bread

Prep. Time: 15 minutes **Cooking Time:** 45 minutes **Servings:** 8

Ingredients:
- 3 ripe bananas
- 1/3 cup of melted vegan butter or coconut oil
- 3/4 cup of granulated sugar
- 1 teaspoon of vanilla extract
- 1 teaspoon of baking powder
- 1 teaspoon of baking soda
- 1/2 teaspoon of salt
- 1 1/2 cups of all-purpose flour
- 1/2 cup of almond milk or other plant-based milk
- 1/2 cup of chopped walnuts (optional)

Instructions:
1. Preheat the oven to 350°F (175°C). Grease a 9x5 inch (23x13 cm) loaf pan with cooking spray or vegan butter.
2. In a large mixing bowl, mash the bananas.
3. Stir in the melted vegan butter or coconut oil, granulated sugar, and vanilla extract.
4. In a separate mixing bowl, whisk together the baking powder, baking soda, salt and all-purpose flour.
5. Add the dry ingredients to the wet ingredients, alternating with the almond milk, stirring until just combined.
6. Fold in the chopped walnuts, if using.
7. Pour the batter into the prepared loaf pan.
8. Bake for 45-50 minutes or until a toothpick inserted into the center comes out clean.
9. Allow to cool in the pan for 10 minutes before removing from the pan and

allowing to cool completely on a wire rack.
Nutritional Value: Calories: 250, Fat: 9g, Carbohydrates: 43g, Protein: 2g, Fiber: 3g.

365. Vegan Strawberry Cheesecake

Prep. Time: 30 minutes **Cooking Time:** 1 hour **Cooling Time:** 3 hours **Servings:** 8
Ingredients:
- Crust:
- 1 cup of graham cracker crumbs
- 1/4 cup of vegan butter, melted
- 2 tablespoons of granulated sugar
- Filling:
- 1 cup of raw cashews, soaked in water for at least 2 hours
- 1/2 cup of vegan cream cheese, at room temperature
- 1/2 cup of granulated sugar
- 1/4 cup of lemon juice
- 1/4 cup of full-fat coconut milk
- 1 teaspoon of vanilla extract
- 1/4 teaspoon of salt
- 1 cup of fresh strawberries, hulled and quartered

Instructions:
1. Preheat the oven to 350°F (175°C). Grease a 9-inch springform pan.
2. To make the crust, mix together the graham cracker crumbs, melted vegan butter, and sugar in a small bowl. Press the mixture into the bottom of the prepared pan.
3. To make the filling, drain the soaked cashews and add them to a blender or food processor. Add the vegan cream cheese, sugar, lemon juice, coconut milk, vanilla extract, and salt. Blend until smooth and creamy.
4. Pour the filling over the crust and smooth the top.
5. Dot the top of the cheesecake with the quartered strawberries.
6. Place the cheesecake in the oven and bake for 50-60 minutes or until the edges are golden brown and the center is set.
7. Remove the cheesecake from the oven and let it cool on a wire rack for 1 hour. Then refrigerate it for at least 2 hours or until completely chilled.
8. Serve chilled and enjoy!

Nutritional Value: Calories: 357, Fat: 24g, Protein: 5g, Carbohydrates: 30g, Fiber: 2g, Cholesterol: 0mg, Sodium: 193mg

366. Vegan Pumpkin Pie

Prep. Time: 20 minutes, **Cooking Time:** 1 hour and 10 minutes **Servings:** 8
Ingredients:
- 1 pre-made pie crust or homemade vegan pie crust
- 1 can of pumpkin puree
- 3/4 cup of granulated sugar
- 1 teaspoon of ground cinnamon
- 1/2 teaspoon of ground ginger
- 1/4 teaspoon of ground nutmeg
- 1/4 teaspoon of salt
- 1/2 cup of coconut cream
- 1/2 cup of almond milk
- 2 tablespoons of cornstarch
- 1 teaspoon of vanilla extract

Instructions:
1. Preheat the oven to 425°F (220°C).
2. Roll out the pie crust and place it in a 9-inch (23cm) pie dish. Trim the edges and prick the bottom of the crust with a fork.
3. In a large mixing bowl, combine the pumpkin puree, granulated sugar, cinnamon, ginger, nutmeg and salt. Mix until well blended.

4. In a separate mixing bowl, whisk together the coconut cream, almond milk, cornstarch and vanilla extract.
5. Add the wet ingredients to the pumpkin mixture and stir until well combined.
6. Pour the mixture into the prepared crust.
7. Place the pie on a baking sheet and bake for 15 minutes.
8. Reduce the oven temperature to 350°F (175°C) and bake for another 55-60 minutes or until the filling is set.
9. Allow to cool to room temperature before refrigerating for at least 2 hours before serving.

Nutritional Value: Calories: 240, Fat: 10g, Carbohydrates: 35g, Protein: 3g, Fiber: 3g.

367. Vegan Chocolate Brownies

Prep. Time: 15 minutes **Cooking Time:** 30 minutes **Servings:** 9

Ingredients:
- 1 cup of all-purpose flour
- 1/2 cup of cocoa powder
- 1 teaspoon of baking powder
- 1/2 teaspoon of salt
- 1/2 cup of vegan butter, melted
- 1 cup of granulated sugar
- 1/4 cup of unsweetened applesauce
- 1 teaspoon of vanilla extract
- 1/2 cup of vegan chocolate chips

Instructions:
1. Preheat the oven to 350°F (175°C). Grease an 8x8 inch square baking pan.
2. In a medium bowl, whisk together the flour, cocoa powder, baking powder, and salt.
3. In a large bowl, mix together the melted vegan butter, sugar, applesauce, and vanilla extract.
4. Gradually add the dry ingredients to the wet ingredients and mix until well combined.
5. Fold in the chocolate chips.
6. Pour the batter into the prepared pan and spread it out evenly.
7. Bake for 25-30 minutes or until a toothpick inserted into the center comes out clean.
8. Remove from the oven and let the brownies cool for 15 minutes before slicing and serving.

Nutritional Value: Calories: 210, Fat: 12g, Protein: 2g, Carbohydrates: 26g, Fiber: 2g, Cholesterol: 0mg, Sodium: 111mg.

368. Vegan Lemon Bars

Prep. Time: 30 minutes, **Cooking Time:** 1 hour **Servings:** 12

Ingredients:
- For the crust:
- 1 and 1/2 cups of all-purpose flour
- 1/2 cup of powdered sugar
- 1/2 cup of vegan butter, chilled and cubed
- For the filling:
- 1 cup of granulated sugar
- 3 tablespoons of cornstarch
- 1/4 cup of lemon zest
- 1/2 cup of fresh lemon juice
- 1/4 cup of aquafaba (the liquid from a can of chickpeas)
- 1/4 cup of vegan butter

Instructions:
1. Preheat the oven to 350°F (175°C) and grease a 9x13 inch (23x33cm) baking dish.
2. In a mixing bowl, combine the flour and powdered sugar.
3. Add the chilled and cubed vegan butter to the flour mixture and use a pastry cutter or your fingers to combine until the mixture resembles coarse crumbs.
4. Press the crust mixture into the bottom of the prepared baking dish and bake for 20-25 minutes or until lightly golden brown.

5. While the crust is baking, prepare the filling. In a separate mixing bowl, whisk together the granulated sugar, cornstarch and lemon zest.
6. Stir in the lemon juice and aquafaba.
7. Cut the vegan butter into small cubes and add it to the mixture, stir until well combined.
8. Once the crust is done baking, pour the filling mixture over the hot crust.
9. Return the baking dish to the oven and bake for an additional 25-30 minutes or until the filling is set.
10. Allow to cool completely before refrigerating for at least 2 hours before cutting into squares.

Nutritional Value: Calories: 250, Fat: 10g, Carbohydrates: 40g, Protein: 2g, Fiber: 1g.

369. Vegan Pecan Pie

Prep. Time: 30 minutes **Cooking Time:** 1 hour **Servings:** 8
Ingredients:
- Crust:
- 1 1/4 cups of all-purpose flour
- 1/4 teaspoon of salt
- 1/4 cup of vegan butter, chilled and diced
- 2-3 tablespoons of ice water
- Filling:
- 1 cup of pecans, chopped
- 1/2 cup of maple syrup
- 1/4 cup of brown sugar
- 2 tablespoons of cornstarch
- 1/4 cup of unsweetened plant-based milk
- 1 teaspoon of vanilla extract
- 1/4 teaspoon of salt
- 1/4 cup of vegan butter

Instructions:
1. To make the crust, in a medium bowl, whisk together the flour and salt. Cut in the vegan butter using a pastry cutter or your fingers until the mixture resembles coarse crumbs. Gradually add the ice water, 1 tablespoon at a time, until the dough comes together. Form the dough into a ball, wrap it in plastic wrap, and refrigerate for at least 30 minutes.
2. Preheat the oven to 375°F (190°C). Roll the dough out on a lightly floured surface to fit a 9-inch pie dish. Press the dough into the dish and trim the edges.
3. To make the filling, in a medium saucepan, combine the pecans, maple syrup, brown sugar, cornstarch, plant-based milk, vanilla extract, salt, and vegan butter. Cook over medium heat, stirring frequently, until the mixture thickens and comes to a boil.
4. Pour the filling into the crust and spread it out evenly.

Nutritional Value: Calories: 340, Fat: 18g, Cholesterol: 4mg, Sodium: 230mg, Carbohydrates: 38g, Protein: 19g

370. Vegan Blueberry Cobbler

Prep. Time: 20 minutes **Cooking Time:** 40 minutes **Servings:** 6
Ingredients:
- For the filling:
- 4 cups of fresh blueberries
- 1/2 cup of granulated sugar
- 2 tablespoons of cornstarch
- 1 tablespoon of lemon juice
- 1 teaspoon of vanilla extract
- For the topping:
- 1 cup of all-purpose flour
- 1/2 cup of granulated sugar
- 1/2 cup of vegan butter, chilled and cubed
- 1 teaspoon of baking powder
- 1/4 teaspoon of salt
- 1/4 cup of unsweetened non-dairy milk

Instructions:
1. Preheat the oven to 375°F (190°C) and grease a 8x8 inch (20x20cm) baking dish.

2. In a mixing bowl, combine the blueberries, sugar, cornstarch, lemon juice and vanilla extract. Pour the mixture into the prepared baking dish.
3. In another mixing bowl, combine the flour, sugar, baking powder and salt. Add the chilled and cubed vegan butter and use a pastry cutter or your fingers to combine until the mixture resembles coarse crumbs.
4. Stir in the non-dairy milk until the dough comes together.
5. Drop spoonfuls of the dough over the blueberry mixture in the baking dish.
6. Bake for 40-45 minutes or until the topping is golden brown and the filling is bubbling.
7. Serve warm with a scoop of vegan ice cream on top, if desired.

Nutritional Value: Calories: 300, Fat: 12g, Carbohydrates: 49g, Protein: 2g, Fiber: 3g.

371. Vegan Ice Cream

Prep. Time: 10 minutes **Freezing Time:** 4 hours
Servings: 4
Ingredients:
- 1 can of full-fat coconut milk
- 1/2 cup of granulated sugar
- 1 teaspoon of vanilla extract
- 1/4 teaspoon of salt
- 2 cups of frozen berries or any other fruit of your choice

Instructions:
1. In a blender or food processor, combine the coconut milk, sugar, vanilla extract, and salt. Blend until the sugar has dissolved.
2. Add the frozen berries or fruit and blend until smooth.
3. Pour the mixture into a loaf pan or any other container that can be frozen.
4. Cover the container with plastic wrap or a lid, and freeze for at least 4 hours or until firm.
5. Before serving, remove from the freezer and let it sit at room temperature for 5-10 minutes to soften.
6. Scoop the ice cream into bowls or cones and enjoy.
7. Note: If the ice cream is too hard after freezing, you can blend or process it again for a few seconds to make it creamier.

Nutritional Value: Calories: 250, Fat: 24g, Carbohydrates: 16g, Protein: 2g, Fiber: 2g.

372. Vegan Tiramisu

Prep. Time: 30 minutes **Cooling Time:** 4 hours
Servings: 8
Ingredients:
- 1 cup of aquafaba (the liquid from a can of chickpeas)
- 3/4 cup of granulated sugar
- 1 teaspoon of cream of tartar
- 1 teaspoon of vanilla extract
- 1/4 cup of strong brewed coffee
- 1/4 cup of Amaretto or marsala wine
- 2 cups of vegan mascarpone cheese
- 1/2 cup of powdered sugar
- 1/4 cup of unsweetened cocoa powder

Instructions:
1. In a large mixing bowl, whisk the aquafaba, granulated sugar, cream of tartar, and vanilla extract until stiff peaks form.
2. In a separate bowl, mix together the coffee and Amaretto or marsala wine.
3. In another bowl, mix together the vegan mascarpone cheese, powdered sugar, and cocoa powder until smooth.
4. Carefully fold the mascarpone mixture into the aquafaba mixture.

5. Dip ladyfingers in the coffee mixture and layer them in the bottom of an 8x8 inch dish.
6. Spread half of the mascarpone mixture over the ladyfingers.
7. Repeat the layers of ladyfingers and mascarpone mixture.
8. Cover and refrigerate for at least 4 hours to allow the flavors to meld together.
9. Dust the top of the tiramisu with cocoa powder before serving.

Nutritional Value: Calories: 338, Fat: 20g, Protein: 2g, Carbohydrates: 33g, Fiber: 1g, Cholesterol: 0mg, Sodium: 113mg

373. Vegan Crème Brûlée

Prep. Time: 15 minutes **Cooking Time:** 45 minutes **Servings:** 4

Ingredients:
- 1 can of full-fat coconut milk
- 1/2 cup of granulated sugar
- 1 teaspoon of vanilla extract
- 1/4 teaspoon of salt
- 2 tablespoons of cornstarch
- 4 tablespoons of granulated sugar for caramelizing

Instructions:
1. Preheat the oven to 300 degrees F (150 degrees C).
2. In a medium saucepan, combine the coconut milk, sugar, vanilla extract, and salt. Cook over medium heat, stirring occasionally, until the sugar has dissolved.
3. In a small bowl, mix the cornstarch with 2 tablespoons of water to make a slurry.
4. Slowly pour the cornstarch mixture into the saucepan with the coconut milk, whisking constantly to prevent lumps from forming.
5. Bring the mixture to a simmer, and continue to cook for 2-3 minutes, or until thickened.
6. Remove the saucepan from the heat and let it cool for a few minutes.
7. Pour the mixture into 4 ramekins or small oven-proof dishes.
8. Place the ramekins in a baking dish and pour enough hot water into the dish to come halfway up the sides of the ramekins.
9. Bake the custards for 45 minutes or until set.
10. Remove the ramekins from the baking dish and let them cool to room temperature. Once cool, refrigerate for at least 2 hours or until chilled.
11. Before serving, sprinkle 1 tablespoon of sugar on top of each custard. Using a kitchen torch, caramelize the sugar until it forms a golden-brown crust.
12. Note: If you don't have a kitchen torch, you can place the custards under the broiler for a minute or two, being careful not to burn the sugar.

Nutritional Value: Calories: 310, Fat: 27g, Carbohydrates: 20g, Protein: 2g, Fiber: 0g.

374. Vegan Peanut Butter Cups

Prep. Time: 10 minutes **Freezing Time:** 20 minutes **Servings:** 12

Ingredients:
- Chocolate Layer:
- 1 cup of vegan chocolate chips
- 2 tablespoons of vegan butter
- Peanut Butter Layer:
- 1/2 cup of smooth peanut butter
- 2 tablespoons of powdered sugar
- 1 tablespoon of vegan butter

Instructions:
1. Line a 12-cup muffin tin with paper liners.

2. In a small saucepan, melt the vegan chocolate chips and vegan butter over low heat, stirring constantly until smooth.
3. Using a small cookie scoop or spoon, divide the melted chocolate among the paper liners, spreading it evenly to cover the bottom of each cup. Place the tin in the freezer for 10 minutes to set the chocolate.
4. In a medium bowl, mix together the peanut butter, powdered sugar, and vegan butter until smooth.
5. Remove the muffin tin from the freezer and divide the peanut butter mixture among the chocolate cups, spreading it evenly on top of the chocolate.
6. Return the tin to the freezer for another 10 minutes to set the peanut butter layer.
7. Remove the peanut butter cups from the tin and store them in an airtight container in the refrigerator until ready to serve.

Nutritional Value: Calories: 164, Fat: 14g, Protein: 3g, Carbohydrates: 8g, Fiber: 1g, Cholesterol: 0mg, Sodium: 63mg

375. Vegan Key Lime Pie

Prep. Time: 30 minutes **Cooking Time:** 1 hour
Servings: 8
Ingredients:
- 1 1/2 cups graham cracker crumbs
- 1/4 cup granulated sugar
- 1/2 cup vegan butter, melted
- 1 can (14 oz) full-fat coconut milk
- 1/2 cup freshly squeezed lime juice
- 1/2 cup granulated sugar
- 1/4 cup cornstarch
- 1/4 teaspoon salt
- 1/2 teaspoon lime zest

Instructions:
1. Preheat the oven to 350°F (180°C).
2. In a mixing bowl, combine graham cracker crumbs, sugar, and melted butter. Press the mixture into the bottom of a 9-inch (23 cm) pie dish.
3. Bake the crust for 10 minutes, then set it aside to cool.
4. In a saucepan, whisk together the coconut milk, lime juice, sugar, cornstarch, and salt. Cook over medium heat, whisking constantly, until the mixture thickens and comes to a boil. Remove from heat and stir in the lime zest.
5. Pour the filling into the cooled crust.
6. Cover the pie with plastic wrap and refrigerate for at least 1 hour to set.

Nutritional Value: Calories: 390, Fat: 28g, Cholesterol: 14mg, Sugar: 8g , Carbohydrates: 32g, Protein: 11g

376. Vegan Chocolate Truffles

Prep. Time: 20 minutes **Cooling Time:** 1 hour and 40 minutes **Servings:** 18-20 truffles
Ingredients:
- 1 cup of vegan chocolate chips
- 1/4 cup of unsweetened plant-based milk
- 1/4 cup of vegan butter
- 1 teaspoon of vanilla extract
- 1/4 cup of cocoa powder or crushed nuts for rolling

Instructions:
1. In a medium saucepan, melt the vegan chocolate chips, plant-based milk, vegan butter, and vanilla extract over low heat, stirring constantly until smooth.
2. Remove the pan from heat and let the mixture cool for 10 minutes.
3. Cover and refrigerate the mixture for at least 1 hour or until firm.
4. Using a small cookie scoop or spoon, form the mixture into 1-inch balls.
5. Place the cocoa powder or crushed nuts in a shallow dish. Roll the truffles in the cocoa powder or nuts, coating them evenly.

6. Place the truffles on a baking sheet lined with parchment paper and refrigerate for at least 30 minutes to set.
7. Store the truffles in an airtight container in the refrigerator until ready to serve.

Nutritional Value (per truffle): Calories: 96, Fat: 8g, Protein: 1g, Carbohydrates: 6g, Fiber: 1g, Cholesterol: 0mg, Sodium: 27mg

377. Vegan Almond Butter Cups

Prep. Time: 15 minutes **Cooking Time:** 15 minutes **Servings:** 12

Ingredients:
- 1 cup vegan chocolate chips
- 1/4 cup almond butter
- 1 teaspoon coconut oil
- flaky sea salt, for sprinkling

Instructions:
1. In a double boiler or a heatproof bowl set over a pot of simmering water, melt the chocolate chips.
2. Line a 12-cup muffin tin with paper liners or silicone cups.
3. Once the chocolate is melted, remove from heat and stir in the almond butter and coconut oil.
4. Using a small cookie scoop or spoon, divide the chocolate mixture among the muffin cups.
5. Sprinkle a pinch of sea salt on top of each cup.
6. Place the muffin tin in the refrigerator for at least 15 minutes to set.
7. Once set, remove the cups from the tin and enjoy!

Nutritional Value: Calories: 456, Fat: 38g, Cholesterol: 182mg, Sugar 8g, Carbohydrates: 38g, Protein: 19g

378. Vegan Berry Crisp

Prep. Time: 15 minutes **Cooking Time:** 30 minutes **Servings:** 8

Ingredients:
- 4 cups mixed berries (such as blueberries, raspberries, and blackberries)
- 1/4 cup granulated sugar
- 2 tablespoons cornstarch
- 1 teaspoon vanilla extract
- 1 cup rolled oats
- 1/2 cup all-purpose flour
- 1/2 cup brown sugar
- 1/2 teaspoon ground cinnamon
- 1/4 teaspoon salt
- 1/2 cup vegan butter, cut into small cubes

Instructions:
1. Preheat the oven to 375°F (190°C).
2. In a large mixing bowl, toss together the berries, granulated sugar, cornstarch, and vanilla extract.
3. Pour the mixture into a 9-inch square baking dish.
4. In the same bowl, mix together the oats, flour, brown sugar, cinnamon, and salt.
5. Using your fingers or a pastry cutter, work the vegan butter into the oat mixture until the mixture is crumbly.
6. Sprinkle the oat mixture over the berries in the baking dish.
7. Bake the crisp for 30 minutes, or until the topping is golden brown and the filling is bubbly.
8. Let cool for 10 minutes before serving. Serve with vegan ice cream or whipped cream, if desired.

Nutritional Value: Calories: 345, Fat: 26g, Cholesterol: 13mg, Sugar: 9g, Carbohydrates: 22g, Protein: 15g

379. Vegan Apple Pie

Prep. Time: 30 minutes **Cooking Time:** 1 hour **Servings:** 8

Ingredients:
- 2 cups all-purpose flour
- 1/2 cup granulated sugar

- 1/4 teaspoon salt
- 1/2 cup vegan butter, cold and cubed
- 1/4 cup ice water
- 6 cups thinly sliced peeled apples
- 1/4 cup granulated sugar
- 1 teaspoon ground cinnamon
- 1/4 teaspoon nutmeg
- 1 tablespoon cornstarch
- 1 tablespoon fresh lemon juice
- 1 tablespoon vegan butter
- 1 tablespoon coarse sugar (optional)

Instructions:
1. To make the crust, in a large bowl, combine the flour, sugar and salt. Cut in the vegan butter until the mixture resembles coarse crumbs. Gradually add ice water, 1 tablespoon at a time, until dough forms a ball.
2. Divide the dough in half so that one portion is slightly larger than the other. Flatten each portion into a disk and wrap in plastic wrap. Refrigerate for at least 1 hour.
3. Preheat oven to 375°F (190°C).
4. In a large bowl, combine the apples, sugar, cinnamon, nutmeg, cornstarch and lemon juice; toss to coat.
5. On a lightly floured surface, roll the larger portion of dough to fit a 9-in. pie plate. Transfer dough to pie plate. Trim even with rim.
6. Add the apple mixture and dot with vegan butter. Roll remaining dough to a 1/8-in.-thick circle; place over filling. Trim, seal and flute edge. Cut slits in top. Sprinkle with coarse sugar if desired.
7. Place pie on a baking sheet and bake for 50-60 minutes or until crust is golden brown and filling is bubbly.
8. Cool on a wire rack.

Nutritional Value: Calories: 399, Fat: 34g, Cholesterol: 13mg, Sugar: 12g, Carbohydrates: 38g, Protein: 18g

380. Vegan Vanilla Cupcakes

Prep. Time: 10 minutes **Baking Time:** 15 minutes **Servings:** 12 cupcakes

Ingredients:
- 1 and 1/2 cups of all-purpose flour
- 1 cup of granulated sugar
- 1 teaspoon of baking powder
- 1/2 teaspoon of baking soda
- 1/2 teaspoon of salt
- 1 cup of unsweetened plant-based milk
- 1/3 cup of vegetable oil
- 2 tablespoons of white vinegar
- 1 teaspoon of vanilla extract
- Frosting:
- 1/2 cup of vegan butter, at room temperature
- 2 cups of powdered sugar
- 2 tablespoons of unsweetened plant-based milk
- 1 teaspoon of vanilla extract

Instructions:
1. Preheat the oven to 350°F (175°C) and line a 12-cup muffin tin with paper liners.
2. In a large mixing bowl, whisk together the flour, sugar, baking powder, baking soda, and salt.
3. In a separate bowl, mix together the plant-based milk, oil, vinegar, and vanilla extract.
4. Gradually add the wet ingredients to the dry ingredients and mix until just combined.
5. Divide the batter evenly among the muffin cups.
6. Bake for 15-20 minutes or until a toothpick inserted in the center of a cupcake comes out clean.

7. Let the cupcakes cool completely before frosting.
8. To make the frosting, in a medium mixing bowl, beat the vegan butter until light and fluffy. Gradually add the powdered sugar, plant-based milk, and vanilla extract, and beat until smooth.
9. Spread the frosting on top of the cooled cupcakes.

Nutritional Value (per cupcake): Calories: 260, Fat: 12g, Protein: 2g, Carbohydrates: 37g, Fiber: 1g, Cholesterol: 0mg, Sodium: 131mg

381. Vegan Pumpkin Cheesecake

Prep. Time: 15 min **Cooking Time:** 1 hr 15 min **Servings:** 8

Ingredients:
- 1 1/2 cups graham cracker crumbs
- 1/4 cup granulated sugar
- 1/4 cup vegan butter, melted
- 1 1/2 cups raw cashews, soaked in water for at least 4 hours or overnight
- 1/2 cup canned pumpkin puree
- 1/2 cup vegan cream cheese
- 1/4 cup maple syrup
- 2 tbsp lemon juice
- 1 tsp vanilla extract
- 1 tsp pumpkin pie spice
- 1/4 tsp salt

Instructions:
1. Preheat the oven to 350°F (175°C).
2. In a bowl, mix together the graham cracker crumbs, sugar, and melted vegan butter. Press the mixture into the bottom of a 9-inch (23cm) springform pan.
3. Drain the soaked cashews and add them to a blender or food processor with the pumpkin puree, vegan cream cheese, maple syrup, lemon juice, vanilla extract, pumpkin pie spice, and salt. Blend until smooth.
4. Pour the mixture over the crust and smooth out the top.
5. Bake for 45-50 minutes or until the edges are set and the center is slightly jiggly. Let the cheesecake cool for at least 15 minutes before removing it from the springform pan.
6. Chill the cheesecake in the refrigerator for at least 1 hour before serving.

Nutritional Value: Calories: 337, Fat: 25g, Saturated Fat: 7g, Carbohydrates: 26g, Fiber: 2g, Sugar: 16g, Protein: 5g.

382. Vegan Chocolate Cake

Prep. Time: 20 minutes **Baking Time:** 40 minutes **Servings:** 8-10

Ingredients:
- 2 cups of all-purpose flour
- 1 and 3/4 cups of granulated sugar
- 3/4 cup of unsweetened cocoa powder
- 1 teaspoon of baking soda
- 1/2 teaspoon of baking powder
- 1/2 teaspoon of salt
- 1 cup of unsweetened plant-based milk
- 1/2 cup of vegetable oil
- 2 teaspoons of white vinegar
- 2 teaspoons of vanilla extract
- Frosting:
- 1 cup of vegan chocolate chips
- 1/2 cup of unsweetened plant-based milk
- 1/2 cup of vegan butter, at room temperature
- 1 and 1/2 cups of powdered sugar

Instructions:
1. Preheat the oven to 350°F (175°C) and grease two 9-inch round cake pans.
2. In a large mixing bowl, whisk together the flour, sugar, cocoa powder, baking soda, baking powder, and salt.
3. In a separate bowl, mix together the plant-based milk, oil, vinegar, and vanilla extract.

4. Gradually add the wet ingredients to the dry ingredients and mix until just combined.
5. Divide the batter evenly between the prepared pans and smooth the tops.
6. Bake for 35-40 minutes or until a toothpick inserted in the center of a cake comes out clean.
7. Let the cakes cool completely before frosting.
8. To make the frosting, In a medium saucepan, melt the chocolate chips and milk over low heat, stirring constantly until smooth. Remove from heat and let it cool.
9. In a medium mixing bowl, beat the vegan butter until light and fluffy. Gradually add the powdered sugar and chocolate mixture, and beat until smooth.
10. Spread frosting on top of one cake layer and place the other layer on top of it. Then frost the top and sides of the cake.

Nutritional Value: Calories: 198, Fat: 29g, Cholesterol: 14mg, Sugar: 5g, Carbohydrates: 38g, Protein: 16g

383. Vegan Chocolate Pudding

Prep. Time: 15 minutes **Cooking Time:** 0 minutes **Servings:** 4
Ingredients:
- 1 cup almond milk
- 1/2 cup coconut cream
- 1/4 cup cocoa powder
- 1/4 cup maple syrup
- 2 Tbsp cornstarch
- 1 tsp vanilla extract
- 1/4 tsp sea salt

Instructions:
1. In a medium saucepan, whisk together the almond milk, coconut cream, cocoa powder, maple syrup, cornstarch, vanilla extract and sea salt until smooth.
2. Cook over medium heat, whisking constantly, until the mixture comes to a boil and thickens, about 5 minutes.
3. Remove from heat and pour the pudding into 4 bowls or cups.
4. Cover the surface of pudding with plastic wrap to prevent a skin from forming.
5. Refrigerate for at least 30 minutes, or until chilled.
6. Enjoy!

Nutritional Value: Calories: 310, Fat: 14g, Cholesterol: 3mg, Sugar: 9g, Carbohydrates: 22g, Protein: 13g

384. Vegan Oatmeal Cookies

Prep. Time: 10 minutes **Cooking Time:** 10 minutes **Servings:** 12
Ingredients:
- 1 cup all-purpose flour
- 1/2 cup rolled oats
- 1/2 cup brown sugar
- 1/4 cup unsweetened applesauce
- 1/4 cup vegetable oil
- 1 tsp vanilla extract
- 1/2 tsp baking powder
- 1/4 tsp baking soda
- 1/4 tsp salt
- 1/2 cup raisins (optional)
- 1/2 cup chopped nuts (optional)

Instructions:
1. Preheat the oven to 350°F (180°C) and line a baking sheet with parchment paper.
2. In a large bowl, whisk together the flour, oats, brown sugar, baking powder, baking soda, and salt.
3. In a separate bowl, mix together the applesauce, vegetable oil, and vanilla extract.
4. Add the wet ingredients to the dry ingredients and mix until just combined.
5. Stir in raisins or nuts if using.

6. Using a spoon or cookie scoop, drop the dough onto the prepared baking sheet.
7. Bake for 10-12 minutes, or until golden brown.
8. Let the cookies cool on the baking sheet for 5 minutes before transferring them to a wire rack to cool completely.

Nutritional Value: Calories: 304, Fat: 15g, Cholesterol: 2mg, Sugar: 8g, Carbohydrates: 28g, Protein: 20g

385. Vegan Cinnamon Rolls

Prep. Time: 30 minutes **Cooking Time:** 2 hours **Servings:** 12
Ingredients:
- 2 cups all-purpose flour
- 2 cups whole wheat flour
- 1/2 cup granulated sugar
- 1 tablespoon active dry yeast
- 1 teaspoon salt
- 1 cup unsweetened almond milk
- 1/4 cup vegan butter, melted
- 1/4 cup aquafaba (the liquid from a can of chickpeas)
- 1/4 cup ground flaxseed
- 1/2 cup vegan cream cheese
- 1/2 cup vegan butter
- 1/2 cup granulated sugar
- 1 tablespoon ground cinnamon
- 1/4 cup maple syrup

Instructions:
1. In a large mixing bowl, combine the all-purpose flour, whole wheat flour, sugar, yeast, and salt.
2. In a separate bowl, mix together the almond milk, melted vegan butter, aquafaba, and ground flaxseed.
3. Slowly add the wet ingredients to the dry ingredients, mixing until a dough forms. Knead the dough for about 10 minutes.
4. Place the dough in a greased bowl, cover with a towel, and let it rise in a warm place for about 1 hour.
5. In a separate mixing bowl, combine the vegan cream cheese, vegan butter, sugar, and cinnamon.
6. Once the dough has risen, roll it out into a large rectangle on a floured surface. Spread the cream cheese mixture over the dough, leaving about 1/2 inch of space around the edges.
7. Roll the dough up tightly, then cut it into 12 equal pieces.
8. Place the rolls in a greased baking dish, cover with a towel, and let them rise for another 30 minutes.
9. Preheat the oven to 350 degrees F.
10. Once the rolls have risen, bake them for 25-30 minutes, or until golden brown.
11. Remove from the oven and drizzle with maple syrup before serving.

Nutrition Value: Calories: 250 Fat: 12g Saturated Fat: 4g Carbohydrates: 34g Fiber: 3g Sugar: 14g Protein: 4g Sodium: 200mg Cholesterol: 0mg

386. Vegan Peach Cobbler

Prep. Time: 20 minutes **Baking Time:** 40 minutes **Servings:** 8
Ingredients:
- 8 cups of fresh peaches, peeled and sliced
- 1/2 cup of granulated sugar
- 2 tablespoons of cornstarch
- 1 teaspoon of ground cinnamon
- 1/4 teaspoon of salt
- 1 cup of all-purpose flour
- 1/2 cup of granulated sugar
- 1/2 cup of vegan butter, chilled and cubed
- 1 teaspoon of baking powder
- 1/4 teaspoon of salt
- 1/2 cup of unsweetened plant-based milk

Instructions:

1. Preheat the oven to 375°F (190°C) and grease an 8x8 inch baking dish.
2. In a large mixing bowl, mix together the peaches, 1/2 cup of sugar, cornstarch, cinnamon, and 1/4 teaspoon of salt.
3. Pour the mixture into the prepared baking dish.
4. In a separate mixing bowl, mix together the flour, 1/2 cup of sugar, baking powder, and 1/4 teaspoon of salt.
5. Using a pastry cutter or your hands, cut in the vegan butter until the mixture resembles coarse crumbs.
6. Gradually add the plant-based milk and mix until a dough forms.
7. Drop spoonfuls of the dough on top of the peach mixture.
8. Bake for 35-40 minutes or until the top is golden brown and the filling is bubbly.
9. Let the cobbler cool for at least 15 minutes before serving.

Nutritional Value: Calories: 322, Fat: 15g, Protein: 3g, Carbohydrates: 45g, Fiber: 2g, Cholesterol: 0mg, Sodium: 231mg

387. Vegan Lemon Tart

Prep. Time: 20 minutes **Cooking Time:** 50 minutes **Servings:** 8

Ingredients:
- 1 1/4 cup all-purpose flour
- 1/4 cup powdered sugar
- 1/2 cup vegan butter
- 2 tbsp ice water
- 1 cup raw cashews, soaked in water for at least 2 hours
- 1/2 cup coconut cream
- 1/4 cup freshly squeezed lemon juice
- 1/4 cup maple syrup
- 2 tsp grated lemon zest
- 1/4 tsp turmeric powder (optional, for color)
- 1/4 tsp salt
- Vegan whipped cream, for serving (optional)
- Lemon zest, for garnish

Instructions:
1. In a large mixing bowl, combine flour and powdered sugar. Add vegan butter and mix until crumbly. Slowly add ice water and mix until dough comes together.
2. Form dough into a ball, flatten it into a disk, and wrap it in plastic wrap. Refrigerate for at least 30 minutes.
3. Preheat the oven to 375°F (190°C). Roll out dough on a lightly floured surface to about 1/4 inch thickness. Press dough into a 9-inch tart pan, trimming off any excess dough. Prick the bottom of the crust with a fork and bake for 15-20 minutes, or until lightly golden. Let it cool.
4. Drain and rinse the soaked cashews. In a high-speed blender or food processor, blend cashews, coconut cream, lemon juice, maple syrup, lemon zest, turmeric powder (if using), and salt until smooth.
5. Pour the filling into the cooled crust and smooth out the top. Chill in the refrigerator for at least 30 minutes.
6. Preheat the oven to 350°F (175°C). Bake for 20-25 minutes, or until the filling is set. Let it cool completely before serving.
7. Serve with vegan whipped cream and garnish with lemon zest, if desired.

Nutritional Value (per serving, based on 8 **Servings**): Calories: 340 Fat: 25g Carbohydrates: 25g Protein: 5g Fiber: 2g Sugar: 10g

388. Vegan Gingerbread Cookies

Prep. Time: 20 minutes **Baking Time:** 10-12 minutes **Servings:** 12

Ingredients:
- 3 cups of all-purpose flour

- 1 and 1/2 teaspoons of ground ginger
- 1 teaspoon of ground cinnamon
- 1/4 teaspoon of ground nutmeg
- 1/4 teaspoon of ground allspice
- 1/4 teaspoon of ground cloves
- 1/2 teaspoon of baking soda
- 1/4 teaspoon of salt
- 1/2 cup of vegan butter, at room temperature
- 1/2 cup of granulated sugar
- 1/4 cup of molasses
- 1 teaspoon of vanilla extract
- 1/4 cup of unsweetened plant-based milk

Instructions:
1. Preheat the oven to 350°F (175°C) and line a baking sheet with parchment paper.
2. In a medium mixing bowl, whisk together the flour, ginger, cinnamon, nutmeg, allspice, cloves, baking soda, and salt.
3. In a separate mixing bowl, beat the vegan butter and sugar until light and fluffy.
4. Add the molasses and vanilla extract and mix until well combined.
5. Gradually add the dry ingredients to the wet ingredients, mixing until well combined.
6. Gradually add the plant-based milk and mix until a dough forms.
7. Roll the dough out to 1/4 inch thickness on a floured surface.
8. Use cookie cutters to cut out the desired shapes and place them on the prepared baking sheet.
9. Bake for 10-12 minutes or until the edges are firm and the cookies are lightly golden brown.
10. Let the cookies cool on the baking sheet for 5 minutes before transferring them to a wire rack to cool completely.

Nutritional Value (per cookie): Calories: 131, Fat: 5g, Protein: 1g, Carbohydrates: 20g, Fiber: 1g, Cholesterol: 0mg, Sodium: 99mg

389. Vegan Pecan Tart

Prep. Time: 30 minutes **Cooking Time:** 1 hour
Servings: 8
Ingredients:
- 1 1/2 cups all-purpose flour
- 1/2 cup pecan pieces
- 1/4 cup granulated sugar
- 1/4 cup brown sugar
- 1/4 teaspoon salt
- 1/2 cup vegan butter, chilled and diced
- 3 tablespoons ice water
- 1/2 cup maple syrup
- 1/4 cup brown sugar
- 1/4 cup cornstarch
- 1/4 teaspoon salt
- 1 cup unsweetened almond milk
- 1 teaspoon vanilla extract
- 1 cup pecan halves

Instructions:
1. In a food processor, pulse together the flour, pecan pieces, granulated sugar, brown sugar, and salt until the pecans are finely ground.
2. Add the vegan butter and pulse until the mixture resembles coarse crumbs.
3. Slowly add the ice water, 1 tablespoon at a time, until the dough comes together.
4. Press the dough into a 9-inch tart pan with a removable bottom.
5. Chill the crust in the refrigerator for at least 30 minutes.
6. Preheat the oven to 350°F.
7. In a saucepan, whisk together the maple syrup, brown sugar, cornstarch, and salt.
8. Stir in the almond milk and bring to a simmer over medium heat.
9. Cook for 2 minutes, or until thickened.
10. Remove from the heat and stir in the vanilla and pecan halves.
11. Pour the filling into the chilled crust.

12. Bake for 40-45 minutes, or until the crust is golden brown and the filling is bubbly.
13. Let cool to room temperature before serving.

Nutritional Value per serving: Calories: 420, Fat: 31g, Saturated Fat: 4g, Cholesterol: 0mg, Sodium: 150mg, Carbohydrates: 35g, Fiber: 3g, Sugar: 17g, Protein: 4g.

390. Vegan Red Velvet Cake

Prep. Time: 30 minutes **Baking Time:** 30-35 minutes **Servings:** 12
Ingredients:
- 2 and 1/2 cups of all-purpose flour
- 1 and 1/2 cups of granulated sugar
- 1 teaspoon of baking powder
- 1/2 teaspoon of baking soda
- 1/2 teaspoon of salt
- 2 tablespoons of unsweetened cocoa powder
- 1 cup of unsweetened plant-based milk
- 1/2 cup of vegetable oil
- 2 teaspoons of white vinegar
- 1 teaspoon of vanilla extract
- 2 tablespoons of red food coloring
- 1 recipe of vegan cream cheese frosting (optional)

Instructions:
1. Preheat the oven to 350°F (175°C) and grease and flour two 9-inch round cake pans.
2. In a large mixing bowl, whisk together the flour, sugar, baking powder, baking soda, salt, and cocoa powder.
3. In a separate mixing bowl, whisk together the plant-based milk, vegetable oil, vinegar, vanilla extract, and red food coloring.
4. Gradually add the wet ingredients to the dry ingredients, mixing until well combined.
5. Divide the batter evenly between the prepared cake pans.
6. Bake for 30-35 minutes or until a toothpick inserted into the center of the cakes comes out clean.
7. Let the cakes cool in the pans for 10 minutes before transferring them to a wire rack to cool completely.
8. Once the cakes are cool, you can frost them with vegan cream cheese frosting, if desired.

Nutritional Value (per slice): Calories: 408, Fat: 17g, Protein: 3g, Carbohydrates: 61g, Fiber: 1g, Cholesterol: 0mg, Sodium: 213mg

391. Vegan Chocolate Chip Muffins

Prep. Time: 15 minutes, **Cooking Time:** 30 minutes **Servings:** 12 muffins
Ingredients:
- 2 cups all-purpose flour
- 2 teaspoons baking powder
- 1 teaspoon baking soda
- 1/2 teaspoon salt
- 1 teaspoon ground cinnamon
- 1/2 cup granulated sugar
- 1/2 cup brown sugar
- 1/2 cup unsweetened applesauce
- 1/2 cup non-dairy milk
- 1 teaspoon vanilla extract
- 1/2 cup vegan chocolate chips
- 1/2 cup chopped pecans (optional)

Instructions:
1. Preheat the oven to 350°F (175°C) and line a muffin tin with paper liners.
2. In a large mixing bowl, combine the flour, baking powder, baking soda, salt and cinnamon.
3. In a separate mixing bowl, beat the granulated sugar, brown sugar, applesauce, non-dairy milk, and vanilla extract together until well mixed.

4. Pour the wet mixture into the dry mixture and stir until just combined.
5. Fold in the chocolate chips and pecans (if using)
6. Spoon the batter into the muffin cups, filling them about 3/4 of the way full.
7. Bake for 25-30 minutes, or until a toothpick inserted into the center of a muffin comes out clean.
8. Let the muffins cool in the pan for 5 minutes before removing them to a wire rack to cool completely.

392.   Vegan Baked Apple

Prep. Time: 15 minutes, **Cooking Time:** 45 minutes **Servings:** 4
Ingredients:
- 4 apples (peeled and cored)
- 1/4 cup brown sugar
- 1 tsp cinnamon
- 1/4 tsp nutmeg
- 1/4 cup rolled oats
- 1/4 cup flour
- 2 tbsp vegan butter
- 1/4 cup chopped pecans (optional)

Instructions:
1. Preheat oven to 350F (175C).
2. In a small bowl, mix together brown sugar, cinnamon, and nutmeg.
3. In a separate bowl, mix together oats, flour, and vegan butter until crumbly.
4. Stuff each apple with the sugar and spice mixture, then top with the oat mixture and chopped pecans.
5. Place apples in a baking dish and bake for 45 minutes or until apples are tender.
6. Serve warm with vanilla non-dairy ice cream if desired.

Nutritional Value: Calories: 298, Fat: 18g, Cholesterol: 3mg, Sugar: 7g, Carbohydrates: 27g, Protein: 14g

393.   Vegan Chocolate Fondue

Prep. Time: 5 minutes **Cooking Time:** 10 minutes **Servings:** 4
Ingredients:
- 1 cup of vegan semisweet chocolate chips
- 1/2 cup of full-fat coconut milk
- 1 tablespoon of maple syrup (optional)
- 1/2 teaspoon of vanilla extract (optional)
- Fresh fruits, pretzels, cookies, or other dipping items of your choice

Instructions:
1. In a small saucepan, heat the coconut milk over medium heat until hot but not boiling.
2. Remove the saucepan from heat and add the chocolate chips, maple syrup, and vanilla extract (if using) and stir until the chocolate is fully melted and the mixture is smooth.
3. Serve the fondue warm, with your choice of fruits, pretzels, cookies, or other dipping items.

Nutritional Value (per serving, without dipping items): Calories: 187, Fat: 15g, Protein: 2g, Carbohydrates: 12g, Fiber: 2g, Cholesterol: 0mg, Sodium: 15mg

394.   Vegan Rice Pudding

Prep. Time: 15 minutes **Cooking Time:** 30 minutes **Servings:** 4
Ingredients:
- 1 cup uncooked white rice
- 2 cups water
- 1 cup unsweetened almond milk
- 1/2 cup maple syrup
- 1 teaspoon vanilla extract
- 1/4 teaspoon ground cinnamon
- 1/4 teaspoon salt
- 1/4 cup raisins (optional)
- 1/4 cup chopped pecans or almonds (optional)

Instructions:
1. Rinse the rice in a fine-mesh strainer until the water runs clear.
2. In a medium saucepan, combine the rice, water, almond milk, maple syrup, vanilla extract, cinnamon, and salt. Bring to a boil over medium-high heat.
3. Reduce heat to low and cover the pot with a tight-fitting lid. Simmer for 18 to 20 minutes, or until the rice is tender and the liquid has been absorbed.
4. Stir in the raisins, if using, and cook for an additional 2 minutes.
5. Remove from heat and let stand for 5 minutes.
6. Fluff the rice with a fork and stir in the chopped nuts, if using.
7. Serve warm or chilled.

Nutritional Value per serving: Calories: 305, Fat: 3g, Carbohydrates: 64g, Protein: 4g, Fiber: 1g, Sugar: 20g, Sodium: 108mg

395. Vegan Chocolate Banana Bread

Prep. Time: 15 minutes **Cooking Time:** 35 minutes **Servings:** 8
Ingredients:
- 3 ripe bananas
- 1/2 cup unsweetened cocoa powder
- 1/2 cup almond milk
- 1/2 cup maple syrup
- 1/3 cup coconut oil, melted
- 2 tsp vanilla extract
- 1 tsp baking powder
- 1 tsp baking soda
- 1/2 tsp salt
- 1 and 1/2 cups all-purpose flour
- 1 cup vegan chocolate chips

Instructions:
1. Preheat the oven to 350F. Grease a 9x5 inch loaf pan with cooking spray.
2. In a medium bowl, mash the bananas with a fork.
3. In a large mixing bowl, combine the mashed bananas, cocoa powder, almond milk, maple syrup, coconut oil, and vanilla extract. Mix well.
4. In another medium bowl, mix together the baking powder, baking soda, salt, and flour.
5. Gradually add the dry ingredients to the wet ingredients and mix until just combined.
6. Fold in the chocolate chips.
7. Pour the batter into the prepared loaf pan.
8. Bake for 35 minutes, or until a toothpick inserted into the center comes out clean.
9. Let it cool for 10 minutes in the pan and then transfer it to a wire rack to cool completely.

Nutritional Value: Calories: 285, Fat: 14g, Carbohydrates: 39g, Protein: 4g, Fiber: 3g, Sugar: 20g

396. Vegan Chocolate Orange Truffles

Prep. Time: 20 minutes **Cooking Time:** 40 minutes **Servings:** 12
Ingredients:
- 1 cup unsweetened cocoa powder
- 1 cup powdered sugar
- 1/2 cup melted coconut oil
- 1 tsp orange extract
- 1 tsp vanilla extract
- Pinch of salt
- 1/4 cup vegan chocolate chips (optional)
- Orange zest (optional)

Instructions:
1. In a medium bowl, mix together the cocoa powder, powdered sugar, melted coconut oil, orange extract, vanilla extract, and salt until well combined.

2. If desired, fold in vegan chocolate chips and orange zest.
3. Cover the bowl with plastic wrap and chill in the refrigerator for at least 30 minutes, or until firm enough to roll into balls.
4. Once chilled, roll the mixture into 12 equal-sized balls.
5. Store the truffles in the refrigerator until ready to serve.

Nutritional Value: Calories: 326, Fat: 9g, Cholesterol: 0mg, Sugar: 14g, Carbohydrates: 38g, Protein: 19g

397. Vegan Scones

Prep. Time: 10 minutes **Cooking Time:** 20 minutes **Servings:** 8
Ingredients:
- 2 cups all-purpose flour
- 2 tbsp granulated sugar
- 2 tsp baking powder
- 1/2 tsp salt
- 1/2 cup vegan butter, chilled and cubed
- 3/4 cup unsweetened almond milk
- 1 tsp vanilla extract
- 1/2 cup vegan chocolate chips (optional)

Instructions:
1. Preheat the oven to 425°F (220°C) and line a baking sheet with parchment paper.
2. In a large mixing bowl, combine the flour, sugar, baking powder, and salt. Mix well.
3. Add the chilled cubed vegan butter to the dry ingredients and use a pastry cutter or your fingers to mix until the mixture resembles coarse crumbs.
4. In a separate small mixing bowl, combine the almond milk and vanilla extract.
5. Gradually add the wet ingredients to the dry ingredients, stirring with a fork until a dough forms.
6. Fold in the vegan chocolate chips, if using.
7. On a lightly floured surface, roll out the dough to about 1/2 inch thickness.
8. Use a round cookie cutter or a glass to cut out the scones.
9. Place the scones on the prepared baking sheet and bake for 15-20 minutes or until lightly golden brown.
10. Serve warm with vegan butter or jam, if desired.

Nutritional Value: Calories: 156, Protein: 2g, Carbohydrates: 20g, Fat: 8g, Cholesterol: 0mg, Sodium: 158mg, Fiber: 1g, Sugar: 3g

398. Vegan Cheesecake

Prep. Time: 30 minutes **Baking Time:** 1 hour, Cooling Time: 1 hour **Servings:** 10
Ingredients: Crust:
- 1 and 1/2 cups of graham cracker crumbs (or any vegan cookie crumbs)
- 1/4 cup of granulated sugar
- 1/4 cup of melted vegan butter
- Filling:
- 16 oz of vegan cream cheese, at room temperature
- 1 cup of granulated sugar
- 1 teaspoon of vanilla extract
- 1/4 cup of cornstarch or arrowroot powder
- 1/4 cup of plant-based milk

Instructions:
1. Preheat the oven to 325°F (165°C) and grease a 9-inch springform pan.
2. In a medium mixing bowl, combine the graham cracker crumbs, sugar, and melted vegan butter. Press the mixture firmly into the bottom and up the sides of the prepared pan.
3. In a large mixing bowl, beat the vegan cream cheese with an electric mixer on medium speed until smooth.

4. Gradually add the sugar, vanilla extract, cornstarch, and plant-based milk, continuing to beat until well combined.
5. Pour the filling into the crust and smooth the top with a spatula.
6. Bake the cheesecake for 1 hour or until the edges are set and the center is just slightly jiggly.
7. Turn off the oven and let the cheesecake cool inside for 1 hour.
8. After an hour, remove the cheesecake from the oven and let it cool to room temperature. Then, cover and refrigerate for at least 2 hours before slicing and serving.

Nutritional Value: Calories: 394, Fat: 33g, Protein: 6g, Carbohydrates: 25g, Fiber: 1g, Cholesterol: 0mg, Sodium: 312mg

399. Vegan Chocolate Hazelnut Tart

Prep. Time: 15 minutes **Cooking Time:** 15 minutes **Servings:** 6
Ingredients:
- 1 1/2 cups all-purpose flour
- 1/3 cup unsweetened cocoa powder
- 1/3 cup sugar
- 1 tsp baking powder
- 1/4 tsp salt
- 1/2 cup vegan butter, chilled and cubed
- 1/2 cup chopped hazelnuts
- 1/4 cup unsweetened almond milk
- 1 tsp vanilla extract
- 1/2 cup chocolate hazelnut spread
- 1/4 cup chopped hazelnuts, for topping

Instructions:
1. In a large mixing bowl, whisk together the flour, cocoa powder, sugar, baking powder, and salt.
2. Add in the vegan butter and using a pastry cutter or your fingers, mix until the mixture resembles coarse crumbs.
3. Stir in the chopped hazelnuts.
4. In a small bowl, mix together the almond milk and vanilla extract.
5. Add the wet ingredients to the dry ingredients and mix until a dough forms.
6. Preheat the oven to 350°F (175°C).
7. Press the dough into a 9-inch tart pan with a removable bottom.
8. Spread the chocolate hazelnut spread over the crust.
9. Sprinkle the chopped hazelnuts over the top.
10. Bake for 20-25 minutes, or until the crust is golden brown.
11. Let cool before removing from the pan and slicing to serve. Enjoy!

Nutritional Value: Calories: 432, Fat: 38g, Cholesterol: 6mg, Sugar: 9g, Carbohydrates: 36g, Protein: 14g

400. Vegan Apple Tart

Prep. Time: 30 minutes **Cooking Time:** 1 hour **Servings:** 8-10
Ingredients: Crust:
- 2 cups of all-purpose flour
- 1/2 cup of granulated sugar
- 1/2 cup of vegan butter, cold and cubed
- 2 tablespoons of ice water
- Filling:
- 6-8 medium apples, peeled, cored, and thinly sliced
- 1/4 cup of granulated sugar
- 1 teaspoon of ground cinnamon
- 1/4 teaspoon of ground nutmeg
- 1 tablespoon of vegan butter
- 1 tablespoon of cornstarch

Instructions:
1. Preheat the oven to 375°F (190°C)
2. In a large mixing bowl, combine the flour and sugar. Add the vegan butter and mix until the mixture resembles coarse crumbs. Slowly add the ice water, one

tablespoon at a time, until the dough comes together.
3. Roll out the dough on a lightly floured surface to a thickness of about 1/8 inch. Transfer it to a 9-inch tart pan with a removable bottom and press it into the bottom and up the sides of the pan.
4. In a separate mixing bowl, combine the sliced apples, sugar, cinnamon, nutmeg, and vegan butter. Mix until the apples are evenly coated.
5. Spread the apple mixture over the crust, leaving about 1/2 inch of crust around the edges.
6. In a small bowl, mix together the cornstarch with 1 tablespoon of water. Brush the mixture over the apples.
7. Bake for 50-60 minutes or until the crust is golden brown and the apples are tender.
8. Let the tart cool before serving.

Nutritional Value: Calories: 365, Fat: 16g, Protein: 4g, Carbohydrates: 57g, Fiber: 3g, Cholesterol: 0mg, Sodium: 119mg

401. Vegan Apple Crumble

Prep. Time: 20 minutes **Cooking Time:** 40 minutes **Servings:** 7
Ingredients:
- 4-5 cups thinly sliced, peeled and cored apples
- 3/4 cup rolled oats
- 1/2 cup all-purpose flour
- 1/2 cup brown sugar
- 1/2 cup chopped hazelnuts or pecans
- 1/4 cup vegan butter, chilled and cubed
- 1 tsp cinnamon
- 1/4 tsp nutmeg
- Pinch of salt

Instructions:
1. Preheat your oven to 375°F (190°C).
2. In a large mixing bowl, combine the apples, cinnamon, nutmeg, and a pinch of salt. Toss to coat the apples evenly.
3. In a separate mixing bowl, combine the rolled oats, flour, brown sugar, and chopped nuts. Mix well.
4. Add the cubed vegan butter to the oat mixture and use your fingers to rub it in until the mixture resembles coarse crumbs.
5. Grease a 9-inch round baking dish with a little bit of vegan butter. Pour the apple mixture into the dish and spread it out evenly.
6. Sprinkle the oat mixture over the apples, making sure to cover the entire surface.
7. Place the dish in the preheated oven and bake for 35-40 minutes, or until the top is golden brown and the apples are tender.
8. Let the crumble cool for a few minutes before serving. Serve warm with a scoop of vegan ice cream or whipped coconut cream, if desired.
9. Enjoy your delicious vegan apple crumble!

Nutritional Value: Calories: 283, Fat: 18g, Cholesterol: 6mg, Sugar: 14g, Carbohydrates: 27g, Protein: 11g

402. Vegan Chocolate Cream Pie

Prep. Time: 30 minutes **Cooking Time:** 90 minutes **Servings:** 8
Ingredients:
Crust:
- 1 and 1/2 cups of graham cracker crumbs
- 1/4 cup of granulated sugar
- 1/4 cup of vegan butter, melted

Filling:
- 1 and 1/2 cups of full-fat coconut milk
- 1/2 cup of granulated sugar
- 1/2 cup of unsweetened cocoa powder

- 1/4 cup of cornstarch
- 1/4 teaspoon of salt
- 1 teaspoon of vanilla extract
- Vegan whipped cream (optional)

Instructions:
1. Preheat the oven to 350°F (175°C).
2. In a medium mixing bowl, mix together the graham cracker crumbs, sugar, and melted vegan butter. Press the mixture into the bottom and up the sides of a 9-inch pie dish.
3. Bake the crust for 10-12 minutes or until lightly golden brown. Let it cool completely before filling.
4. In a medium saucepan, whisk together the coconut milk, sugar, cocoa powder, cornstarch, and salt. Cook over medium heat, whisking constantly, until the mixture comes to a simmer and thickens.
5. Remove the saucepan from heat and stir in the vanilla extract.
6. Pour the filling into the cooled crust and smooth the top.
7. Let the pie cool to room temperature before refrigerating for at least 1 hour or until firm.
8. Serve the pie chilled, topped with vegan whipped cream, if desired.

Nutritional Value (per slice): Calories: 456, Fat: 29g, Protein: 5g, Carbohydrates: 49g, Fiber: 2g, Cholesterol: 0mg, Sodium: 324mg

403. Vegan Mango Sorbet

Prep. Time: 15 minutes **Freezing Time:** 4 hours
Servings: 5
Ingredients:
- 2 cups frozen mango chunks
- 1/4 cup sugar
- 2 tablespoons fresh lime juice
- 1 tablespoon honey or agave nectar (optional)
- 1/4 teaspoon salt

Instructions:
1. In a blender or food processor, combine the frozen mango, sugar, lime juice, honey or agave nectar (if using) and salt.
2. Blend or process until smooth and creamy.
3. Taste and adjust the sweetness or acidity as desired.
4. Pour the mixture into a loaf pan and cover with plastic wrap, making sure the plastic wrap is touching the surface of the sorbet to prevent ice crystals from forming.
5. Freeze for at least 4 hours or until firm.
6. To serve, let the sorbet sit at room temperature for a few minutes to soften before scooping into bowls or cones.

Nutritional Value: Calories: 107, Fat: 4g, Cholesterol: 0mg, Sugar: 6g, Carbohydrates: 13g, Protein: 6g

404. Vegan Raspberry Sorbet

Total Time: 3 hours and 30 minutes, **Prep. Time:** 30 minutes, **Cooking Time:** 3 hours
Servings: 8
Ingredients:
- 4 cups of fresh raspberries
- 1 cup of granulated sugar
- 1/2 cup of water
- 1 tablespoon of freshly squeezed lemon juice

Instructions:
1. In a medium saucepan, combine the sugar and water and bring to a boil over medium-high heat.
2. Reduce the heat to low and let the mixture simmer for 2-3 minutes or until the sugar is completely dissolved. Remove from heat and let it cool.
3. In a blender or food processor, puree the raspberries until smooth.
4. Strain the puree through a fine-mesh sieve to remove the seeds.

5. In a large mixing bowl, combine the raspberry puree, cooled sugar syrup, and lemon juice.
6. Pour the mixture into a 9x13 inch baking dish and place it in the freezer.
7. Every 30 minutes, use a fork to scrape the edges and stir the mixture, breaking up any ice crystals that have formed. Do this for 2-3 hours or until the sorbet is firm and scoopable.
8. Serve the sorbet immediately or transfer it to an airtight container and store it in the freezer for up to 2 weeks.

Nutritional Value: Calories: 111, Fat: 0g, Protein: 1g, Carbohydrates: 29g, Fiber: 3g, Cholesterol: 0mg, Sodium: 1mg

405. Vegan Banana Cream Pie

Prep. Time: 20 minutes **Cooking Time:** 20 minutes **Servings:** 7
Ingredients:
- Crust:
- 1 1/2 cups all-purpose flour
- 1/2 cup vegan butter
- 1/4 cup granulated sugar
- 1/4 teaspoon salt
- 2-3 tablespoons ice water
- Filling:
- 3 ripe bananas
- 1 can (14 oz) full-fat coconut milk
- 1/4 cup granulated sugar
- 1/4 cup cornstarch
- 1 teaspoon vanilla extract
- Pinch of salt
- 1 vegan pie crust

Instructions:
1. Preheat the oven to 350°F.
2. To make the crust, mix together the flour, sugar, and salt in a large bowl. Add the vegan butter and cut it into the flour mixture using a pastry cutter or your fingers until the mixture resembles coarse crumbs.
3. Add 2-3 tablespoons of ice water and mix until the dough comes together.
4. Roll out the dough on a lightly floured surface and press it into a 9-inch pie dish. Prick the bottom of the crust with a fork and pre-bake it for 8-10 minutes.
5. To make the filling, peel and mash the bananas in a separate bowl.
6. In a medium saucepan, heat the coconut milk, sugar, cornstarch, vanilla extract, and salt over medium heat. Stir constantly until the mixture thickens, about 5-7 minutes.
7. Remove from heat and stir in the mashed bananas.
8. Pour the filling into the pre-baked pie crust and smooth out the top.
9. Chill the pie for at least 2 hours before slicing and serving.

Nutritional Value: Calories: 388, Fat: 26g, Cholesterol: 0mg, Sugar: 22g, Carbohydrates: 42g, Protein: 7g

406. Vegan Blueberry Muffins

Prep. Time: 15 minutes **Cooking Time:** 30 minutes **Servings:** 12
Ingredients:
- 2 cups of all-purpose flour
- 1/2 cup of granulated sugar
- 2 teaspoons of baking powder
- 1/2 teaspoon of salt
- 1 cup of unsweetened almond milk
- 1/3 cup of vegetable oil
- 1 teaspoon of vanilla extract
- 1 and 1/2 cups of fresh blueberries

Instructions:
1. Preheat the oven to 350°F (175°C) and grease a 12-cup muffin tin.
2. In a large mixing bowl, combine the flour, sugar, baking powder, and salt.

3. In a separate mixing bowl, whisk together the almond milk, vegetable oil, and vanilla extract.
4. Pour the wet ingredients into the dry ingredients and stir just until combined.
5. Gently fold in the blueberries.
6. Spoon the batter into the prepared muffin cups, filling each about 2/3 full.
7. Bake the muffins for 25-30 minutes or until a toothpick inserted into the center of a muffin comes out clean.
8. Allow the muffins to cool in the tin for 5 minutes before transferring them to a wire rack to cool completely.

Nutritional Value (per muffin): Calories: 156, Fat: 7g, Protein: 2g, Carbohydrates: 22g, Fiber: 1g, Cholesterol: 0mg, Sodium: 135mg

407. Vegan Chocolate Macarons

Prep. Time: 25 minutes **Cooking Time:** 15 minutes **Servings:** 5
Ingredients:
- 1 cup (120g) powdered sugar
- 3/4 cup (90g) almond flour
- 1/4 cup (20g) cocoa powder
- 3 tablespoons aquafaba (the liquid from a can of chickpeas)
- 1/4 teaspoon cream of tartar
- 1/4 cup (50g) granulated sugar
- 1/2 teaspoon vanilla extract
- 1/4 teaspoon salt
- Chocolate Ganache Filling:
- 1/2 cup (90g) vegan chocolate chips
- 1/4 cup (60ml) coconut cream or non-dairy milk
- 1 tablespoon (15g) coconut oil (optional, but recommended)

Instructions:
1. Preheat the oven to 350°F (175°C). Line two baking sheets with parchment paper.
2. In a food processor, grind the powdered sugar, almond flour, and cocoa powder together until fine and well combined.
3. In a stand mixer or using a hand-held mixer, beat the aquafaba, cream of tartar, and granulated sugar together until stiff peaks form. This should take about 5-7 minutes.
4. Add the vanilla extract and salt to the aquafaba mixture, and beat for another minute.
5. Gently fold the dry ingredients into the aquafaba mixture, being careful not to deflate the mixture.
6. Transfer the mixture to a piping bag fitted with a round tip. Pipe 1-inch circles onto the prepared baking sheets.
7. Tap the baking sheets firmly on the counter to remove any air bubbles. Allow the macarons to sit at room temperature for 30 minutes to an hour, or until a skin forms on the surface.
8. Bake the macarons for 12-15 minutes, or until set. Allow the macarons to cool completely on the baking sheet before filling.
9. To make the chocolate ganache filling, melt the chocolate chips, coconut cream, and coconut oil together in a double boiler or in the microwave.
10. Once the macarons are cooled, pipe a small amount of the chocolate ganache onto one macaron shell, then sandwich it with another shell. Repeat with the remaining macaron shells and ganache.
11. Allow the macarons to set in the refrigerator for at least 30 minutes before serving.
12. Enjoy your Vegan Chocolate Macarons!

Nutritional Value: Calories: 244, Fat: 32g, Cholesterol: 3mg, Sugar: 12g, Carbohydrates: 14g, Protein: 6g

408. Vegan Chocolate Banana Ice Cream

Prep. Time: 5 minutes **Freezing Time:** 6 hours
Servings: 2
Ingredients:
- 3 ripe bananas, peeled and frozen
- 2 tablespoons of cocoa powder
- 1 teaspoon of vanilla extract (optional)
- 1 tablespoon of maple syrup or sweetener of your choice (optional)

Instructions:
1. Cut the frozen bananas into small chunks and place them in a food processor.
2. Add the cocoa powder, vanilla extract, and maple syrup (if using) to the food processor.
3. Process the ingredients until smooth and creamy, scraping down the sides of the bowl as needed. This may take a few minutes.
4. Transfer the ice cream to a lidded container and freeze for at least 6 hours or until firm.
5. Scoop and serve the ice cream immediately or store it in the freezer for up to 2 weeks.

Nutritional Value: Calories: 110, Fat: 1g, Protein: 2g, Carbohydrates: 30g, Fiber: 3g, Cholesterol: 0mg, Sodium: 1mg

409. Vegan Blackberry Sorbet

Prep. Time: 15 minutes **Freezing Time:** 3 hours
Servings: 5
Ingredients:
- 4 cups fresh blackberries
- 1/2 cup granulated sugar
- 1/4 cup water
- 1 tablespoon fresh lemon juice

Instructions:
1. In a medium saucepan, combine the blackberries, sugar, and water. Bring to a boil over medium-high heat, then reduce the heat and simmer for 5 minutes, or until the blackberries are soft and the sugar is dissolved.
2. Remove from heat and let cool for a few minutes.
3. Transfer the mixture to a blender and puree until smooth.
4. Strain the puree through a fine-mesh sieve into a bowl, pressing on the solids to extract as much juice as possible. Discard the solids.
5. Stir in the lemon juice.
6. Taste and adjust sweetness if needed.
7. Pour the mixture into an ice cream maker and churn according to the manufacturer's Instructions.
8. If you don't have an ice cream maker, you can pour the mixture into a container and freeze for about 2 hours. Then, using a fork, scrape the mixture to break up any ice crystals. Repeat this process every 30 minutes for 2-3 hours, or until the mixture is frozen and the desired consistency is reached.
9. Serve and enjoy!

Nutritional Value: Calories: 177, Fat: 2g, Cholesterol: 0mg, Sugar: 14g, Carbohydrates: 38g, Protein: 4g

410. Vegan Orange Tart

Prep. Time: 30 minutes **Cooking Time:** 1 hour
Servings: 8
Ingredients:
- Crust:
- 1 and 1/2 cups of all-purpose flour
- 1/4 cup of granulated sugar
- 1/4 teaspoon of salt
- 1/2 cup of vegan butter
- 2 tablespoons of cold water
- Filling
- 1 cup of freshly squeezed orange juice

- 1/4 cup of cornstarch
- 1/4 cup of granulated sugar
- 1/4 teaspoon of salt
- 1 tablespoon of grated orange zest
- 2 tablespoons of vegan butter

Instructions:

1. Preheat the oven to 350°F (175°C) and grease a 9-inch tart pan with a removable bottom.
2. To make the crust, combine the flour, sugar, and salt in a mixing bowl. Cut the vegan butter into small pieces and add it to the bowl.
3. Use a pastry cutter or your fingers to work the butter into the flour mixture until it resembles coarse crumbs.
4. Add the cold water to the bowl and stir until the dough comes together.
5. Press the dough evenly into the bottom and up the sides of the prepared tart pan.
6. Prick the bottom of the crust with a fork and bake for 15-20 minutes or until lightly golden brown.
7. To make the filling, combine the orange juice, cornstarch, sugar, and salt in a medium saucepan. Cook over medium-high heat, whisking constantly, until the mixture comes to a boil and thickens.
8. Remove the saucepan from heat and stir in the orange zest and vegan butter.
9. Pour the filling into the cooled crust and smooth the top with a spatula.
10. Bake the tart for an additional 25-30 minutes, or until the filling is set and the crust is golden brown.
11. Remove the tart from the oven and let it cool completely on a wire rack before removing the sides of the pan.
12. Serve the tart chilled or at room temperature, garnished with additional orange zest or fresh berries if desired.

Nutritional Value: Calories: 240, Fat: 13g, Protein: 2g, Carbohydrates: 30g, Fiber: 1g, Cholesterol: 0mg, Sodium: 150mg

30-Days Meal Plan

DAY	BREAKFAST	LUNCH	SNACKS	DINNER	DESSERTS
1	Vegan Breakfast Waffles	Avocado And Tomato Toast	Vegan Lentil And Vegetable Curry Pizza	Tomato And Eggplant Gratin	Vegan Scones
2	Vegan Breakfast Tacos	Grilled Vegetable Wrap	Vegan Lentil And	Cauliflower And Pea Curry	Vegan Blueberry Cobbler
3	Vegan Breakfast Tacos	Creamy Tomato And Basil	Roasted Cauliflower And	Roasted Cauliflower Bites	Vegan Lemon Bars
4	Vegan Breakfast Strata	Vegetable And Chickpea	Vegan Lentil And	Lentil And Vegetable Curry	Vegan Chocolate Truffles
5	Mushroom And Goat Cheese	Vegetable And Black Bean	Spinach Apple Smoothie	Stuffed Okra With Peanut	Vegan Chocolate Cake
6	Vegan Breakfast	Vegetable And Quinoa Fried	Cucumber Melon Smoothie	Stuffed Bell Peppers With	Vegan Orange Tart
7	Vegetable Frittata	Grilled Portobello	Chocolate Banana	Quinoa And Black Bean	Vegan Banana Cream Pie
8	Vegan Breakfast Sausage	Lentil Soup	Avocado Lime Smoothie	Falafel Balls With Tahini	Vegan Tiramisu
9	Eggplant And Mozzarella	Vegetable Paella	Pineapple Coconut	Vegetable Jalfrezi	Fruit Sorbet
10	Lentil And Sweet Potato Hash	Vegetable Korma	Strawberry Basil Smoothie	Lentil And Beetroot Patty	Vegan Lemon Tart
11	Carrot And Ginger Breakfast	Vegetable And Lentil Soup	Blueberry Almond	Grilled Eggplant Rolls With	Vegan Chocolate Fondue
12	Veggie Omelette	Vegetable And Black Bean	Chickpea And Avocado	Roasted Brussels Sprouts	Vegan Chocolate Orange
13	Vegan Breakfast Omelette	Vegetable Lasagna	Baked Sweet Potato Fries	Lentil And Pumpkin Curry	Vegan Apple Crumble
14	Tomato And Basil Breakfast	Vegan Chili	Vegan Chili Cheese Fries	Sweet Potato And Black	Vegan Apple Crisp
15	Zucchini And Feta Fritters	Roasted Vegetable And	Cucumber And Dill Yogurt	Carrot And Ginger Soup	Vegan Strawberry
16	Vegan Breakfast Sandwich	Spaghetti With Marinara	Creamy Tomato And Lentil	Lentil And Vegetable	Vegan Key Lime Pie
17	Vegan Breakfast Sandwich	Vegetable Pad Thai	Eggplant Parmesan Bites	Vegetable And Lentil Pot	Vegan Blackberry Sorbet
18	Vegan Eggless French Toast	Vegetable And Tofu	Vegan Mac And Cheese	Vegetable Lasagna	Vegan Rice Pudding
19	Sweet Potato And Kale	Vegetable Pot Pie	Indian-Style Lentil And	Vegetable Moussaka	Vegan Berry Crisp
20	Chia Seed Pudding	Spicy Sweet Potato And	Sweet Potato And Black	Pan-Seared Portobello	Vegan Chocolate Banana
21	Vegan Breakfast Tofu	Creamy Mushroom And Wild	Vegan Lentil And	Vegetable And Lentil Soup	Vegan Apple Pie
22	Vegan Breakfast Enchiladas	Vegetable And Tofu Lettuce	Vegetable And Lentil	Eggplant Parmesan	Vegan Baked Apple
23	Breakfast Polenta With	Vegetable And Lentil	Vegan Lentil And	Spinach And Ricotta	Vegan Red Velvet Cake
24	Vegan Breakfast Risotto	Caprese Salad With Grilled	Black Bean And Corn	Tomato And Eggplant	Vegan Chocolate Pudding
25	Vegan Breakfast Chia	Vegetable And White Bean	Tomato And Basil	Vegetable And Paneer	Vegan Chocolate Chip
26	Vegan Breakfast Parfait	Lentil And Vegetable Stew	Stuffed Portobello	Vegetable And Lentil Dal	Vegan Gingerbread
27	Vegan Breakfast Casserole	Chickpea And Spinach Stew	Vegetable And Lentil Curry	Vegetable And Paneer	Vegan Chocolate Mousse
28	Avocado Toast	Roasted Vegetable And Fete	Roasted Portobello	Black Bean And Sweet	Vegan Apple Tart
29	Chickpea And Spinach	Vegetable And White Bean	Grilled Zucchini And Bell	Stuffed Eggplant With	Vegan Pumpkin Pie
30	Vegan Breakfast Waffles	Pasta Primavera	Mango Madness Smoothie	eggplant parmesan	Vegan Pecan Pie

Support my Work

If you enjoyed the contents of this book and want to help me in a simple, accessible, and fast way, I warmly invite you to leave an honest review directly on the Amazon product page. That way, other people looking for vegetarian recipes and other vegetarian diet-related content will find my book and all of my work. To do this, use the camera on your smartphone to scan the QR code or click on [this link](#) if you have the reader in the digital version.

Thank you, Katy.

Conclusion

A vegetarian diet is a healthy and balanced food choice following some basic guidelines, such as the intake of plant proteins, the inclusion of a wide range of foods, including fruits, vegetables, grains, and seeds, and the limitation of processed or rich foods of fats and sugars. Furthermore, it is important to pay attention to the supply of essential nutrients that may be deficient in the vegetarian diet, such as vitamin B12, and to integrate them through alternative sources or supplements. A vegetarian diet, when followed correctly, can provide a wide range of health benefits, including a reduction in the risk of cardiovascular disease, diabetes, and some cancers.

Eating vegetable proteins is essential to ensure a balanced and nutrient-rich vegetarian diet. These proteins can be obtained from quinoa, tofu, legumes, chia and flax seeds, and dried fruit. These foods provide a complete supply of essential amino acids. They are also rich in other vital nutrients such as fiber, iron, magnesium, and potassium. Therefore, it is necessary to include a variety of protein sources in your diet to ensure a total nutrient intake and prevent any deficiencies. Additionally, these plant-based protein sources are often low in saturated fat and cholesterol-free, making them healthier than animal protein.

The variety of foods in the vegetarian diet is essential to ensure a balanced and nutrient-rich diet. Fruits, vegetables, grains, seeds, and legumes are all important foods to include in your diet to ensure a complete supply of nutrients. Fruits and vegetables provide vitamins, minerals, and antioxidants, and whole grains and legumes provide complex carbohydrates and proteins. Seeds, like chia and flax, are rich in essential fatty acids and minerals. Therefore, it is important to include a wide range of foods in your diet to prevent deficiencies and ensure that you eat a balanced and healthy diet. In addition, varying food choices help prevent food boredom and maintain interest in the diet over the long term.

Limiting processed foods high in fat and sugar is essential to ensure a balanced and healthy diet. These foods are often high in empty calories and lacking in essential nutrients, and can increase the risk of obesity, cardiovascular disease, and diabetes.

Instead of opting for these foods, choosing natural and whole foods, such as fruits, vegetables, grains, and legumes, is essential to ensure a complete supply of nutrients. Also, limiting or avoiding condiments and sauces high in fat and sugar is necessary. Instead, choose healthier options like spices, herbs, and lemon juice to flavor foods. These small choices can have a significant impact on your long-term health.

The vegetarian diet can be adapted to many cultures and lifestyles, making it an accessible choice for many people. Many cultural recipes and ingredients can be easily adapted to meet the requirements of a vegetarian diet. For example, Indian cuisine offers many vegetarian options, such as dal and naan bread. In contrast, Mexican cuisine provides opportunities such as vegetable fajitas and bean tacos. It's essential to experiment with different recipes and ingredients to keep the diet exciting and ensure a wide range of nutrients. Furthermore, the vegetarian diet can be personalized according to individual preferences, such as using products of biological origin or excluding certain foods, such as milk or eggs. This flexibility makes a vegetarian diet a healthy and sustainable choice for many people.

A vegetarian diet can have many positive health and well-being benefits. According to numerous studies, a vegetarian diet can reduce the risk of chronic diseases such as diabetes, cardiovascular disease, and obesity. Additionally, the vegetarian diet is rich in antioxidants and protective nutrients that can help prevent cancer and other diseases. A vegetarian diet is also associated with a higher quality of life and increased longevity. These positive benefits are why a vegetarian can be a healthy and sustainable choice for many people. However, it is essential to remember that each person is unique and that the most suitable diet can vary according to individual needs. Therefore, it is always important to speak to your doctor or health care professional before making any changes to your diet.

I wish you much joy and happiness in your kitchen with vegetarian recipes.

Manufactured by Amazon.ca
Bolton, ON